THE DECOLONIZATION OF QUEBEC

THE
DECOLONIZATION
OF
QUEBEC

AN ANALYSIS OF
LEFT-WING NATIONALISM

Henry Milner
Sheilagh Hodgins Milner

MCCLELLAND AND STEWART LIMITED

Aislin cartoons reproduced by
permission of the artist

The Canadian Publishers
McClelland and Stewart Limited
25 Hollinger Road, Toronto

PRINTED AND BOUND IN CANADA

Carleton
Contemporaries

A series of books designed to stimulate
informed discussion of current and
controversial issues in Canada, and to
improve the two-way flow of ideas
between people and government.

ISSUED UNDER THE EDITORIAL
SUPERVISION OF THE INSTITUTE OF
CANADIAN STUDIES, CARLETON
UNIVERSITY, OTTAWA.
INTERIM DIRECTOR OF THE INSTITUTE,
N.H. LITHWICK

TABLE OF CONTENTS

PREFACE

The original focus of this study was to investigate what seemed to be a unique phenomenon in North America. While trade unionism on this continent has, over the years, been increasingly characterized by conservatism, in Quebec the Confederation of National Trade Unions has led an apparent move by the labour movement toward radicalism in recent years. The progressively more socialist and militant position of organized labour in Quebec, however, proved impossible to study without consideration of the context in which this movement was taking place. A major change in the CNTU suggested that Quebec itself was undergoing a significant transformation.

The conventional wisdom of political science suggests that, in terms of the "left-right" spectrum, nationalism is reactionary or "rightist" while internationalism is progressive or "leftist." Yet the CNTU, among other progressive elements has shared Quebec's growing indépendentiste spirit. On the whole, it became clear to us during the course of our investigations that the contemporary transformations in Quebec were the result of a particular inter-weaving of class and nation, colonialism and capitalism. An historical analysis of the structure of Quebec society was required.

In approaching such analysis we were not neutral, "objective" and detached. Our socialist leanings lead us to favour greater power for the workers of Quebec as elsewhere. Nor were we passive in our appraisal of the colonized status of Les Québecois; on the contrary we sympathize with and share the growing determination of the people of Quebec to liberate themselves from external domination.

Our purpose in writing, then, is to make social analysis meaningful and – in this period of growing realization in English Canada of the fact that French Canada is awakening, and of English "backlash" against such awakening – to elicit at least greater awareness if not solidarity among English-speaking Canadians for Quebec's struggle for decolonization.

Events in Quebec have been moving so rapidly that is it now clear we are witnessing not merely a change in the thinking of a few union leaders, but a major transformation in Quebec society, one with implications far wider than any provincial boundaries. Because of the press of time we have perhaps left out much which needs to be said; yet we have attempted to integrate and to make sense of many seemingly unrelated facts and events. Elaboration can come later. It seems to us that some sympathetic interpretation of the entire question of Quebec's objective condition, present orientation and future possibilities must be made available to English-speaking Canadians – and right now. Whether our understandings, as English-speaking residents of Quebec, are accurate must be left to your, the reader's, judgment.

Along the way the authors received a great deal of help. It would be impossible to acknowledge all those whose suggestions proved in one way or another way useful. We can just mention a few who have been particularly helpful in the process of the development of this book.

First of all we extend our thanks to John Porter of Carleton University. As thesis advisor he was instrumental in getting the basic work off the ground and into manuscript shape. We are indebted, also, to Stanley Ryerson, Jon Alexander, Marcel Rioux, David Brooks, Pauline Jewett and Hubert Guindon for their advice and assistance. The manuscript was prepared for press in its various stages by Maggie Waller and Linda Alexander whom we gratefully acknowledge. Finally, we must add an apology to our infant son Paul and to Debbie Hodgins who looked after him those last few rather hectic and trying months.

The various people who helped the work along might be very surprised at the final form it has taken; though we hope they won't be disappointed. Nevertheless, none of them are, of course, in any way responsible for the errors, omissions, etc. in this text – rather they are laid firmly at the foot of each author by the other.

"I know of no national distinctions marking and continuing a more hopeless inferiority . . . if they prefer remaining stationary, the greater part of them must be laborers in the employ of English capitalists. In either case it would appear that the great mass of French Canadians are doomed, in some measure, to occupy an inferior position, and to be dependent on the English for employment. The evils of poverty and dependence would merely be aggravated in a ten-fold degree, by a spirit of jealous and resentful nationality which should separate the working class of the community from the possessors of wealth and employers of labor. . . ."

Lord Durham, 1838.

INTRODUCTION

As we write these words, Quebec has just passed through its latest "crisis" – this time in the form of a public service strike and its aftermath – and people are wondering about the form of this year's "fall offensive" which usually comes after the summer as the next step toward political and economic self-determination. For over ten years now, English Canadians have been asking "What does Quebec want from us?" What Quebec wants from them today is nothing: finally the people of Quebec are simply responding directly to their colonized existence.

The issue of Quebec can no longer be attributed, no matter what our politicians may say, to the cries in the wilderness of a few separatists or the subversive propaganda of foreign ideologues and ideologies. What is happening in Quebec is actually the product of concrete, objective conditions, coupled with a growing critical awareness of these conditions. Simply put, Quebec has produced a popular and powerful movement united by aims fundamentally opposed to the continuation of the socioeconomic status quo. An independent, socialist Quebec is a goal for many Québecois, and a seriously considered possibility for perhaps a majority. These facts become significant, even staggering, when we compare Quebec to the United States, and incredibly so when we remember the Quebec of the thirties and before.

Quebec has recently witnessed the largest strike in Canadian history, one which sent more than 210,000 public and para-public employees onto the picket lines, striking for job security, a minimum wage of $100.00 a week, and fair salary increases. The strikers came from professional and manual laboring groups, and every sector in between. The strike action impelled the formation of a cohesive common front of the three major trade union federations. When, after two weeks, the workers were legally forced back to work – and the leaders of the common front jailed for disobeying court injunctions – a week-long revolt broke out spontaneously throughout the province. Spontaneous actions by workers in every kind of job (including private industry) virtually closed down the province. In the end the actions died down, but the militancy and sense of purpose shown by the workers remained, and no one can guess how long the calm will prevail this time. And these are by no means isolated actions, but rather the culmination of a decade of growing ferment in the ranks of labour, and of a growing class analysis among its leaders, activists and thinkers. This ferment constitutes the latest stage in a struggle that has been gradually intensifying.

What makes this sequence of events all the more remarkable is that in the thirties, when the rest of North America turned toward the left and was swept by a current of radical innovation, Quebec stood unaffected, more strongly than ever the traditional society it had always been. While the political elite sold out Quebec's resources (and workers' interests) to American and English-Canadian capitalists, the people were kept in check by an ideological elite, at the centre of which was the Church. Because this group controlled thought through education and practically all media outlets it was able to contain frustration and anger within the local community, to brand progressive reforms as immoral, and to channel any excess resentment upon scapegoats such as the Jews. While English North America's opinion leaders preached (though seldom really practiced) New Deals and One Big Union and a New Society, Quebec's elite glorified a feudal theocracy – an ideal which, however noble it might have sometimes been, remained irrelevant to the causes and solutions of the desperate problems of the Depression.

In the sixties the pattern came to be almost reversed. While the U.S.A. and Canada have both been the scene of important and well-publicised radical activities, the effect of the movement which arose in this period has been limited by its inherent weakness. Its appeal has been restricted, basically, to students, youth in general, some women's groups, intellectuals and certain elements among Black and Chicano Americans. It has been unable to win significant middle class and, especially, working class support. Organized labour has been particularly cold to this movement and has mostly opposed its struggle against the war in Vietnam and its goal of participatory democracy. This attitude was manifested and symbolized in the extreme by the "hard hat" mentality of some construction workers. When the centre of the movement left the campus in the late sixties in an effort to find roots in the communities, it met with meagre success; and now much of that energy is going into the establishment of new communities and counter-institutions. In the long run, these kinds of alternative structures and the cultural critique they evoke may prove to be instrumental in guiding reconstruction of a system which will have become ecologically desperate; but for now, English North American capitalism has survived the onslaught. It survived because its contradictions were felt to be intolerable only to a marginal group; its masses have found in it, if not fulfillment, at least sufficient distraction for them to remain docile.

Among Quebec's youth a similar, if somewhat more restrained, cultural revolution took place in the sixties, influenced greatly by North American and even world-wide developments. In addition, there was the same move toward community organizing and a corresponding proliferation of citizens' committees and welfare rights groups, etc. But there was something more. The movement in Quebec, as was nowhere else the case in North America, crossed class lines and grew strong in the ranks and cadres of (of all places) organized labour.

When in 1971 students and some teachers at the Université de Montréal launched a campaign against the university's Institute of Criminology because of its role in the training of police in Brazil and in other countries, they received the support and even active participation of some university workers. When the University's 1,500 workers went on strike the same year for better working conditions, students refused to cross the picket lines, and it was this solidarity which forced the administration to make major concessions. In Quebec many students who had become politicized on the campus in the mid-

3

sixties found alliances and some even found jobs with trade union centrals and locals. The Montreal Council of the CNTU led the fight for the release of revolutionary "terrorists" Pierre Vallières and Charles Gagnon; for an analogy, one might (try to) imagine the AFL-CIO intervening on behalf of the "Weathermen."

In 1972 the Societé St. Jean Baptiste, the patriotic semi-establishment and very traditional French-Canadian order, met in June, and, among other things, extended fraternal greetings to the union movement – one which had just engaged in actions that led establishment figures to accuse the movement of trying to topple the government and institute an independent socialist Quebec. In sum, the change in Quebec has been a profound one; the movement has done very little to divide workers from students, and it has narrowed rather than widened the gap between the intellectuals and the masses.

We do not wish to glorify les Québecois; nor do we wish to imply that the situation here is fully ripe for the introduction of a socialist system. There are still numerous differences, still uncertainties, still internal conflicts. Yet the fact remains that in the past forty years, and especially in these last ten years, the people of Quebec have come to an awareness of their exploited condition under international capitalism and are developing a determination to oppose it and build something new.

Why? Why here and not elsewhere? Two facile answers immediately present themselves and each is partially correct. First, the cultural revolution of Quebec's youth took place at the same time as, rather than some thirty (and more) years after, the growth of organized trade union militancy among workers. Having noted this, however, we are still far from an adequate explanation. Second, there is the often-made assertion that the old quasi-feudal mentality of Quebec, since it lasted so long, was never really replaced by the culture of economic liberalism, or individualism, which dominated English North America. Thus Quebec could move almost directly from the social solidarity of a traditional, hierarchical, peasant society to the class solidarity of a socialist collectivity without being trapped at the stage of competitive laissez-faire capitalism and its concomitant cultural and social patterns.

Again, there is some validity in this argument, but it is

hardly sufficient either. A complex process of change took place in those forty years and only by understanding this process in its depth and specificity can we begin to account for the direction this movement has taken and will take. Furthermore these changes must be seen as the concrete responses to the objective situation in which les Québecois found themselves – how they came to understand their condition and to understand that it had to be transformed and transcended.

What is crucial is Quebec's being a colony, not in the political-geographical sense of the term, but in the human, social and economic senses. It is an entity controlled from outside, a society which can act and decide only within limits circumscribed by the colonizer. This has been the reality of Quebec since its founding; this has been its reality, though more subtly, after the gradual takeover by American-based capitalism in this century.

One can generally discern roughly three stages in the history of a colonized people. The first is the old order under which the people find solace in their traditions and culture and collectively submit to socioeconomic inferiority and powerlessness. This is followed by a far briefer stage where progressive elements of the colonized group attempt to deny their collective origins – instead calling for individuals to integrate themselves to the colonizing society in order to win the benefits of integration. A third and deeper stage emerges when the demand for individual equality is exposed as illusory and a more realistic assertion of the right to collective equality and self-determination comes to the fore.

Among American Blacks, the three stages can be sharply identified: one, with the terrorization and consequent submissiveness of the coloured people in the early days; two, with the Negro civil rights movement for desegregation in the fifties and early sixties; and, three, with the appearance of a "Black Power" movement and the growing demands by Blacks for control of the most important social and economic institutions in their neighbourhoods. The latter sections of this book explore each of these stages as they developed among the "White Niggers of America," les Québecois.

The book is divided into two parts. The first is an analytical statement of the effects of imperialism on Quebec's economy and culture. We attempt, in some detail, to describe Quebec's economy, its strengths and weaknesses, patterns of trade and ownership. We also take a look at the socioeconomic status of French Canadians in Quebec and its evolution.

The second part might be labelled an historical analysis of the interrelation between ideas and events, from the thirties to the present. It provides a description and analysis of the major factors which gradually have led to the development of a nationalism on the left in both the ideas and actions of contemporary Quebec.

This book is not put forth simply as scholarship, but rather as a contribution to the very struggle described (not in the form of propaganda, though we may be accused of this) by providing theoretical analysis which may allow people involved in the struggle or related struggles to reach a better understanding of the roots and strategic possibilities. Most of all, it is written for people on the fringes of the movement, who are perhaps somewhat sympathetic to the movement, but harbour doubts and fears – to the many English-speaking people in Quebec who are not part of nor linked to the English business elite, and to all Canadians who, justifiably, think the events and lessons of Quebec will be crucial in the future political directions of Canada.

Finally, we are convinced that the attitudes of English Canadians (especially those in Quebec) and the future role they will play will be important in the directions the movement will take, and perhaps will significantly affect its achievements; and we sincerely hope that, if nothing else, readers of this book will subsequently approach the present condition of Quebec and its liberation efforts, both more critically and sympathetically – and with greater understanding.

Part One

**THE
ECONOMY
OF A
COLONIZED
SOCIETY**

CHAPTER 1

THE
AMERICAN
METROPOLIS

Quebec lies geographically on the northern border of the United States; economically, Quebec lies firmly within the grasp of that nation whose arms consist of dollars as well as the weapons of war. Subservience may be bought often more cheaply by money than by Marines. In this latter aspect Quebec's position is not unlike that of many other societies, especially in the Western hemisphere. The U.S.A. is the most powerfully developed capitalist society yet to emerge upon this planet. Not only its actual foreign economic and political policies, but its very internal socio-political system directly affect people and nations well outside its political boundaries. Or, one might say in other words that the political boundaries of the United States extend far beyond its national geographical boundaries, and this simple fact is one of utmost importance to Quebec.

As manager of the "free" capitalist world, the United States behaves toward other nations in ways which are to a great extent a reflection and outgrowth of the economic structures and social system inside its borders. The basis of this system we understand to be the American class structure and the organizational and cultural means whereby this class structure is maintained. Hence the apparent paradox: in order to understand many of the most important aspects of everyday experience in Quebec, we must understand some of the crucial facts of life in the United States – beginning with its internal class structure and the culture which sustains this structure. It is only after we reach some understanding of what in the United States is increasingly referred to as simply "The System," that we can go on to analyze the colonial question with special reference to Quebec. In addition, the insight thus gained into the capitalist state writ large can, to some degree, be applied to our analysis of capitalism in Quebec. Let us therefore, begin at the beginning.

The United States is a monopoly capitalist state: that is, the economy is dominated by giant corporations.

> [These] great corporations are the very important units of wealth, to which individuals of property are variously attached. The corporation is the source, and the basis of the continued power and privilege of wealth. All the men and families of great wealth are now identified with large corporations in which their property is seated.[1]

These "men and families of great wealth" form the basis of the American ruling class. They constitute ". . . a social upper class which owns a disproportionate amount of a country's wealth, receives a disproportionate amount of a country's yearly income, and contributes a disproportionate number of its members to the controlling institutions and key decision making groups of the country."[2] Despite the American creed and its myth of equality of opportunity for all, this ruling class is in fact not recruited from all social classes in the society. Rather, it perpetuates itself in a very conscious fashion: there are special schools, special clubs, special resort areas, special modes of speech and mannerism and comportment – all explicitly designed to prepare the children of this class eventually to take their presumedly "rightful" (and privileged) place in society. This homogeneity in the socialization process gives the ruling class not only a special incentive for cooperation, but also added solidarity, for similar values, attitudes, and styles of life are engendered in the children at a very tender age. The members of this class are not to be looked upon as a group of idle, hedonistic parasites; rather they are, for the most part, not only well educated but also both industrious and competent.

Many modern authors have assumed that the growing use of a managerial class and the dispersal of ownership through various forms of securities since Marx's time have created a division between the ownership on the one hand, and, on the other, the control of industry. Dahrendorf is one of the most effective proponents of this commonly held viewpoint. The thesis, in his words, is that "The separation of ownership and control has replaced one group by two whose positions, roles and outlooks are far from identical [and therefore] the homogeneous class predicted by Marx has in fact not developed. Capital – and thereby capitalism – has dissolved and given way, in the economic sphere, to a plurality of partly agreed, partly competing, and partly simply different groups."[3]

In fact this conclusion is not warranted by Dahrendorf's premise. The creation of a large group of professional managers and the increasing spread of what may be termed a managerial outlook are readily observable phenomena which, far from dissolving its power, have instead served to increase the vitality and viability of the owning class. What has occurred is an alteration in the form and expression of that power in such a way as to make it more consonant with the long-term interests of the ruling class in a period of technological change and organizational innovation. This is perhaps the final stage in the transition from laissez-faire to monopoly capitalism.

The facts show that owners are managers and managers owners in sufficient numbers to result in the long-term interests of both groups converging to such degree as to make any remaining differences so slight as to be virtually imperceptible. As Domhoff has shown: "successful managers become owners themselves with the help of stock options and stock tips, and . . . they are assimilated socially into the upper class [and] a considerable number of corporate executives are of the upper class originally even when they are not majority owners in a given corporation."[4] The evidence marshalled by Domhoff in support of this assertion is impressive. Further, we note with Baran and Sweezy that if any conflict at all persists, it is between managers and small stockholders rather than large stockholders. Specifically:

It is generally assumed that the desire of managers, . . . to generate the largest feasible volume of internal corporate funds leads to an interest in a low dividend payout rate, while stockholders' concern to maximize their disposable cash income leads to an interest in a. higher payout rate. Actually, this is much too simple. Most managers are themselves big owners of stock (in their own and other compa-

11

nies) and as such have the same interest in dividends as other big stockholders. This interest is neither in a minimum nor maximum payout rate but somewhere in between: (for managers this is particularly important as a guarantee of family security after they retire or die); on the other hand, they should also steadily appreciate in value. . . . Nevertheless, the special managerial interest in a low payout rate does exist and is undoubtedly important. But the point to be emphasized is that this makes managers the allies of the very largest stockholders for whom a minimum payout rate is a desideratum. The reason of course is that the very rich save a large part of their incomes in any case, and it is to their advantage for the corporation in which they own stock to do the saving for them. . . .[5]

Each generation of managers recruits its own successors and trains, grooms and promotes them according to its own standards and values. The new managers are not recruited equally from all strata of the population, but whatever their social origins, their styles of life, objectives and interests quickly become those of the managerial class. This ideology seems to be the result of a socialization process which stresses the importance of material wealth and access to decision-making positions. Frequently the managers themselves come from upper class families. There is certainly a modicum of mobility into this ruling class from the lower segments of the population. Socialists (and sociologists) from Marx on have recognized the necessity for this upper class to co-opt the brightest individuals from the lower classes so as both to ensure maintenance of the quality of the ruling class, and also to rob other classes of potential leaders. The few instances of mobility into the ruling classes from lower segments of the population are important: they tend to mask the essential homogeneity of the class. Nevertheless, ". . . higher education at the best institutions perpetuates the advantages of wealth in succeeding generations, while among the poor, vast reservoirs of talent and creativity go unexploited."[6]

There is no suggestion here that the wealthy and powerful conspire to oppress the remaining population. Life in the most totalitarian society must be more complex. It is clear, however, that the American upper class forms the nucleus of the ruling class; that separate social and educational institutions exist to ensure maintenance of the ruling class; and that this maintenance is further facilitated through great influence upon or actual control over the major institutions of American society – institutions which do allow (difficult) access to individuals from different backgrounds; and that when these individuals have sufficiently integrated their values and social perspectives with that of the upper class they come to be accepted as members of the elite. In these non-conspiratorial ways, the ruling class is perpetuated and revitalized while its hegemony remains intact.

Because so many individuals within the ruling class own stock in many different corporations it might be expected that they are more concerned, at this stage in the development of American capitalism, with the success of the system as a whole rather than with the short-run success of their own company or companies. This dispersal of stock and the death of family capitalism has tended to free the hereditary rich to go into government service, the professions, and the arts, contributing further to the stability of the system as a whole. The particularly vicious competition of nineteenth-century capitalism has been replaced by co-operation in a general way to protect a particular system, its myths, and the privilege it allows its ruling class.

In sum, the expansion of American capitalism into an economy dominated by large managerially-run corporations with some dispersal of stock ownership has not fundamentally altered the ruling structure of American society. It has moderated, consolidated and polished it. It has allowed the ruling class to identify correctly its interests with the stability and growth of the various industrial sectors and even the economy as a whole, rather than simply with the more shortsighted interests of the particular enterprises owned by individual families within this class. Through such means as interlocking directorships combined with the dispersal of stock ownership among different ruling-class individuals and especially among corporations dominated by them (in particular, financial institutions such as banks, insurance companies, savings and loan companies, brokerage houses and mutual funds) the ruling class has been able to reap direct financial benefit as well. Finally, the above developments have enabled members of the business elite to portray themselves before the public as "good corporate citizens" ready and willing to sacrifice the interests of their own firms for the sake of general economic well-being. It is thus beyond this polished exterior that we must penetrate if we wish to grasp the real dynamic at work in the system of monopoly capitalism.

Monopoly capitalism is a self-contradictory system in that it tends to generate ever more surplus, for which it must provide consumption and investment outlets to absorb this surplus and allow the smooth operation of the system. The surplus is the difference between the total revenue of a corporation and its costs of production. It is profits in the widest sense of the term, rather than in its official restricted usage. Unless this surplus is absorbed, reinvested, the market becomes flooded, the system stagnates, and the myth of scarcity is exposed.[7]* If the supply of goods is too great, the demand is by definition too small. But, instead of cutting back supply, corporations aim at stimulating demand. Cutting prices is generally ruled out; this would introduce elements of uncertainty, even instability, and make rational planning – a necessity for huge, modern corporate structures – impossible. Without rational planning, profits could diminish to well below acceptable levels; then corporate heads

---

* "Administrative prices in the short and medium run increase profits, and enable thereby increased capital accumulation. But price and market control imply a strictly limited growth of output. This is the basic contradiction which monopoly capitalism adds to the fundamental contradictions of the capitalist mode of production, revealed by Karl Marx. This contradiction implies that all profits realized through price and market control cannot be reinvested in the monopolized sector, without undermining the monopoly profit itself. If they are fully reinvested there, they will lead to a declining capacity utilization, i.e. to a rapidly declining rate of profit. . . .

Of course, capitalism never knows "absolute" over-capitalization: there is always too much capital only from the point of view of obtaining an average rate of profit considered normal by the capitalists. In that sense it is, of course, true that if more possibilities for increased surplus-value production existed, there would be no surplus capital, i.e. that a scarcity and not an abundance of surplus-value is at the root of the problem. But this statement in no way conflicts with the dialectical development of the process. Because previously produced surplus-value, transformed into capital, cannot obtain the average rate of profit, it appears as surplus capital in desperate search for additional fields of investment. Whereas initially the problem arose from too little surplus-value, it thereupon takes the appearance of too much capital." — Ernest Mandel, "The Driving Force of Imperialism in Our Era," paper presented at the Bertrand Russell Symposium on "Imperialism", Linz, Austria, September 1972, pp. 3-4.

would roll and competition could become brutal – endangering the stability of the entire economy. The perpetuation and growth of these corporations and thus of the economy as a whole, depends upon their ability to stimulate demand, to create and expand markets. This task, then, becomes the pressing need of both business and government. It becomes important to the ruling class as a whole that no corporation (of a size sufficient to effect the general economy) should be either too profitable or too unprofitable. The state thus necessarily assumes responsibility under monopoly capitalism to ensure stable prices and profit margins among the giant corporations.

The system of monopoly capitalism is one where there is but a small number of firms comprising one industry and where competition is neither according to price nor according to quality, but simply through advertising. The standard form this takes is for there to be an industry "leader" – e.g., General Motors, or General Electric, or Standard Oil of New Jersey – who dominates the industry and whose changes in price and quality are followed by the other firms. In such a situation there is no compulsion to lower prices and improve quality. The goal is not to increase demand simply for one product, but to maintain and increase the *aggregate* demand for what this industry produces. The reality is that the industry behaves as a monopoly, though it maintains some of the formalities and appurtenances of competition.

It is clear that advertising plays a key role in such a system, but a new and different role. In the automobile industry, for instance, the massive sales campaign has four goals. Most importantly it seeks to convince buyers to spend a large proportion of income on consumer goods. Secondly, it seeks general acceptance of the total automobile-centered American system of transportation. Thirdly, it seeks to engender desires to buy the kind of cars American manufacturers most wish to sell – large, expensive, soon-obsolete but "loaded with extras." The final, and, for two of the "Big Three," least compelling goal is to convince the buyer to buy the particular car advertised. At this level the competition based on sales campaigns rather than prices is seen as a useful incentive; there is fundamentally no difference between the rivalry of Chevrolet and Ford (G.M. vs. Ford) and that between Chevrolet and Pontiac (both G.M.). What advertising must do is maintain the rate of expansion of the industry, keep highways being built, block alternative means of transport. This is one expression of rational self-interest in monopoly capitalism. Now it should be clear that only in a situation of monopoly capitalism is such a massively complex sales campaign either necessary or possible. Except during short periods of disequilibrium, a firm in a competitive industry simply cannot afford saturation advertising. Putting aside the historical chicken-egg question, we may say that modern advertising techniques and monopoly capitalism are interdependent.

Yet although it is "rational" for monopolistic entrepreneurs to engage in massive advertising, the effect of a system based on its concomitant techniques is to diminish rationality among the populace of consumers. The newer techniques of advertising appeal to the most base and least conscious aspects of man's emotional make-up; they are aimed not at informing man about product X as compared to product Y, but rather at altering the mental context through which he or she makes rational/ irrational judgments.[8]

Politics too has become the domain of the ad-man with equally pernicious results. In 1960 the Democrats pioneered the new campaign technology. Simulmatics Inc. statistically proved to John F. Kennedy that, despite prevailing opinion to the contrary, he could use his religion as an issue to his advantage; he did and became America's first Catholic president. Computer simulation was also used by Johnson in 1964 and by both parties in 1968. Perhaps the most telling description of the sale of candidates can be found in Joe McGuiness' vivid and frightening portrayal of the 1968 Nixon campaign in *The Selling of the President.*

Advertising has penetrated much of the political arena beyond election campaigns, as is apparent in the different levels and branches of government. Ronald Reagan, for instance, did not dismiss his high-powered advertising firm once it had elected him Governor of California; rather he used its personnel and techniques to govern. In sum, American politics bears as much resemblance to an informed and active democracy as its economy bears to a competitive laissez-faire market. Using the very techniques perfected by corporate ad-men, political leaders, through administrative and electoral manipulation (with the complicity of a press and other media almost totally in the hands of the ruling class), sell the American system as a whole. The difference between the Democrats and Republicans, Nixon and Humphrey, is like the difference between a Ford and a Chevrolet: miniscule, but played up to the hilt so that Americans buy the entire economic and political system. It should be little wonder then that key U.S. governmental institutions very frequently serve, to use Marx's words, simply as committees for managing the common affairs of the ruling class.[9]

Baran and Sweezy demonstrate that, given the inability of corporations within a monopoly capitalist system to provide for the absorption of surplus, it is in the interest of all classes that government should constantly increase its taxing and spending. Most elements of the lower classes derive sufficient benefits from increased spending to outweigh the disadvantages of increased taxes. To the corporation, increased government spending means increased demand, for there tends to be little problem in shifting most of the associated taxes onto the consumers or the workers so that a relatively constant profit margin is maintained.[10]

Thus government and industry in effect collaborate to stimulate demand so that the surplus is absorbed and the stagnation of the system is prevented. As Herbert Marcuse puts it, the result of such a system is that "people recognize themselves in their commodities; they find their soul in their automobile, hi-fi set, split-level home, kitchen equipment."[11] Thus, "the profit system is oppressive not because relatively trivial luxuries are available, but because basic necessities are not. The locus of oppression resides in the production function: people have no control over what commodities are produced (or services performed), in what amounts, under what conditions, or how they are distributed."[12]

This necessity to stimulate demand on the part of government and industry has profound effects, even to the extent of creating "new needs" which operate similarly to the need for food or sex. "Most of the prevailing needs to relax, to have fun, to behave and consume in accordance with the advertisements, to love and hate what others love and hate, belong to this category of false needs. Such needs have a societal content and function which are determined by external powers over which the individual has no control."[13] In such a situation, in which the consumerist propaganda is so powerful and efficient, the lower classes, though without power and real wealth, are unable to distinguish themselves as a class with interests different from and opposed to those of the ruling class.

The internalization of these new needs tends to hide social class distinctions, and in this way foster the myth of equality. For if "the worker and his boss enjoy the same television program and visit the same resort places, if the typist appears to be as attractively made-up as the daughter of her employer, if the Negro owns a Cadillac, if they all read the same newspaper, then this assimilation indicates not the disappearance of classes, but the extent to which the needs and satisfactions that serve to perpetuate the Establishment are shared by the underlying population."[14]

Because government and the large corporations have essentially the same interests, there are no bodies equally as powerful to protect the consumers. It can be documented that higher labour costs are passed on in the form of higher prices. Levinson notes the following: "While collective economic power may be effective in raising the price of labor, the potentialities of redistribution out of profits are very slight so long as producers remain free to adjust their prices, techniques, and employment so as to protect their profit position."[15] Again, what we are defining as the interests of the lower classes – to equalize wealth and services – are directly opposed to those of the ruling class who seek to maintain the system as a whole and the rate of corporate profit and growth. The necessity on the part of both government and industry to stimulate demand, so as to prevent stagnation of the economic system, thus results in the creation of new needs in the population as a whole. Being unable to distinguish their new needs, the powerless take on themselves some of the outward trappings of the powerful. This prevents them from seeing the socio-economic system as it is: oriented primarily toward the long-term interests of the upper class. It obscures the fact that this class holds disproportionate amounts of wealth and thereby assures its continuance and removes any possibility of the equalization of wealth and services within this system. For as Kolko notes: "Most low income groups live substantially better today, but even though their real wages have mounted, their percentage of the national income has not changed."[16]

To put it another way: "The pleasure of eating an ice cream

cone may be minor compared to the pleasure of meaningful, autonomous work, but the former is easily available and the latter is not. A poor family would undoubtedly rather have a decent apartment than a new TV, but since they are unlikely to get the apartment, what is to be gained by not getting the TV?"[17]

One of the reasons this system has remained unchallenged lies in the nature and dominant philosophy of the American labour unions. Unlike in Europe and elsewhere, the main focus of the leadership has seldom been that of serving the long-term needs of the working class, but has been directed towards preserving economic stability and hence the class structure. In recent years the union has become almost indistinguishable in its own eyes from the corporation. Unions and corporations can be seen lobbying together for bigger missile contracts and trying to get other defense industries into the area. Sometimes they appear before Congress and jointly ask that missiles instead of bombers should be built or bombs instead of missiles, depending on what contract they happen to hold. Such "demands" are perfectly suited to upholding the system as it is. Some large unions even pay their permanent staff six-figure salaries to emphasize their equality of stature with the heads of the large corporations. It should be added that large segments of labour, especially in marginal economic areas, remain unorganized, thereby being without any protection outside of very minimal government regulations.[18]

The impotence of the lower classes derives from their inability to distinguish between myth and reality (which is totally comprehensible in light of the power of the media and advertisements). As long as organized workers continue to build missiles and bombers, self-destructive automobiles, useless gadgetry and all the rest, rather than uniting to demand a change in government spending priorities, they will have inadequate housing, insufficient medical care, polluted air, poor schools, etc. For the priorities of production are not based on the needs of the society as a whole, but rather upon maintaining economic growth and the profit margin.[19] Hence, class inequality persists, in terms of material possessions but more important, in terms of disease and death rates, life span, nutrition, emotional tensions, educational facilities and opportunities for self-satisfaction. The consequences are everywhere visible: "with commodities being priced not according to their costs of production but to yield the maximum possible profit, the principle quid pro quo turns into the opposite of a promoter of rational economic organization and instead becomes a formula for maintaining scarcity in the midst of potential plenty."[20] For only under monopoly capitalism does over-production appear as a constant threat to the continued operation of the system. Thus, in American cities abject poverty is found only minutes away from opulence and luxury, when there need be no poverty at all.

There is of course another option – another way to organize an economy – but this would end the hegemony and privileges of the American ruling class. A prominent New York banker describes this other alternative, with distaste, for he recognizes that it is completely incompatible with the present system of inequality and consumerism:

> Clothing would be purchased for its utility value; food would be bought on the basis of economy and nutritional value; automobiles would be stripped to essentials and held by the same owners for the full ten to fifteen years of their useful lives; homes would be built and maintained for their characteristics of shelter, without regard to style or neighborhood. And what would happen to a market dependent upon new models, new styles, new ideas?[21]

The whole system would have to collapse. . . .

A second way in which the American ruling class provides for the necessary absorption of surplus is through the production of higher levels and the greater quantities of weaponry. The "Cold War" provided the stimulus so that the military system that had been put together in World War II could be maintained and in time expanded.

Recent historians have shown that the Cold War did not just "happen" nor was it foisted on a peaceful and innocent U.S.A. by the evil Russians. Rather each side reciprocated with equal vigor.[22] The Americans *chose* to adopt a military posture toward the USSR after the war. The Truman Doctrine enunciated in 1948, was a major symbolic step in this direction.[23] The torpedoing of the disarmament talks of 1959-60 was another major step.[24] The Russians too promoted the Cold War. Nevertheless, the general American sentiment that eternal vigilance against a Soviet threat is all that is possible and always has been, is a Cold War mythology growing out of fears deliberately fostered by the ruling class among the American population.[25]

Because the ideological rationale behind the military defence of the Cold War was so powerful, it was only after 1968 and the introduction of the Anti-Ballistic Missile system that a sizeable opposition was heard. The result of this ideology predominating unquestioned for almost twenty years is the military-industrial complex. This complex is a growing sector within the ruling class. Retired Pentagon officials and top military brass are hired by companies seeking defense contracts. Over the past twenty-five years a powerful group of "security managers" has been created, linked to the propagation and continuance of the Cold War. This very closely knit group then makes decisions which fundamentally affect the populace at large. They veil them in arguments of technological necessity – we can make this, therefore we must[26] – add a few, at best questionable, statistics about the build-up of Russian and Chinese arms, and, with the arm twisting of the chairmen of the Congressional Armed Services Committees, the expenditures are passed, the money spent, and the weapons built. The complex is not military, the generals and admirals do not exert major power; rather it is a growing element of corporate power using weapons and military "needs" as its source of authority. "For businessmen and their political cohorts have defined the limits within which the military formulates strategy, extending their values and definitions of priorities over essentially docile generals."[27]

The contradictions of the system, the lengths to which it must go to keep "growing," are most evident and terrifying, in the reality behind its military posture and ideology. Marcuse poignantly asks,

Does not the threat of an atomic catastrophe which could wipe out the human race also serve to protect the very forces which perpetuate this danger? . . . If we attempt to relate the causes of the danger to the way in which society is organized and organizes its members, we are immediately confronted with the fact that advanced industrial society becomes richer, bigger, and better as it perpetuates the danger. . . . And yet this society is irrational as a whole. Its productivity is destructive of the free development of human needs and faculties, its peace maintained by the constant threat of war, its growth dependent on the repression of the real possibilities for pacifying the struggle for existence – individual, national and international.[28]

But a large, technologically advanced military is needed for another reason: to protect the great amount of investment in foreign countries from nationalization or Soviet or Chinese influence. For as Kolko says, "military power is the instrument American political leaders utilize to advance their enormous and ever-increasing objective, and that they require a vast Military Establishment is the logical, necessary effect . . . of the basic objectives and momentum of American foreign policy since 1943."[29]

A third way to absorb the surplus is foreign investment. This is especially important in understanding the colonial position of both Canada and Quebec vis-a-vis the United States. As the *U.S. News and World Report* tells us, "Businessmen increasingly are deciding that markets abroad . . . offer the biggest potential for future growth. The feeling grows that the U.S. market, while huge, is relatively 'saturated.' It is overseas that businessmen see the big, untapped market with hundreds of millions of customers wanting – and increasingly able to buy – all kinds of products and services."[30] Their survey reported: one, that foreign sales of American companies are growing much faster than sales of the same companies in this country; two, that profit rates abroad are generally higher than those in similar activities in the U.S.A.; and three, that foreign markets usually can best be tapped by an on-the-scene operation. A plant abroad can avoid tariff and other barriers erected against American exports.*

Baran and Sweezy conclude that between 1950 and 1963 American corporations were able to take in, as income, $12 billion more than they sent out as capital, while at the same

---

* This was true before the imposition, in the fall of 1971, of the Domestic International Sales Corporation (DISC) program by the Nixon administration. This program was designed to encourage investment within the U.S.A. It was one of several measures to stem the increasing American balance of payments deficits and to increase employment.

time expanding their foreign holdings (through reinvesting profits earned abroad, borrowing from foreign banks and investors, etc.) by $28.8 billion.[31]

Thus foreign investment is a most effective method for transferring surplus generated abroad to the investing country. The only mechanism to increase absorption of surplus is to stimulate demand in the foreign markets just as is done at home. This necessity to stimulate demand in the less developed countries, so as to reinforce American economic penetration was frankly asserted by the late President J. F. Kennedy: "Not enough attention has been paid to the part which an early exposure to American goods, skills and American ways of doing things can play in forming the tastes and desires of newly emerging countries."[32]

The above does not constitute a total explanation of American foreign policy. Obviously each of the many cases of American involvement abroad, whether military, economic, or whatever, requires investigation in its own right and in relation to the particular circumstances surrounding it. Nevertheless this much can be said: the workings of the economy of the United States and the need by the ruling class to perpetuate this system lies at the root of most of the fundamental policies of the United States toward other nations and of the spread of the attitudes underlying these policies. The manner in which these policies have evolved and the form they have taken in particular countries has been the result of several second-order factors, such as the race of the population of the country, its strategic importance, and its class structure. Such factors account for the difference between, say, a military form of American intervention in Viet Nam as compared to one limited basically to foreign investment and economic control in Quebec and Canada. At the root of both policies and their rationalizations lie the imperatives of monopoly capitalism at home in the U.S.A. In every significant case of American involvement abroad, the effect has been the same – to take the control of economic and social destiny out of the hands of the people in the "colonies" and place it in the hands of an elite which serves the interests of American corporations. This elite works jointly with American "advisors" whether corporate, political or military. This activity, which can only be called imperialism, has ensured the stability of monopoly capitalism at home both through maintaining a more or less constant level of employment and creating and bringing out when needed a paranoid, anti-communist, militarist psychology which threatens all non-conformity and treats the expression of class consciousness as subversion and treason. Its effect abroad, as we shall see, has been more varied and explosive.

Conclusion

In this chapter we have argued that the American economic system depends for its continued existence upon the continual expansion of existing markets and the creation of new ones to absorb the economic surplus of monopoly capitalist industry. The ruling class, whose power derives from its control of huge corporations, co-operates to increase demand and, thereby, maintain the system as a whole. To stimulate demand the ruling class depends heavily on the media of mass communication and the advertising industry. These powerful tools of persuasion implant in the population as a whole "new needs" which, when the system is successful, become indistinguishable from the individual's basic instinctual needs such as food and sex.

The result of the creation of these "new needs" is a society in which inequality becomes hidden. The lower strata of the population possess potential power and strength only through an awareness of their common position. However, when a proliferation of consumer goods superficially obscures their differences from the upper classes, and when their interest in equalizing wealth in the society is felt to be both unrealizable and un-American, the lower classes become impotent. They lack a consciousness of their own objective situation, finding it instead, falsely, in mass consumption.

To absorb the remainder of the ever-increasing economic surplus the American ruling class utilizes two other principal means. The first is the constant development and construction of technologically advanced weapons utilizing and exaggerating the military threat of the Soviet Union and China.[33] The second is foreign investment. In the less developed countries, where the American ruling class finds investment most profitable, similar mechanisms for stimulating demand and creating markets are used as in the United States.

Yet while the Americans have seldom failed to win the allegiance of a comprador class within these countries, they have nonetheless had to build their economic activities on a military basis – whether through the use of their own forces or through building up, training, indoctrinating, and equipping local military and police castes. Only in this way could the great majority of the population of the developing nations be "pacified" so that they too could enjoy the benefits of American economic control.

This lack of success in the third world heralded by the increasing success of the Vietnamese and the incredible proliferation of national liberation struggles around the world, can be attributed to several causes. Among these is the clear distinction which is evident to everyone between the national culture in these countries and the values and structures that result from Americanization.

It is hard to make a man with brown skin look like one with white, to make a man of a different, but deeply felt natural culture, "think American." In other words, in most of the less developed countries where there is a great deal of American intervention, the mass of the population is of a different race, nationality and culture than the foreign investors. Because the class lines so closely parallel these other divisions the creation of "new needs" does not conceal the inequality and class distinctions. The lower classes of the society become aware of their common position vis-a-vis the imperial power. This, we suggest, helps them come to understand their class relationship vis-a-vis their indigenous ruling class who serve the needs of American capital.

In the U.S.A. itself there is evidence of the formation of a new class, or "counter culture," whose composition transcends the old classes but whose consciousness of being apart from and opposed to the destructive consumerist culture of America has been steadily growing. While no real threat to the American ruling class in itself, this new class is important in that it is making common cause with the movements of National Liberation around the world against American-based imperialism. Yet it is in the colonies, where class realities are clearest, that the first line of the attack on international capital will be found.

This suggestion is one that we will explore, test, and utilize in the due course of the description and analysis of Quebec which we are about to begin.

Footnotes to Chapter 1

1. C. Wright Mills, *The Power Elite* (New York: Oxford University Press, 1956), p. 116. See also, G. W. Domhoff, *Who Rules America?* (Englewood Cliffs, N.J.: Prentice-Hall, 1967), p. 156.
2. Domhoff, *ibid.*, p. 5. Our description of the American upper class, its institutions, and the mechanisms by which it forms the nucleus of the ruling class owes much to this important work.
3. Ralf Dahrendorf, *Class and Class Conflict in Industrial Society* (Palo Alto: Stanford University Press, 1959), p. 47.
4. Domhoff, *op. cit.*, p. 148.
5. Paul Baran and Paul M. Sweezy, *Monopoly Capital* (New York: Monthly Review Press, 1966), p. 35.
6. Gabriel Kolko, *Wealth and Power in America* (New York: Praeger, 1962), p. 128.
7. See Baran and Sweezy, *op. cit.* Theirs is the best and fullest exposition of the workings of the present-day monopoly capitalist economy in the U.S.
8. On the actual techniques and their bases, see: J. H. Meyers and W. H. Reynolds, *Consumer Behavior and Marketing Management* (New York: Houghton Mifflin, 1967). On their effects, see: Giancarlo Buzzi, *Advertising: Its Cultural and Political Effects* (Minneapolis: University of Minnesota Press, 1968), and Perry London, *Behavior Control* (New York: Harper and Row, 1971).
9. To document this assertion, one may draw upon a truly immense body of literature. The following works are a mere sampling.
   1. Re: ADMINISTRATIVE AGENCIES:
   Hobart Rowen, *The Free Enterprisers: Kennedy, Johnson and the Business Establishment* (New York: Putnam's Sons, 1964); Theodore Lowi, *The End of Liberalism* (New York: Norton, 1969); Robert Sherrill, *Why They Call it Politics* (New York: Harcourt Brace Jovanovich, 1972); Clark Mollenhoff, *Washington Cover-up* (New York: Popular Library, 1962); Gary Greenberg, "Revolt at Justice," in Charles Peters and Timothy Adams (eds.), *Inside the System* (New York: Praeger, 1970); Blair Bolles, *How To Get Rich in Washington: Rich Man's Division of the Welfare State* (New York: Dell, 1952); Andrew Tully and Milton Britten, *Where Did Your Money Go?* (New York: Simon and Schuster, 1964); Barbara and John Ehrenreich, *The American Health Empire: Power, Profits, and Politics* (New York: Vintage Books, 1971); Martin & Susan Tolchin, *To the Victor . . .: Political*

Patronage from the Clubhouse to the Whitehouse (New York: Vintage Books, 1971); Ferdinand Lundberg, *The Rich and the Super-Rich: A Study in the Power of Money Today* (Toronto: Bantam, 1968); Grant McConnell, *Private Power & American Democracy* (New York: Knopf, 1966); Fred Krinsky, *Democracy and Complexity: Who Governs the Governors?* (Toronto: Collier-Macmillan, 1968); Jack Anderson and Carl Kalvelage, *American Government . . . Like It Is* (Morristown, N.J.: General Learning Press, 1972); William W. Boyer, *Bureaucracy on Trial: Policy Making by Government Agencies* (Indianapolis: Bobbs-Merrill, 1964); Phillip Stern, *The Great Treasury Raid* (New York: Signet, 1964); Marvin Gettleman & David Mermelstein (eds.), *The Great Society Reader: The Failure of American Liberalism* (New York: Vintage, 1967); Clark Holmes, "The Plot Against Law Reform," *Washington Monthly* (June, 1970); Andrew Hacker, "Liberal Democracy and Social Control," in Leonard Fein (ed.), *American Democracy: Essays on Image and Realities* (New York: Holt, Rinehart & Winston, 1964); William O. Douglas, "The Corps of Engineers: The Public be Damned," in Walt Anderson (ed.), *Politics and Environment* (Pacific Palisades, Calif.: Goodyear, 1970).

2. Re: INDEPENDENT REGULATORY AGENCIES:

Marver Bernstein, *Regulating Business by Independent Commission* (Princeton, N.J.: Princeton University Press, 1955); David Frier, *Conflict of Interest in the Eisenhower Administration* (Ames: Iowa State University Press, 1969); Samuel Krislov & Lloyd Muslof (eds.), *The Politics of Regulation* (Boston: Houghton Mifflin, 1964); Ernest Gruening, *The Public Pays, and Still Pays: A Study of Power Propaganda* (Toronto: Copp Clark, 1959); John C. Esposito & Larry Silverman (& the Ralph Nader Study Group on Air Pollution), *Vanishing Air* (New York: Grossman, 1970); Robert Fellmeth (& the Ralph Nader Study Group on the Interstate Commerce Commission and Transportation), *The Interstate Commerce Omission: The Public Interest and the ICC* (New York: Grossman, 1970); Louis Kohlmeier, Jr., *The Regulators: Watchdog Agencies and the Public Interest* (New York: Harper and Row, 1969).

3. Re: PRESIDENTIAL COMMISSIONS:

Phillip Meranto (ed.), *The Kerner Report Revisited* (Urbana: Institute of Government and Public Affairs, University of Illinois, June 1, 1970); Howard Shulman, "Behind the Scenes and Under the Rug: One Man's Presidential Commission," (National Commission on Urban Problems) in Peters & Adams (eds.), *op. cit.*

4. Re: CONGRESSIONAL COMMITTEES:
Ronald Steel, "The Congressional Check," in Henry Kariel (ed.), *The Political Order* (New York: Basic Books, 1970); Nick Datz, *Let Them Eat Promises: The Politics of Hunger in America* (Englewood Cliffs, N.J.: Prentice-Hall, 1969); Lee Metcalf & Vic Reinemer, *Overcharge* (New York: McKay, 1967); Drew Pearson & Jack Anderson, *The Case Against Congress* (New York: Simon & Schuster, 1968); Arthur Maass, "Congress and Water Resources," in Alan Altschuler (ed.), *Politics of the Federal Bureaucracy* (New York: Dodd, Mead, 1968).

10. *Op. cit.,* p. 149.

11. Herbert Marcuse, *One Dimensional Man* (Boston, Beacon, 1964), p. 9.

12. Ellen Willis, "Consumerism and Women," (Toronto: Hogtown Press, undated pamphlet), pp. 2-3.

13. Marcuse, *op. cit.,* p. 5.

14. *Ibid.,* p. 8.

15. Quoted in Baran and Sweezy, *op. cit.,* p. 78.

16. *Op. cit.,* p. 3.

17. Willis, *op. cit.,* p. 3.

18. Solomon Barkin, "The Decline of the Labor Movement," in Andrew Hacker (ed.), *The Corporation Takeover* (Garden City, N.Y.: Anchor, 1965).

19. Duane Lockard, *The Perverted Priorities of American Politics* (Riverside, N.J.: The Macmillan Co., 1971).

20. Baran and Sweezy, *op. cit.,* p. 337.

21. Quoted in *ibid.,* p. 124.

22. See, for instance, William A. Williams, *The Tragedy of American Diplomacy* (New York: Dell, 1959). A more recent and sophisticated "revisionist" historical analysis is Gabriel Kolko, *The Roots of American Foreign Policy* (Boston: Beacon, 1969).

23. See Richard Barnet, *Intervention & Revolution* (Cleveland: World, 1968), pp. 116-21.

24. Fred Cook, *The Warfare State* (New York: Collier, 1964). The relatively friendly Khruschev visit to Camp David caused a 1959 "peace jitters" downturn in the stock market larger than any in almost four years. In 1960, when the Paris Summit was spoiled by the U-2 incident, Cook noted, the financial page of the *New York Times* headlined: "Summit Failure a Market Tonic", p. 181. The 1972 Peking and Moscow Summit meetings had no such effect; investors' attitudes had changed. One explanation: Vietnam. "That there are shrewd businessmen who recognize that at times one must cut one's

losses should hardly come as a surprise. The surprise is that it has taken them so long to awaken to the reality of a lost war and its social and economic consequences". Harry Magdoff, "The Logic of Imperialism," *Social Policy* (September/October, 1970), p. 21.

25. Edward Herman and Richard Du Boff, *America's Vietnam Policy: The Strategy of Deception* (Wash., D.C.: Public Affairs Press, 1966); Clark Mollenhoff, *The Pentagon: Politics, Profits & Plunder* (New York: Putnam's Sons, 1967); J. W. Fulbright, *The Pentagon Propaganda Machine* (New York: Knopf, 1971); and Nathan Miller, "The Making of a Majority; Safeguard and the Senate," in Peters and Adams, *op. cit.*

26. "Our future planning is based on long-term contracts. One must believe in the Long Term Threat," (James Ling, Director of LTV) quoted, along with other munitions supply executives in Bernard Nossitter, "Arms Firms See Postwar Spurt," *Washington Post* (December 8, 1968), p. 16. See also John McDermott, "Technology: The Opiate of the Intellectuals," *New York Review of Books* (July 31, 1969), and Nigel Calder, "So Technically Sweet," in his *Technopolis: Social Control of the Uses of Science* (London: Panther Books, 1970), Part 1.

27. Gabriel Kolko, *The Roots of American Foreign Policy* (Beacon Press, 1969), p. xiii. See also: George W. Brown, *Generals and the Public: Recent Policymaking in Civil-Military Relations* (Lawrence: University of Kansas Governmental Research Series, No. 29, 1964); and, for an example of rebellion on the part of the military, see Robert J. Art, *The TFX Decision: McNamara and the Military* (Boston: Little, Brown, 1968). Various articles in David Horowitz (ed.), *Corporations and the Cold War* (New York: Monthly Review Press, 1969) constitute probably the most thorough analysis to date of this phenomenon.

28. Marcuse, *op. cit.*, p. ix.

29. Kolko, *The Roots of American Foreign Policy, op. cit.*, p. 27.

30. Quoted in Baran and Sweezy, *op. cit.*, p. 198. For a very interesting argument that U.S. capitalists are looking less and less toward the Third World and more and more toward the relatively developed countries (but not the most highly developed countries – with which the U.S. now must compete), see S. M. Miller, Roy Bennett and Cyril Alapatt, "Does the U.S. Economy Require Imperialism?", *Social Policy* (September/October, 1970). The significance of this argument for Quebec seems obvious, yet the authors inexplicably decline use of the term "imperialism", as is ably pointed out in Harry Magdoff's fine rebuttal in the same issue.

29

31. Baran and Sweezy further note that: "In interpreting these figures – which it should be remembered do not include management fees, royalties, and various forms of hidden remittances – it is important to bear in mind that according to the same sources total direct foreign investment expanded from $11.8 billion in 1950 to $40.6 billion in 1963, an increase of $28.8 billion." *Op. cit.,* p. 107. By 1968 the figure had increased to $64.8 billion, up $24.2 billion in five years. Source: *Survey of Current Business* (October, 1969), p. 28.

32. Quoted in Ian Lumsden's article, "Imperialism and Canadian Intellectuals," in Lumsden (ed.), *Close the 49th Parallel, etc.: The Americanization of Canada* (Toronto: University of Toronto Press, 1969), p. 324.

33. See, for instance Richard Barnet, *The Economy of Death* (New York: Atheneum, 1969).

CHAPTER 2

QUEBEC:
AN
ECONOMIC
SATELLITE

From the mother country to the colony. Quebec, like the
U.S.A., can be described as monopoly capitalist, though not in
nearly so "advanced" a stage as its powerful neighbor; its
economy too is controlled by large corporations. However,
these corporations are not owned by an indigenous class as they
are in the United States. Just the contrary, the Quebec economy
is externally controlled; its industry and commerce controlled
by Anglo Canadians and Americans. We use the word "external" to refer to English-Canadian capitalists as well because in
relation to Quebec society that is fundamentally what they are.
Those who happen to reside within Quebec's provincial boundaries, and this number is decreasing, have built for themselves
English-language enclaves almost completely isolated from
Quebec society – its traditions, language, culture, and aspirations.

Below the reader will find facts and statistics demonstrating
the reality of foreign control. Following, there is an analysis of
Quebec's underdevelopment using Ontario for purposes of
comparison; for, while Ontario or Canada may be regarded as
economically colonized in relation to the U.S.A., Quebec is
doubly colonized, by the U.S.A. and by English Canada. The
economic development of Quebec which began in earnest at
the end of the last century is a classic example of the colonial
pattern. Based almost totally on foreign capital and entrepreneurship, key aspects of Quebec's economy such as labour
use, wage scales, technological capacity, resource development,

and market distribution were organized not to be independent or competitive, but rather complementary to the Canadian and American economies, to serve the interests of the Anglo-American ruling classes rather than the needs of its own people.

Eighty percent of Quebec is French speaking, and yet Anglophones control the economy. Within the entire Canadian economic elite, as defined by Porter, only 51 (6.7 percent) are Francophones,[1] although the latter compose almost one-third of the country's population. Looking at business establishments in Quebec, the Royal Commission on Bilingualism and Biculturalism reported that 47 percent of the province's labour force is employed by Francophones; 24 percent of this is in agriculture and service industries. Anglophone Canadian establishments employed 37.7 percent of the work force with foreign interests employing the remaining 15 percent.[2]

Table 2-1 describes the size of corporations owned by

TABLE 2-1

Size of establishments owned by Francophone Canadians, Anglophone Canadians, and foreign interests in selected industrial sectors, measured by numbers employed — Quebec, 1961.

	Employees	Percentage of labour force in establishments owned by			
	Number (thousands)	Franco-phone Canadians	Anglo-phone Canadians	Foreign interests	Total
Agriculture	131.2	91.3	8.7	0.0	100
Mining	25.9	6.5	53.1	40.4	100
Manufacturing	468.3	21.8	46.9	31.3	100
Construction	126.4	50.7	35.2	14.1	100
Transportation and communications	102.4	37.5	49.4	13.1	100
Wholesale trade	69.3	34.1	47.2	18.7	100
Retail trade	178.7	56.7	35.8	7.5	100
Finance	62.2	25.8	53.1	21.1	100
Services	350.9	71.4	28.6	0.0	100
All industries[1]	1,515.3	47.3	37.7	15.0	100

Source: Raynauld, "La propriété des entreprises au Québec."
From the *Report of the Royal Commission on Bilingualism and Biculturalism,* Vol. 3, p. 54.
[1] Excludes forestry, fishing and trapping, the public sector, and unspecified industries.

Francophone Canadians, Anglophone Canadians and foreign interests in selected industrial sectors, as measured by the numbers employed. "Roughly half of the labour force working for Francophone Canadian interests (24 percent of the total Quebec labour force) was concentrated in agriculture and service industries."[3] We shall further note the fragility of the industrial sectors in which French-Canadian enterprises do employ a large percentage of the work force. Francophone Canadian establishments are concentrated in industrial sectors which pay the lowest wages, and which essentially produce for a local market, being responsible for only 5 percent of total sales outside the province. They are smaller in terms of the number of employees than either the Anglo-Canadian, or the American firms; their workers are less productive than those in the foreign-owned establishments, and their methods and machinery are less technologically advanced.[4]

The largest industrial sector by far is that of manufacturing which accounts for 27 percent of the total labour force. Francophone Canadian manufacturers employed only 22 percent of those working in this sector; and these firms accounted for only 15 percent of the total value added* by manufacturing industries in Quebec. (See Table 2-2.) These figures become particularly relevant when it is noted that Anglophone Canadian firms employ 47 percent of the labour force and yet produce 43 percent of the total value added. Foreign controlled firms employed only 31 percent of the labour force and yet they produced 42 percent of the value added.[5] The recent "leaked" Gray Report on foreign ownership provides additional, up to date and even starker figures. For instance, 60.3 percent of taxable income earned by companies in manufacturing in Quebec from 1965 to 1968, went to predominantly foreign-owned corporations.[6]

It is important to again emphasize the different sorts of products produced by establishments under the control of Francophone or Anglo-Canadian, or foreign interests.

---

* "Industrial output is measured by the statistical concept of 'value added'. This is the value of the produced goods less the cost of energy and raw materials: it represents the transformation wrought by an establishment upon the products or material it produces." *Report of the Royal Commission on Bilingualism and Biculturalism*, volume 3, p. 53.

TABLE 2-2

Size of manufacturing establishments owned by Francophone Canadians, Anglophone Canadians, and foreign interests, measured by value added — Quebec, 1961.

	Percentage of total value added in establishments owned by			
	Francophone Canadians	Anglophone Canadians	Foreign interests	Total
Food	30.9	32.0	38.1	100
Beverage	4.7	64.9	30.4	100
Tobacco products	0.9	31.2	67.9	100
Rubber	8.0	37.5	54.5	100
Leather	49.4	46.3	4.3	100
Textile	2.1	68.3	29.6	100
Knitting mills	24.7	53.2	22.1	100
Clothing	8.2	88.6	3.2	100
Wood	84.0	13.2	2.8	100
Furniture and fixtures	39.4	53.6	7.0	100
Paper	4.8	53.3	41.9	100
Paper products	22.0	41.2	33.8	100
Printing and publishing	28.2	65.7	6.1	100
Iron and steel	11.7	28.9	59.4	100
Non-ferrous metals	3.7	11.6	84.7	100
Metal fabricating	23.7	35.9	40.4	100
Machinery	18.3	17.0	64.7	100
Transportation equipment	6.4	14.4	79.2	100
Electrical products	6.6	58.0	35.4	100
Non-metallic mineral products	14.8	51.2	34.0	100
Petroleum and coal products	0.0	0.0	100.0	100
Chemical and medical products	6.5	16.4	77.1	100
Precision instruments	4.6	23.5	71.9	100
Miscellaneous	24.5	41.3	34.2	100
All industries	15.4	42.8	41.8	100

Source: André Raynauld, "La Propriété des Entreprises au Québec," from the *Report of the Royal Commission on Bilingualism and Biculturalism*, volume 3, p. 56.

There are, as we see, only two sectors, wood and leather, in which 50 percent or more of the value added by the enterprises is controlled by Francophone Canadians. On the other hand, "there were nine sectors – including the clothing, textile, printing and publishing, and beverage industries – in which Anglophone Canadian interests accounted for 50 percent or more of the industrial output. In another nine – including the industries manufacturing petroleum products, non-ferrous metals, transportation equipment, and chemical products – the foreign interests had a comparable representation."[7]

Foreign controlled establishments are essentially heavy industries, depending upon export markets for sales, while the Francophone and to a lesser extent the Anglophone Canadian firms are dependent upon high levels of domestic consumption. The latter two are, therefore, more affected by phenomena such as unemployment, inflation, and the monetary policies of the Canadian government. Furthermore, the types of manufacturing firms that are owned by French-Canadians, a good example are many small and medium sized shoe factories, make up the most static and slow-developing industrial segment. They are tied to a limited market and unchanging economic structure. It is in the area of heavy industry, in producers goods, as well as the more complex and expensive consumer goods such as electric appliances, that one can reasonably expect economic growth through industrial expansion and technological development. And it is these very sectors that are now predominantly outside Quebec's control. What this means is simply that under the present system Quebec's economic future lies in foreign hands.

Looking at Table 2-3 we note that foreign controlled industries export more than 50 percent of the total product exported in the sectors of tobacco, rubber, primary metals, metal products, machinery, transportation materials, non-metallic mineral products, and chemical products. In no manufacturing sector do enterprises under French-Canadian control export more than 50 percent of the total product exported. English-Canadian controlled firms handled more than 50 percent of the exports of textiles, hosiery, clothing, furniture, paper, printing and publishing, and electrical appliances.

In all, Francophone manufacturing firms sold 22 percent of their output outside of Quebec, Anglophone firms sold 49 percent, and foreign owned firms 60 percent of their production outside Quebec.[8] Again the absence of French-Canadian control over the economy of Quebec is evident. Anglophone Cana-

35

TABLE 2-3

Exports from firms controlled by Francophone Canadians, Anglophone Canadians, and foreigners, as a percentage of the total exports in each manufacturing sector.

Exports	Francophone Canadians		Anglophone Canadians		Foreigners	
	to other provinces	to other countries	to other provinces	to other countries	to other provinces	to other countries
Food and beverage	4.67	5.67	30.22	74.30	65.11	20.02
Tobacco	0	0	30.37	16.13	69.63	83.87
Rubber	2.50	9.40	37.30	32.82	60.20	57.77
Leather	44.38	40.83	49.65	25.51	5.97	33.66
Textiles	1.06	0.36	78.50	80.71	20.44	18.93
Hosiery	14.17	0.32	68.38	99.36	17.45	0.32
Clothing	6.05	3.91	91.41	88.88	2.54	7.21
Wood	62.36	29.88	30.64	60.06	7.00	10.07
Furniture	30.04	6.85	62.30	79.81	7.66	13.34
Paper	3.36	2.45	53.60	67.19	43.04	30.36
Printing & Publishing	21.27	0	64.27	100.00	14.46	0
Primary Metal Industry	1.35	0.07	41.24	41.78	57.41	58.15
Metal products	6.39	1.91	43.22	48.85	50.40	49.24
Machinery	7.61	2.85	12.48	5.73	79.91	91.42
Transportation equip.	5.61	1.85	13.58	0.70	80.81	97.44
Electrical Appliances	2.08	1.03	57.98	14.62	39.94	84.35
Non-metallic mineral products	0.78	0	52.98	5.12	46.24	94.88
Petroleum & oil	0	0	0	0	100.00	100.00
Chemical products	1.21	0.09	13.68	5.44	85.11	94.46
Diverse industries	9.88	28.77	29.52	11.58	60.60	59.66
Total exports of all manufacturing industries	5.58	2.27	42.20	47.48	52.22	50.25

Source: André Raynauld, "La Propriété des Entreprises du Québec," study done for the *Royal Commission on Bilingualism and Biculturalism*, p. 175.

dians and foreign interests use Quebec's raw materials, and its labour, which is cheaper than in most other parts of North America, to produce for markets outside the province.

André d'Allemagne aptly describes the situation and its effects. Quebec's economy is characterized by:

a strong concentration on primary industry which results in Quebec exporting raw materials and importing manufactured products which often could have been produced within Quebec.

the exploitation of different economic sectors according to foreign priorities without concern for the collective interests of the population. This leads to a strong concentration in some sectors and a profound disequilibrium in the growth of the different economic sectors.

the rating of regions based upon their immediate profitability to foreign capital, which results in a strong regional concentration of industry and a serious disequilibrium in the evolution of different regions of the country.

a strong preoccupation with profits arising from the exploitation of the nation's resources which are mostly exported to foreign countries where they are even sometimes used in the processing of goods competitive with those from Quebec.

a general dependence upon external policies and decisions which determine the evolution of the Quebec economy.[9]

It is not only who owns the products exported but also the actual products which are exported and imported that indicate the great degree of foreign control over Quebec's natural resources and heavy industry. Table 2-3 further informs us that Quebec exports to the United States the products from its most productive industries (paper, aluminum, refined metals, etc.). It exports to English Canada essentially simple goods of mass consumption; these industries are only poorly accommodated to such a small market. Hence, their productivity is weak and on the decline for they require mass production to prosper.[10] Quebec imports from Ontario goods from the very highly protected industries such as household and other electrical appliances of all kinds, automobiles, rugs, etc., for which it pays dearly.

It is not only foreign ownership of crucial industries, but also the Canadian tariff structures which retards the development of the Quebec economy. From the situation described above, Rodrigue Tremblay concludes that the citizens of Quebec are essentially subsidizing the highly protected industries of Ontario. Ontario accounts for 68 percent of the most highly protected Canadian industries, Quebec has 24 percent, while 9 percent are divided equally between the two.[11] Tremblay concludes: "we can sum up . . . by saying that the Canadian tariff structure functions basically to the advantage of Ontario, also that these tariffs even diminish exports from Quebec and in addition squeeze many Quebec enterprises into a market too narrow for efficient production."[12]

Industries engaged in manufacturing break down into three more or less distinct types: (1) industries tied to the extraction of natural resources – pulp and paper, primary metals, etc. – the primary sector; (2) light secondary industry characterized by being labour intensive, paying low salaries, and using little modern technology. It includes food, beverages, textiles, leather, clothing, tobacco, etc.; (3) heavy secondary industry which pays relatively high wages, and utilizes advanced technology. This group includes chemical products, metal products, products derived from petroleum, transportation equipment, electrical apparatus, machinery, etc.

Since 1935, the industrial evolution of Quebec has been characterized by a rapid development of the industries related to natural resources, the primary sector. In 1961, 41 percent of the production of this sector was exported. Light and heavy secondary industry are directed toward the Canadian markets, while primary industry finds markets usually in the United States.[13]

Looking at Table 2-4 we see that after the food industry the second and third largest manufacturing industries in Quebec (as measured by total value of production) are those of pulp and paper and primary metals. Both of these industries export most of their products to the United States, further depriving Quebec of natural resources or the potential for development. It is these natural resources that represent Quebec's bargaining power for bringing in foreign capital and goods. This bargaining power increases in value if the materials are processed within the province before being exported and sold. Industry concentrated on the extraction of raw materials rather than on the processing of finished goods (as is found in Quebec and Canada) is capital rather than labour intensive; there are fewer jobs, and the preoccupations and concerns of the industry are remote from the needs of the people in the region in which it is located.

TABLE 2-4

The five largest manufacturing industries in Quebec (as measured by the total value of production) and the destination of the products. 1966.

	Total Production (in millions of dollars)	Market
1. food & beverage	1,895	Quebec (76.5%)
2. pulp & paper & connected industries	1,132	U.S. (54.0%)
3. primary metals	848	U.S. (43.9%)
4. clothing	739	Canada (56.1%)
5. textiles	731	Canada (38.3%)

Source: Rodrigue Tremblay, *Indépendance et Marché Commun Québec-Etats-Unis* (Montreal: Editions du Jour, 1970), p. 41, p. 42.

Taking the pulp and paper industry as an example, we can begin to understand the effects of an industry being controlled by foreigners (English Canadians and Americans) and being oriented to a foreign market. Between 1956 and 1966 the pulp and paper mills in Quebec did not increase their total production while that of the Western countries increased by 41 percent. This discrepancy can be explained in part by the fact that the production procedures and the methods of lumbering of these foreign interests did not aim at conserving the forest, maintaining the balance of nature, etc., thereby reducing the ratio of raw materials to finished product.[14] André d'Allemagne concludes: "Quebec's forests are thus exploited or more exactly pillaged by foreigners without consideration for national interests and in a manner which assures neither the full yield nor the continued existence of this nationally vital natural resource."[15]

A particularly fine example of the ravage of Quebec's forests by foreign-owned firms in the pulp and paper industry has very recently come to light. A short digression on the facts of this case – the I.T.T.-Rayonier project[16] – is merited at this point as an illustration of just exactly what is meant by "resource development" in the context of a foreign dominated monopoly capitalist economy. The I.T.T.-Rayonier case may be more dramatic but the basic pattern is repeated again and again by other corporations in primary industry.

I.T.T.-Rayonier is a wholly owned subsidiary of I.T.T. (International Telegraph and Telecommunications) now the eighth largest American company. A true conglomerate, it controls Sheraton Hotels, Wonder Bread, Hartford Insurance, and many other varied corporations around the world. With a yearly revenue larger than that of Quebec or many countries, I.T.T. has itself intervened in the internal political affairs of different nations. It was revealed for instance that its Puerto-Rican operations (which run the local telephone company) maintained complete files on every member of Puerto Rico's national assembly. In April, 1972 Washington syndicated columnist Jack Anderson exposed I.T.T.'s even more spectacular involvement with an attempt to overthrow the Allende government in Chile.

Recently the Bourassa government leased to I.T.T.-Rayonier forested land on Quebec's North Shore four times the size of New Brunswick so that it could produce cellulose acetate, a rather unfinished pulpwood product, to sell to its European subsidiaries. The governments (provincial and federal) have put up one quarter of the 160 million dollar initial investment in interest-free loans; and millions more in services and allowances have been promised by the Bourassa government making it a particularly lucrative deal for I.T.T. The company is expected, by conservative estimates, to gain a full return on its investment within eight years of operation giving it another seventy-two years on its lease to deplete Quebec's forests and send its profits out of Quebec to its American owners. Aside from less than two thousand jobs and a few million in taxes, the people of Quebec gain nothing in compensation.[16] The processing and usage of the cellulose acetate will probably create somewhere around ten thousand jobs in secondary manufacturing – not in Quebec but in Europe and the United States. Meanwhile the people of Quebec continue to be deprived of the opportunity to develop the resources of their province for their own benefit. (This is not to mention the part I.T.T., based on its past record, is likely to play in any future political initiatives among the people of Quebec toward their liberation.)

The next largest manufacturing enterprise in Quebec is that of mining or the industry of primary metals. Twenty-five of the fifty largest mining companies in Quebec have their headquarters in Toronto, while nine others are controlled from outside of Canada. Only six of the mining enterprises are controlled by Francophones, and these are not among the largest nor the most profitable.[17] Again, natural resources are exploited and exported and Quebec's potential for development is diminished.[18] The fourth and fifth largest manufacturing industries are clothing and textiles and they serve a predominantly English-Canadian market. In chapter 4, when we analyse the relationship of a satellitic economy to that of a metropolis, the significance of these factors as highlighted in the descriptions of both the pulp and paper industry and the mining industry will be made clear and set into a larger context.

In this section we have attempted to demonstrate the satellitic nature of the Quebec economy. The two largest manufacturing industries in the province outside of the food industry are primarily controlled by foreigners and have always been so. Both of these industries depend upon the extraction of certain of Quebec's natural resources which they then export to the U.S.A. The areas of the economy which are expanding and prospering are controlled by non-Francophones. These industries are usually capital intensive, paying relatively high wages, and using modern technology. As early as 1938, Stuart Jamieson described much the same phenomenon: "the English-speaking group, owners and directors as well as gainfully employed, predominate in highly specialized and corporate-controlled industries requiring heavy investments of capital and depending on a wide market."[19]

Firms owned by Francophones display opposite characteristics: they are found in sectors of the economy which are in decline; they are labour intensive, pay low wages, and are less productive than the foreign owned firms. Again the situation was much the same in the late thirties: "French-Canadian companies produce for a local market . . . the majority of the plants are small in capital investment and labour force."[20]

At the beginning of this chapter it was suggested that the Quebec economy does not respond to the needs of the population partially because few of its people have any significant influence over the economy. This is not to suggest that if the

French-Canadian elite were to become the most powerful element in the society, a fundamental change in the economic relationships would occur. As noted in chapter one, the United States is blessed with an indigenous ruling class and yet its economy operates primarily in the interests of this class rather than the population as a whole. There is inequality in both societies the roots of which can be found in the same "multinational" system of monopoly capitalism. Nevertheless the relative under-development of Quebec to the U.S.A., or even to Ontario as we shall see in the next section, attests to the fact that the foreign element of economic control in Quebec is significant.

The standard of living generally in Quebec is 25 percent lower than the Canadian mean, and 50 percent lower than the American mean.[21] For the period 1926 to 1958 the average personal per-capita revenue for Quebec was 72.49 percent that of Ontario. For the period 1935 to 1948 the average personal revenue per worker in Quebec was 80.18 percent that in Ontario. The difference between these two figures (72.49 and 80.18 percent) is accounted for by the fact that the working population is 36.41 percent of the total population in Quebec, but 41.30 percent in Ontario.[22] High unemployment in Quebec is a factor here. Further, the year by year statistics lead Raynauld to suggest an increase in the discrepancies in average revenue between the two provinces.[23] Since 1926 Quebec's condition in comparison to Ontario has deteriorated.

These facts are especially discomforting when we consider that the growth rate of industrial production for the years 1935 to 1955 is actually greater in Quebec than in Ontario.[24] After the war, however, the Quebec economy began to slow down. In the years 1947 to 1957, the growth rate for Quebec is 0.8 percent lower than that of Ontario, the actual figures are as follows: Canada, 8.6 percent; Quebec, 8.3 percent; and Ontario, 9.1 percent.[25] By the early fifties the rapid expansion of the earlier period seems to have subsided and the growth rate of the Quebec economy fell behind both the Ontario and Canadian averages. Nevertheless, on the whole Quebec's rate of economic growth has been reasonably healthy. The causes of the low revenue of its people lie elsewhere.

The disparties between the mean personal revenue in Ontario and Quebec are also not accounted for by the distribution of the labour force in primary, secondary, and tertiary industry. The percentage of the labour force in each sector has historically been almost the same in both provinces.[26] Only now Quebec shows signs of falling behind in this area as well. The Castonguay-Nepveu Commission found that in 1967 the figures were the following: Primary sector, Ontario – 7.5% of its labour force, Quebec – 8.4%; Secondary, Ontario – 36.6%, Quebec – 30.3%; Tertiary, Ontario – 55.8%, Quebec – 61.3%.[27] It is interesting to note the lack of importance of agriculture in Quebec as compared to other provinces. In Ontario, agriculture accounts for 7.4 percent of total production while in Quebec it accounts for 6.3 percent.[28] The unimportance of agriculture in Quebec is partially explained by its lack of profitability to the individual farmer. Between 1950 and 1965, the price of farm products increased by 5 percent, but the costs of production increased by 40 percent. This means that even if the farmer had augmented his gross revenue by

TABLE 2-5

Personal per capita income in Quebec as a percentage of that in Ontario 1926 to 1958.

1926	74.07	1943	67.65
1927	73.91	1944	66.93
1928	74.57	1945	66.73
1929	74.73	1946	70.64
1930	74.28	1947	72.97
1931	74.27	1948	72.87
1932	74.72	1949	70.44
1933	72.99	1950	70.72
1934	72.77	1951	70.03
1935	71.42	1952	70.56
1936	73.28	1953	71.76
1937	72.14	1954	73.23
1938	71.27	1955	71.34
1939	71.18	1956	72.08
1940	68.19	1957	72.49
1941	67.02	1958	72.58
1942	67.62		

Source: A. Raynauld, *Croissance et Structures Economique de la Province du Québec* (Québec: Ministrée de L'Industrie et Commerce, 1962).

increasing the volume of production, his net revenue did not increase. The result was that Quebec, in 1965, imported three times more foodstuffs from Ontario than it exported to Ontario.[29]

TABLE 2-6

Hourly wages in the manufacturing industries in Quebec as a percentage of those in Ontario, 1938 to 1957.

1938	79.82	1954	86.08
1939	80.56	1955	85.47
1941	84.29	1956	85.33
1942	84.71	1957	85.29
1943	87.36		
1944	87.48		
1945	89.90		
1946	89.19	NOTE: For the years 1938 to 1944,
1947	86.34	only male and female wage earners
1948	86.43	were counted. Comparable figures
1949	86.64	for 1940 are not available.
1950	84.91		
1951	84.47		
1952	84.30		
1953	85.00		

Source: A. Raynauld, *Croissance et Structures Economique de la Province de Québec, ibid.,* p. 59.

It can be seen from Table 2-9 that while heavy industry – iron and steel products, transportation equipment – became by far the most important of Ontario's manufacturing industries by 1955, this sector ranked fifth in importance in Quebec, accounting for only 12.59 percent of total manufacturing. Tables 2-10 and 2-11 demonstrate that it was in these sectors and others such as electrical equipment that Quebec's development fell even further behind that of Ontario in the years 1947-1963. What seems to be happening is that the industries which are most important in the Quebec economy are expanding slowly, while the industries which are most important to the Ontario economy are expanding rapidly. Those industries which grow more rapidly in Quebec have comparatively little impact on the performance of the Quebec economy as a whole.

This is summed up rather graphically in Table 2-11 which

speaks for itself. The Castonguay-Nepveu report points to what this means in terms of the availability of work for the people of Quebec: "Between 1961 and 1965, employment in the manufacturing industry in Canada registered a variation of 15.5 percent; in Quebec the variation was only 9.3 percent, while Ontario was clearly ahead with an increase of 21 percent."[30] As the CNTU document "Ne Comptons Que Sur Nos Propres Moyens" points out, if Quebec had experienced the Ontario rate of growth rather than its own, 51,350 more jobs would have been created in that period. "If we admit that the manufacturing structure has stayed approximately the same between 1965 and 1970, (actually it has probably deteriorated in Quebec and improved in Ontario) there would have been another 50,000 jobs created for Quebec. Thus, over a period of ten years it would have been necessary to create at least 100,000

TABLE 2-7

Growth rate of industrial production in Canada and the Provinces 1947 to 1957.

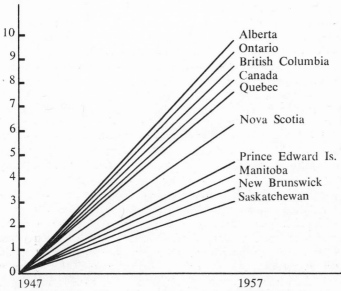

Source: André Raynauld, *Croissance et Structures Economique de la Province de Québec, ibid.,* p. 70.

TABLE 2-8

The relative importance of different economic sectors in Quebec, Ontario, and Canada, 1935 and 1955.

	Quebec 1935	Quebec 1955	Ontario 1935	Ontario 1955	Canada 1935	Canada 1955
	(percent)		(percent)		(percent)	
Agriculture	12.4	6.3	13.5	7.4	25.3	16.5
Forests	3.8	5.2	1.5	1.9	2.6	4.3
Fishing and trapping	0.5	0.1	0.4	0.2	1.1	0.7
Mineral industries	3.6	6.2	9.0	4.0	7.1	6.9
Electricity	8.0	3.8	5.2	3.3	5.1	3.2
Manufacturing	57.5	62.8	58.7	68.2	45.8	51.9
Construction	14.2	15.6	11.7	14.9	12.5	16.4

Source: André Raynauld, *Croissance et Structures Economiques de la Province de Québec,* p. 71.

more new jobs, *not just in total, but in the manufacturing sector alone.*"[31]

Quebec's record of economic growth is thus misleading. First, as we saw, the above average rate of economic growth that characterized Quebec in the thirties and forties, was replaced in the fifties by a growing deceleration of the expansion of Quebec's economy when compared to Ontario or Canada as a whole. Moreover, the actual growth that did occur was too often in those economic sectors least beneficial to long-term development and to increased and better-paid employment. In these sectors, such as heavy industry and the production of technologically advanced consumer goods, external influences have held back Quebec's economy from the beginning and continue to do so. This is the most fundamental cause of the perceptively lower revenue of its people, and of its comparative underdevelopment which we shall discuss in the chapters to follow. Some prefer to call it foreign control; we, along with many people in Quebec, call it colonialism.

Doubly colonized, Quebec's economic disadvantage when compared to Ontario is starkly and unmistakably evident. Because Quebec was developed by outside forces to fit outside interests it has become a society whose major industries are tied to resource extraction – mining, pulp and paper, etc. The entire economy was built around the requirements of these industries and their foreign owners. Hence significantly lower wages and higher unemployment than in Ontario and even Canada as a whole have resulted.

The higher standard of living of the people of Ontario, where the economy has benefited from its relationship to Quebec and other areas in the Canadian hinterland, and from comparatively greater autonomy,* stands as a constant re-

TABLE 2-9

Relative importance of manufacturing industries in Quebec and Ontario, 1935 and 1955 (in percentage).

	1935		1955	
	Quebec	Ontario	Quebec	Ontario
Food & beverage	20.40	22.61	16.03	15.12
Tobacco & tobacco products, rubber products, leather products	9.28	7.11	5.35	4.79
Textiles & clothing	23.89	11.50	15.24	5.84
Products of pulp & paper, publishing, printing & connected industries	18.08	13.11	19.29	13.42
Iron & steel products, transportation equipment	8.42	20.79	12.59	31.21
Non-ferrous metal products, derivatives of petroleum & coal, non-metallic mineral products	13.02	15.16	20.26	14.59
Electrical appliance, chemical & parachemical products	6.18	8.53	9.84	13.16

Source: André Raynauld, *Croissance et Structures Economiques de la Province de Québec*, p. 97.

* Quebec's overall rate of foreign ownership is a little short of Ontario. The Grey Report (*op. cit.*, p. 3) showed that the 1965-1968 average of taxable income by non-resident owned companies was 60.3 percent in Quebec, 70.0 percent in Ontario, and 63.8 percent in Canada as a whole. Most other sectors were comparable though Quebec's figures in transportation, utilities, and services were greater than Ontario's. If, as we have argued, Anglo Canadian control is also treated as foreign control in Quebec, then the figures, it is estimated, rise to approximately 90 percent in manufacturing, mining and various other sectors of the Quebec economy — making the situation far more serious even than in Ontario. See Chapter 4.

minder of those special aspects of Quebec's colonial situation which make it unique and significant in North America.

An economy is comprised of more than large corporations and gross statistics. It is made up of people who work and live

TABLE 2-10

Breakdown of the production value of manufacturing industries, 1964, ($000,000).

	Quebec	Ontario
1. *Industries related to natural resources*		
Wood, paper & related ind.	1,202	1,171
Primary Metals	671	1,498
Non-metallic minerals	268	461
	2,131	3,130
	(24%)	(20%)
2. *Light Industry*		
Food & Beverages	1,629	2,543
Textiles, Leather, Clothing, etc.	1,652	959
Other	636	912
	3,917	4,414
	(45%)	(28%)
3. *Heavy Industry*		
Chemical products	491	1,084
Metal products	541	1,265
Petroleum derivatives	400	487
Transport ind.	377	2,616
Electrical equipment	421	1,201
Machinery	185	788
Other	296	857
	2,716	8,296
	(31%)	(52%)

Source: The Parti Québécois, *Souveraineté et économie,* pp. 14-15. For a more recent breakdown, expressed in terms of productivity, see the Castonguay-Nepveu Report (Vol. 3, Book 1, on development, p. 104).

and survive within it. We turn next to the breakdown of the income of the people of Quebec, comparing the different ethnic and linguistic groups and analyzing the differences in light of what we have seen so far.

TABLE 2-11

*Growth of manufacturing industries in Quebec and Ontario —
(1949-1963) (in %).*

| | Total Growth | | Avg. rate of growth | | Difference |
	Québec	Ontario	Québec	Ontario	(Qué.-Ont.)
1. Food & Bvgs.	150.8	131.6	6.43	6.23	+0.20
2. Tobacco & related prod.	82.3	448.1	4.52	12.86	—8.34
3. Rubber prod.	134.4	72.5	6.18	3.65	+2.54
4. Leather prod.	71.0	69.2	3.54	3.38	+0.16
5. Textiles	74.6	70.5	4.02	4.31	—0.29
6. Clothing & Hosiery	63.6	26.7	3.61	1.78	+1.83
7. Wood Prod. furniture housewares	114.6	76.4	6.10	4.18	+1.92
8. Paper & related prod.	90.2	109.9	4.39	5.31	—0.92
9. Prtg & Pub.	180.0	158.8	7.26	6.82	+0.44
10. Primary metal ind., metal prod. & mach.	111.0	142.0	5.17	6.48	—1.31
11. Transport	92.3	158.8	5.22	7.50	—2.28
12. Misc. electrical equipment	162.4	192.7	6.16	7.23	—1.07
13. Non-metallic mineral prod.	251.0	175.9	8.97	8.08	+0.89
14. Chemicals & related prod.	195.7	222.3	8.37	8.61	—0.42
TOTAL	117.3	141.4	5.76	6.75	—0.99

Source: Chateau, J. P., "Croissance et structures des industries manu-
facturières au Québec et en Ontario, 1949-1963: *Actualité économique,*
Vol. 44, no. 3, Oct.-Dec., 1968, p. 495 (From: *Quebec Labour,* Montreal: Black Rose, 1972, p. 130).

Footnotes to Chapter 2

1. John Porter, *The Vertical Mosaic* (Toronto: University of Toronto Press, 1966), p. 286.
2. *Report of the Royal Commission on Bilingualism and Biculturalism,* Vol. 3, p. 53.
3. *Ibid.,* p. 54.
4. *Ibid.,* p. 57.
5. *Ibid.,* p. 55.
6. *A Citizen's Guide to the Gray Report* (Toronto: New Press, 1971), p. 32. See Chapter Four below.
7. *Report of the Royal Commission on Bilingualism and Biculturalism,* Vol. 3, p. 55.
8. *Ibid.,* p. 57.
9. André d'Allemagne, *Le Colonialisme du Québec* (Montréal: Editions R-B, 1966), p. 48. (Authors' translation.)
10. Rodrigue Tremblay, *Indepéndance et Marché Commun Québec-Etats-Unis* (Montréal: Editions du Jour, 1970), p. 64.
11. *Ibid.,* p. 64.
12. *Ibid.,* p. 46. (Authors' translation.)
13. Mario Dumas, "L'Evolution Economique du Québec: 1940-1965," in *Economie Québecoise* (Montréal: Les Presses de l'Université de Quebec, 1969), p. 226.
14. André d'Allemagne, *op. cit.,* p. 49.
15. *Ibid.,* p. 49. (Authors' translation.)
16. See CNTU, *Québec Labour* (Montréal: Black Rose, 1972), pp. 183-93.
17. André d'Allemagne, *op. cit.,* p. 54.
18. An example as revealing in this industry as I.T.T.-Rayonier is in pulp and paper is Iron Ore of Canada. See CNTU, *Québec Labour* (Montréal: Black Rose, 1972) pp. 175-81.
19. Stuart Jamieson, "French and English in the Institutional Structure of Montreal," M.A. Thesis, McGill University, 1938, p. 74.
20. *Ibid.,* pp. 77-78.
21. André d'Allemagne, *Le Colonialisme du Québec* (Montreal: Editions R-B, 1966), p. 55.
22. André Raynauld, *Croissance et Structures Economiques de la province de Québec* (Québec: Ministère de l'Industrie et Commerce, 1962), p. 201.
23. *Ibid.,* p. 57.
24. *Ibid.,* p. 68. The figures in annual rate of growth of industrial production 1935 to 1955 are: Canada as a whole, 10.0; Québec, 10.2; Ontario, 9.6.
25. *Ibid.,* p. 70.

26. Mario Dumas, *op. cit.,* p. 222.
27. CNTU, *Québec Labour, op. cit.,* p. 128.
28. André Raynauld, *op. cit.,* p. 72.
29. André d'Allemagne, *op. cit.,* p. 51.
30. Cited in CNTU, *op. cit.,* p. 134.
31. *Ibid.,* p. 135.

CHAPTER 3

LES QUEBECOIS: AN OPPRESSED MAJORITY

Quebec like the United States fails to utilise her natural resources, labour, technological abilities, etc., in the interests of the society as a whole. As in all other capitalist societies, areas of abject poverty practically adjoin areas of conspicuous consumption, attesting to the maldistribution of wealth and even of necessities such as food, shelter, and warmth.* Quebec is far less productive than Ontario or the industrialized regions of the United States. At present, as is often the case, the provincial government is in a difficult financial position despite the fact that it provides insufficient social amenities while taxing its people heavily. None of the cities of Quebec treat even a good portion of their sewage; there are overcrowded schools and hospitals; there are fewer public housing units in Montreal than in Ottawa – a city one quarter its size. The people of Quebec spent 18.8 percent of their budgets on housing on the average in 1960, 15 percent higher than Canada as a whole and twice as high as in Sweden.[1] In all, Quebec has more poverty and slum housing, higher infant mortality rates, etc., than one should expect in a society with such productive potential.

---

* In fourteen municipalities on the Island of Montreal with a majority of French inhabitants, family incomes range from $4,500 to $6,500; in thirteen predominantly English Canadian municipalities, the family incomes range from $7,200 to $17,000. Stanley Ryerson, "Technology, Nationalism and the Canada/Quebec 'Problematic'," *Horizons Research Newsletter,* no. 4, January, 1970, p. 5.

Quebec has consistently had a 20 to 50 percent higher unemployment rate than the Canadian average – usually twice as high as in Ontario. Quebecers comprised about one-quarter of Canada's labour force, but 40 percent of its unemployed in 1971. This phenomenon is not new; it was the same in 1970 and previous years. The figures are as follows: 1969 – Quebec 6.9% unemployed, Canada as a whole 4.7%; 1968 – Quebec 6.5%, Canada 4.8%; 1967 – Quebec 5.3%, Canada 4.1%; 1966 – Quebec 4.7%, Canada 3.6%.[2] Selected years in the previous twenty year period show the same breakdown: 1961 – Quebec 9.3%, Canada 7.2%; 1956 – Quebec 5.0%, Canada 3.4%; 1951 – Quebec 2.9%, Canada 2.4%; and 1946 – Quebec 4.0%, Canada 3.4%.[3]

Four out of ten of the unemployed in Quebec are under twenty-five years of age. For several years now Quebec's youth has been exploding onto the labour market at the rate of 75,000 new workers a year – one of the highest per capita rates in the industrialized world. In each of the ten years to come another 75,000 young Quebecers will be looking for their first job.[4]

The discussion of unemployment brings us to the issue of poverty. The actual figures tell the following story. The bottom 40 percent of wage earners in Canada earned 16.2 percent of the total Canadian income in 1951. This figure diminished gradually to 13.3 percent in 1965. The upper 20 percent of the population earned 40.3 percent of all income in 1951 and 42.9 percent in 1965. The relevant figures when applied to *all* individuals are very similar: the total income appropriated by the bottom two-fifths of the population decreased from 12.4 percent in 1951 to 10.4 percent in 1965, while the top fifth of the population increased their share of the total income from 45.0 percent in 1951 to 46.8 percent in 1965.

Only when family income as a whole is considered is there the slightest sign of an improvement in the distribution of income. In 1951 the bottom two-fifths of families earned 19.0 percent of the total income while in 1965 they received 19.9 percent. The top fifth earned 41.1 percent in 1951 and 38.6 percent in 1965.[5] Hence not only do we have a terrible maldistribution of income in this country between the poor and the rich, but also it is clear that in relative terms the poor are at best staying where they are and probably getting poorer.

This is occurring despite the relatively significant number of welfare programs begun and extended during the period under consideration. In fact, if we were able to include farmers and farm families, the proportionate incomes of the wealthy would probably be significantly higher than the figures indicate. Furthermore, unlike the poor, the wealthy have access to many kinds of legal loopholes and financial technicalities so that their real income turns out to be much higher than their declared income on which these statistics are compiled. In fact estimates by Statistics Canada place unreported investment income at approximately 50 percent – and only the wealthy invest.

No comparable data is available for Quebec alone. There is no reason to asume that Quebec is unlike Canada as a whole in the distribution of wealth; if anything, judging by some of the statistics below, there is even greater inequality.

In sum the system in Canada/Quebec is best described as socialism for the rich and capitalism for the poor. While those at the bottom must beg for "handouts" from the governments in the form of welfare, unemployment benefits, etc., the corporate rich are the beneficiaries of numerous sources of public funds, gaining directly from the free services provided to them by the government without stigma or question of repayment.* There is no need here to go into all the various incentives, tax holidays, depreciation allowances, grants, interest-free loans and so on which governments allocate out of tax revenue to the corporate rich. What is less well-known is that all this is happening when at the same time the taxation burden is being lifted from the corporations and passed on to individuals in the form of personal income tax and various hidden sales taxes. Statistics Canada figures reveal that in 1950, for instance, corporate taxes accounted for 50 percent of federal government revenue while today it is down to 12 percent. Personal income tax accounted for 25 percent in 1950, now it is up to 50 percent. Then of course the government trade and commerce officials act as unpaid salesmen for the corporations, the science ministry does their research and development, we build highways for the cars they produce and airports for a commercial air transportation system predominantly used by businessmen

* See for example, "Jean Marchand's Business in Business," *Last Post,* Vol. 2, No. 6, pp. 34-46.

to sell their wares. Socialism for the rich ensures that they stay rich; capitalism for the poor ensures that they stay poor.[6]

Income, however, is only the tip of the iceberg of poverty. A study conducted by Jack Siemiatycki for the Point St. Charles medical clinic in Montreal and reported in *Québec Presse* (April 30, 1972) dramatizes the medical side of poverty. Comparing the working class areas in and around Point St. Charles served by the clinic with middle class areas in the North End, the study found that with age kept constant, the mortality rate in the "Point" area was double that of the North End. Cancer was 70 percent more prevalent, infectious diseases like hepatitis were 50 percent more common. Close to 50 percent of all people examined in the lower class area had teeth in terrible condition; the children all suffered some degree of malnutrition. The manifest presence of all forms of serious medical ailments corresponded to the absence of proper medical services. Psychological tension was understandably found to be

TABLE 3-1

Average labour income of male salary and wage earners, by ethnic origin — Quebec 1961.

	Labour Income	
	Dollars	Index
All Origins	3,469	100.0
British	4,940	142.4
Scandinavian	4,939	142.4
Dutch	4,891	140.9
Jewish	4,851	139.8
Russian	4,828	139.1
German	4,254	122.6
Polish	3,984	114.8
Asiatic	3,734	107.6
Ukranian	3,733	107.6
Other European	3,547	102.4
Hungarian	3,537	101.9
French	3,185	91.8
Italian	2,938	84.6
Indian	2,112	60.8

Source: *Report of Royal Commission on Bilingualism and Biculturalism*, Vol. 3, p. 23.

widespread. We might add that this part of the city suffers from the highest level of industrial pollution and urban blight. In all, the life of the poor is hellish, destructive and self perpetuating.

Inequality among Canadians takes on a different complexion when we compare the annual incomes of the different ethnic groups within Canada as a whole and especially within Quebec (see Table 3-1). The incomes of French-Canadians average at 80 percent of those of Canadians of British origin within Canada; but, looking just at Quebec, we note that the proportionate revenues of the French-Canadians are even less, only 65 percent of those of British origin.

There is no doubt that the region in which the ethnic group lives affects the income level. Some areas are more highly industrialized than others, and hence these regions and the ethnic groups residing there are at an economic advantage. But, regional factors are not nearly sufficient to explain all of the disparities among the revenues of different ethnic groups. For example, we find that the average income of the Canadians of British origin within each province exceeds the provincial mean by 10 percent except in Quebec where the figure is 42.4 percent. On the other hand, the average income of the Canadians of French origin is 12.3 percent lower than the national mean, and almost the same with respect to each provincial mean.[7]

The figures in Table 3-1 are painfully clear. The Québecois, the original settlers and founders of Quebec, who constitute the great majority, 80 percent, of its population are at the bottom of the scale. Above them we find eleven ethnic groups; below them the Indians and Italian-Canadians. It is those ethnic groups whose income puts them at the top of the scale, near the English, that have, for the most part, integrated themselves into the English linguistic and cultural milieu. It was the Italians who, more than any group, adopted in some measure the language of the French-Canadian majority. Hence their low incomes; hence too, no doubt, their recent concerns that their children be educated in English. The colonization and exploitation suffered by the Indians at the hands of the North American White Man need scarcely be pointed out.

If we now look at the role of bilingualism within Quebec we find again that the Canadians of British origin maintain their superior economic position regardless of their level of knowledge of French. Table 3-2 clearly demonstrates the irrelevance, from an economic point of view, of bilingualism to those of British origin. Within a province where English is the first language of only 13.3 percent of the population, those of British origin who are unilingually English have a higher income than bilinguals of either French or English origin. Still, it is worth noting that bilinguals of British origin earn $1,406 more on the average than those of French origin.

Only in a colony are the majority disadvantaged and the minority privileged. Only when the language of economic control is foreign and when its organizational objectives are remote from the needs of the great majority of the population and lie in the hands of an external elite does such a situation arise. To view it in greater detail we must separate income, the variable used up to this point, into its constituent parts – that

TABLE 3-2

The total average income of the male work force according to language and ethnic group — Quebec 1961.

	Distribution in Percent	Number in Thousands	Avg. Income in dollars
All ethnic groups			
unilingual English	11.1	122	5502
unilingual French	36.7	403	3099
bilingual, English & French	52.2	574	4772
Total	100.0	1099	4227
Canadians of British origin			
unilingual English	53.7	72	6049
unilingual French	2.2	3	2783
bilingual, English & French	44.0	59	5929
Total	100.0	134	5918
Canadians of French origin			
unilingual English	0.4	3	5775
unilingual French	45.8	386	3107
bilingual, English & French	53.8	453	4523
Total	100.0	842	3880

Source: A. Raynauld, G. Marion, R. Beland, "La Répartition des revenus entre les groupes ethniques du Canada," Study done for the Royal Commission on Bilingualism and Biculturalism, p. 235.

is, we must look separately at each of the social characteristics which together account for an individual's level of income.

If we analyse the factors affecting the income disparities between the Canadian of French and of British origin, it will appear that the level of schooling is most influential (as might be expected), but variables such as age distribution of the work force, the type of industry, amount of unemployment, occupation and "ethnicity" are also important in explaining the differences. If the Canadians of French origin were as highly educated as those of British origin the distance between their average incomes would be reduced from $960 to $439. This means in fact that "French-Canadians benefit least from education. They obtain even fewer economic advantages than the Italians in their progress from elementary school to high school to university."[8] Hence 45.7 percent of the difference between the two is attributable to the lower level of schooling of those of French origin. For Montreal this figure is 41.9 percent. (With regard to each of the variables below: unemployment,

TABLE 3-3

Percentage of salaried men who worked between 49 and 52 weeks, as a measure (in dollars and percentage) of the labour income disparity attributable to underemployment, by ethnic origin — Montreal metropolitan census area, 1961.

	Percent of total who worked 49-52 weeks	Contribution of Underemployment	
		$	%
English-Scottish	85.2		
French	73.9	240[1]	13.2
Irish	82.0	125	30.0
Northern European	83.1	90	38.0
Italian	65.2	283	11.6
Jewish	74.8	402	72.5
Eastern European	75.0	239	15.5
German	80.6	92	9.2
Other	72.8	291	16.0

1. If the same proportion of Canadians of French origin as of English-Scottish origin had been working 49-52 weeks in 1961, their average income would have been $240 higher.
Source: *Report of Royal Commission on Bilingualism & Biculturalism*, Vol. 3, p. 72.

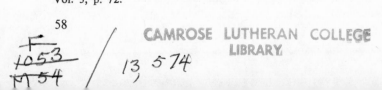

age, etc., we use only those figures for metropolitan Montreal. These data are applicable to Quebec as a whole but with some limited distortion.)

By looking at Table 3-3 we can see the effect of under-employment on the different ethnic groups within the Montreal area. This table also documents the unusually high unemployment among the Canadians of French origin as compared to other ethnic groups in the same locale. When the ethnic groups are ranked as to the percentage which worked 49 to 52 weeks out of the year, the French-Canadians placed seventh of nine. Table 3-4 describes the effects of age distribution of the different ethnic groups on their annual incomes. If, for example, the

TABLE 3-4

Net contribution of age[1] to the labour income of salaried men, by age group — Montreal metropolitan census area, 1961.

Age Group	Dollars
15-19 years	$-1,610$
20-24	-808
25-29	-187
30-34	$+227$
35-39	$+460$
40-44	$+620$
45-49	$+538$
50-54	$+494$
55-59	$+371$
60-64	$+242$
65 and over	-347

1. "Net contribution of age" means the increase $(+)$ or decrease $(-)$ in dollars to the average wage and salary which is attributable to age, all other factors held constant.
Source: *Report of Royal Commission on Bilingualism & Biculturalism*, Vol. 3, p. 73.

French working population is significantly younger than the British, the income disparity could be explained by the fact that the French were more often making the salaries of new recruits while the English were at the height of their careers. The average age for salaried Montrealers of French origin is 37; for those of English-Scottish origin, 40; for those of Jewish origin, 41; for those of Italian origin, 36. Since the average salaried Montrealer of French origin is younger by 2.8 years than one of English-Scottish origin, it can be calculated that a French Montrealer loses $258 because of his relative youth, which represents about 5 percent of the average wage and salary earnings and 15 percent of the income disparity, between the two groups.[9] To what extent this factor is purely demographic and to what extent it reveals that Francophone Quebecers must be younger to get hired at all is unclear.

As we noted previously, individual bilingualism does not necessarily result in economic reward. When bilingual and unilingual persons are compared for each ethnic group, it seems that Canadians of French origin have a moderate advantage in knowing both English and French. This advantage does not show up for the Canadians of English or Scottish origin, suggesting that it is not the bilingualism *per se* which is economically advantageous to the French-Canadian but the fact that he speaks English. In fact, though the number of French-Canadians who are unilingually English is too small to allow certainty, it appears from Table 3-2 that a French-Canadian gains far more through total assimilation, i.e. becoming English, than by competence in both languages ($5,775 per year to $4,523). On the other hand those few English-Canadians who assimilated into the French milieu are found at the absolute bottom of the ladder ($2,783 per year). For those of other ethnic origins, nevertheless, bilingualism *per se* is an advantage – especially for those listed as Jewish, who benefit almost as much as do the French.[10] It was also found that the industries in which people worked did not significantly affect salary and wage distribution of the ethnic groups.[11]

Table 3-5 describes the contribution of "ethnicity" to the income disparities among the groups. As used in the analysis "ethnicity" is the "effect of ethnic origin when all other factors are held constant; it is the expression of a complex phenomenon composed of many elements which are impossible to separate: among these are the quality of schooling; work attitudes; occupational choice; motivations and values; the quality, orientation, effectiveness of institutions; obstacles to mobility; discrimination; and the weight of the past."[12]

In comparison with other factors examined, ethnicity appears to be somewhat less important than underemployment, age, schooling, and occupation. Except in Montreal, we find two major income categories: one including Canadians of English-Scottish, Irish and Northern European origin, where ethnicity increases average earnings, and the other including Canadians of French, Italian, Eastern European and other origins where ethnicity reduces average earnings.[13] Here, it would appear as if an element of discrimination explains, at least partially, this schism between essentially Northern and Southern Europeans, between those closest in appearance and manner to the dominant w.a.s.p. stereotype and those furthest from it.

TABLE 3-5

Net contribution of ethnic origin[1] to labour income of salaried men, by ethnic origin — Montreal metropolitan census area, 1961.

	Deviation from observed average of $4,443	Net contribution of ethnic origin
English-Scottish	+$1,319	+$606
Irish	+ 1,012	+ 468
French	— 330	— 267
Northern European	+ 1,201	+ 303
Italian	— 961	— 370
Jewish	+ 878	+ 9*
Eastern European	— 100	— 480
German	+ 387	+ 65*
Other	— 311	— 334

1. "Net contribution of ethnic origin" means the increase (+) or decrease (—) in dollars to the average wage and salary which is attributable to ethnic origin, all other factors being held constant.
* Not significant.
Source: *Report of Royal Commission on Bilingualism & Biculturalism,* Vol. 3, p. 77.

Judging by the income of its inhabitants, Quebec's economy operates in favour of a small minority of people who are of British origin and who speak English. This is graphically apparent in the physical landscape of Quebec and Montreal. Predominantly English areas are consistently those with disproportionately large numbers of parks, public libraries, as well as adequate housing and services. These areas are less densely populated than others, and because of their usual status as separate municipalities, are able to remain free from industrial and commercial disturbances and thus are less subject to both noise and air pollution. These individuals benefit from, and help cause, the urban degradation of the inner city and yet, unlike most French Canadians, are able to live sheltered from it. In addition, because they tend to own disproportionately large homes, and therefore pay high property taxes, their school boards have greater than average budgets so as to provide above average educational facilities and in this way help perpetuate the inequality.

On the other hand, the French-Canadian population of Quebec includes disproportionately large numbers of individuals on welfare, living in slums, without adequate housing or health care.* Their schools are not on the whole up to the standard of those of the English, for their property taxes provide less money to the school boards. The very high rate of unemployment in Quebec is thus a reflection of the status of French Canadians and does not reflect the situation of English Canadians. And, under the system as it is, little improvement can be expected. It has been estimated that just to keep the unemployment situation from growing worse, Quebec needs over four billion dollars of new investment each year for the balance of the decade. This is more than was invested in Quebec in either 1969 or 1970. To cut the jobless rate to a still intolerably high 6 percent, Quebec would need to attract roughly seven billion dollars a year for the next ten years.[14]

When we look at the very great income disparities between the English and French of Quebec, the fact that the economy is owned and operated to a very large degree by Anglo Canadians and Americans must be seen as crucial. There is no doubt that the elitist notions about education – the structure of the educational system and the role of the clergy – significantly affected the economic status of the French Canadian; but we saw that even the best education means less in terms of dollars to a French than an English Canadian, and that the unilingual English-Canadians are better off economically than bilinguals. It was noted that the French Canadian is worse off in Quebec

---

* The infant mortality rate indices stood at 16 for non-French and 24 for French within Quebec. The maternal mortality index for Montreal as a whole is 1.4; in the working class areas of the south-west part of the city — the French areas — it is 4.7. Stanley Ryerson, "Social and National Factors in the Quebec 'Awakening'," paper presented at the Seventh World Congress of Sociology, 1970, p. 4.

where he comprises 81.2 percent of the population than in the rest of Canada where the French Canadians are only one among many ethnic groups. And, regional characteristics could not explain the disparity. Finally, attention was called to the factor called "ethnicity" as being of some importance (see Table 3-6).

TABLE 3-6

Measure of the influence of certain factors on the income disparities between Canadians of French origin and those of British origin in Montreal ($1,898), in Toronto ($1,093) and in Ottawa ($1,496).

Factors	Influence (%)		
	Montreal	Toronto	Ottawa
Age	5.9	16.1	10.7
Industry	4.2	4.4	7.6
Occupation-schooling	45.1	44.1	62.4
Unemployment	6.3	13.0	9.2
Other (ethnicity, discrimination, etc.)	38.5	22.4	10.1
Total	100.0	100.0	100.0

Source: A. Raynauld, G. Marion, R. Beland, "La répartition des revenus," Study done for the Royal Commission on Bilingualism & Biculturalism, p. 69-70.

"Ethnicity" is a rather neutral word, hence, no doubt, it was chosen by the Bi and Bi Commissioners. However, what it expresses is by no means neutral. It is a mathematical measure of the *direct* socio-economic consequences of Quebec's colonial status, the oppression of its people. Table 3-6 shows that almost 40 percent of the wide disparity in income between French- and English-speaking Quebecers living in Montreal can only be accounted for by the fact that the Québecois are subjected to direct discrimination in the English-controlled economic sector and, conversely, by the fact that Francophones have subjectively accepted their status as inferiors. This acceptance of the inferior status attributed to them by the English, has been and is still in some cases manifested in the attitudes toward work, motivation, competitiveness and aspirations of Francophone Quebecers.

Moreover, the factors accounting for the remaining 60 percent of the income disparity between the French and English are themselves for the most part expressions of the *indirect* consequences of Quebec's colonial status. The relative lack of education among the Québecois, their under-employment, their tendency to enter the job market earlier and to find employment in relatively low paying industries – all these patterns developed at certain historical moments as concrete responses by a colonized people to their state of being. In Part Two we will consider this historical process in some detail.

The choice for the French Canadians has been to assimilate or to be poor. Refusing the first choice, they built a society around submission to the latter. The research done for the Royal Commission on Bilingualism and Biculturalism showed that half of the Francophones in management positions in the large corporations who were studied, believed that "a French

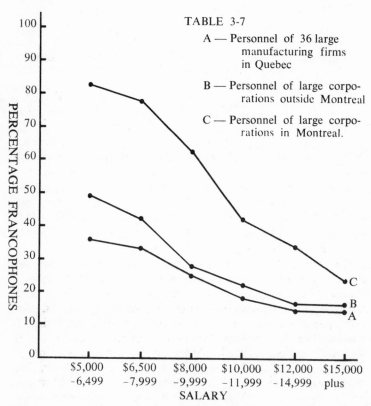

TABLE 3-7

A — Personnel of 36 large manufacturing firms in Quebec

B — Personnel of large corporations outside Montreal

C — Personnel of large corporations in Montreal.

Canadian who is successful is more English than French. Forty-five percent of the sample believed that a French Canadian who received many promotions in a large English corporation must protect the interests of the English Canadians to the detriment of those of the French Canadian."[15] One writer concludes the following:

> Some of these young Francophone graduates will try to break through this 'cultural barrier' which separates them from the industrial world. Business (except in cases of flagrant discrimination which are not all that rare) will be ready to hire them. However, there will be three conditions:
>
> 1 the candidate must have perfect mastery of the English language;
>
> 2 he must be willing to be transferred outside of Quebec;
>
> 3 he must function inside the enterprise in the same manner as his English counterparts; that is to say, for all useful purposes, to think and act in English, and to considerably alter his system of values.[16]

Lysiane Gagnon is not merely voicing journalistic rhetoric, nor are the opinions of Francophone managers based on mere rumors. The facts, here too, are quite explicit. In a study reported by the Royal Commission on Bilingualism and Biculturalism, the investigators assessed the participation of Francophones at the various income levels in a carefully selected sample of corporations in Montreal and the rest of Quebec. The results are graphically displayed in Table 3-7 above. The actual figures are provided in Table 3-8. As the income level goes up, the percentage of Francophones goes down. It is as simple as that.

The solution to Quebec's colonial state is not better paid Francophone corporation managers; it is decolonization. Nevertheless, the inability of the Québecois to place their own technocratic elite, their university and CEGEP graduates, into positions commensurate with their training and expectations – without those individuals having to subject themselves to a thorough process of Anglicization – is an added dimension of Quebec's colonial position. Let it not be thought, however, that the opening up of a few more public service jobs in Ottawa or the hiring of a few Francophone managers in various "pro-

TABLE 3-8

Personnel of 36 large manufacturing firms of Quebec according to salary and language.

Salary	Francophones (percent)	Anglophones (percent)
$5,000 - $6,499	36	64
6,500 - 7,999	35	65
8,000 - 9,999	25	75
10,000 - 11,999	19	81
12,000 - 14,999	15	85
15,000 - and more	15	85
Total	31	69

Personnel of large corporations (outside of Montreal) according to salary and language.

Salary	Francophones (percent)	Anglophones (percent)
$5,000 - $6,499	82	18
6,500 - 7,999	76	24
8,000 - 9,999	61	39
10,000 - 11,999	42	58
12,000 - 14,999	35	65
15,000 - and more	23	77
Total	70	30

Personnel of large corporations in Montreal according to salary and language.

Salary	Francophones (percent)	Anglophones (percent)
$5,000 - $6,499	49	51
6,500 - 7,999	41	59
8,000 - 9,999	27	73
10,000 - 11,999	23	77
12,000 - 14,999	17	83
15,000 - and more	17	83
Total	37	63

Source: Lysiane Gagnon, "Les Conclusions du Rapport B.B.": *Economie Québecoise* (Montréal: Les Presses de l'Université du Québec, 1969), pp. 247, 248.

gressive" corporations, as is being suggested and to some extent instituted at this moment, somehow meets Quebec's real needs and demands. We shall see why not.

In sum the French Canadian within Quebec is greatly disadvantaged. He is often unemployed; even with the same experience, education and bilingual abilities as a Canadian of British origin he earns appreciably less money. Education does not reward him in economic terms to the same extent that it does Canadians of other ethnic groups. A unilingual Canadian of British origin is better off economically than a bilingual of either ethnic origin.

The disparity between the incomes of the Canadians of British and French origins can only partly be explained by factors of schooling, occupation, age, industry and underemployment. The cultural values and attitudes which developed in Quebec in response to its colonial position and discrimination account for at least a part of the income disparity. Within a province, their homeland where they comprise 81.2 percent of the population, French-Canadians are penalized for their language and cultural values, for their very collective existence. This is the societal consequence of Quebec's economic colonial status. This fact is crucial in understanding Quebec and allows us to make significant comparisons with the economic conditions in other nations. Les Québecois too understand the situation. An oppressed majority is not the same as a silent majority.

Footnotes to Chapter 3

1. L. Favreau, *Les Travailleurs Face au Pouvoir* (Montréal: Centre de Formation Populaire, 1972), p. 48.
2. Michel Pelletier et Yves Vaillancourt, *Du Chomage à la Libération,* (Montréal: Editions Québecoises, 1972), p. 32.
3. *Ibid.*
4. Diane Cohen, CBC "Viewpoint," October 20, 1970.
5. *Income Distributions: Incomes of Non-Farm Families and Individuals in Canada in Selected Years, 1951-1965.* (Dominion Bureau of Statistics, June 1969.) See also Special Senate Com-

mittee on Poverty, (Report) *Poverty in Canada,* (Ottawa: Information Canada, 1971), especially pp. 11-23.

6. For a discussion of the shift of the tax burden and related matters, see Rick Deaton, "The Fiscal Crisis and the Public Employee in Canada," *Our Generation* (October, 1972).

7. A. Raynauld, G. Marion, R. Beland, "La Répartition des Revenus entre les Groupes Ethniques du Canada," study done for the Royal Commission on Bilingualism and Biculturalism, Section I.

8. Lysiane Gagnon, *La Presse* (October 26, 1968).

9. A. Raynauld, *op. cit.,* Section II.

10. *Ibid.,* p. 75.

11. *Ibid.,* p. 73.

12. *Ibid.,* p. 63.

13. *Ibid.,* p. 77.

14. Diane Cohen, *op. cit.*

15. Lysiane Gagnon, "Les Conclusions du Rapport B.B.: De Durham à Laurendeau-Dunton: Variation sur le Thème de la Dualité Canadienne," *Economie Québecoise* (Montréal: Les Presses de l'Université de Québec, 1969), p. 251, (authors' translation).

16. *Ibid.,* p. 251, (authors' translation).

CHAPTER 4

THE
SATELLITE
AND THE
METROPOLIS

As an American society that is neither English speaking nor Protestant, Quebec can be identified with the nations of South and Central America. Its colonized state too is reminiscent of Latin America as is the growing consciousness of its people.* In terms of total American investment abroad, Latin America receives 23 percent while Canada with only twenty million people is first with 31 percent.[1] Quebec receives something like a proportionate share of that 31 percent. But there is another similarity between the economic situation of Canada/Quebec and that of the Third World. The "composition of Canadian trade closely resembles that of underdeveloped countries. Exports are composed largely of raw materials or semi-processed materials, while imports are mostly finished manufactured goods."[2] Comparing the U.S.A., Canada, and the nations of the European Economic Community in 1962, we find that Canada imported 31.7 percent raw products and 68.3 percent manufactured ones. For the U.S.A. and the Common Market the totals of raw products were 37.6 and 40.2 percent respectively; for manufactured products the percentage was 62.4 and 59.8. Canada exported 74.3 percent raw products and 25.7 percent manufactured ones. For the U.S.A. the totals were 37.7 primary and 62.3 percent manufactured; for the Common Market countries they were 33.3 and 66.7 percent.[3]

* Quebec was in fact to be one of the areas to be studied for counterinsurgency purposes in the infamous and abortive project Camelot, along with Chile and others.

André Gunder Frank, in a very important analytical work on underdevelopment in Latin America, has presented a model for the workings of a satellitic economy as part of the system of international monopoly capitalism.[4] In its general formation, Frank's model can be usefully applied to other societies that are in somewhat analogous positions – such as Quebec. In the remainder of this chapter we shall attempt to do just that.

Inherent in capitalist economic development are three basic contradictions – that is, three built-in mechanisms working against and distorting genuine economic growth. Frank sets these out as follows:

– the expropriation of economic surplus from the many and its appropriation by the few,

– the polarization of the capitalist system into metropolitan center and peripheral satellites,

– the continuity of the fundamental structure of the capitalist system throughout the history of its expansion and transformation due to the persistence or re-creation of these contradictions everywhere and at all times.[5]

The result, he asserts, is clear and undeniable: "these capitalist contradictions and the historical development of the capitalist system have generated underdevelopment in the peripheral satellites whose economic surplus was expropriated, while generating economic development in the metropolitan centers which appropriate that surplus."[6]

The first contradiction is of course the central assertion of the Marxist critique of capitalist society. Modern Marxist theorists such as Paul Baran have shown that it is the monopoly form of contemporary capitalism that accounts for the fact that the surplus* acquired by the few is not productively invested and often wasted through luxury consumption. A monopoly or quasi-monopoly industrial structure allows the owning class to do with the surplus as it sees fit, rather than having to put it back into their respective companies to make them more productive in order to meet competition. If the ownership class is external, as is the case with Chile and Quebec, then the surplus is, in part if not in whole, expropriated to the metropolis.

* See Chapter 1.

At the apex of the economic structure of Quebec we find three elites, or sub-elites, it would seem arranged hierarchically, who appropriate the economic surplus produced by the Québecois. The French-Canadian elite is the smallest and the least wealthy and powerful of the three with the Anglo-Canadian second and the American being the most powerful in terms of the number and size of enterprises under their control. To focus briefly on the French-Canadian elite we look at those Quebec firms controlled by French Canadians, borrowing the results of a study which selected from these firms a sample of the two largest banks, the two largest trust companies, the six largest industries, the three largest insurance companies, and the three largest finance companies.[7]

There are 216 positions on the boards of directors of these enterprises held by 163 persons. Of these 163 persons, 65 (40 percent) hold 118 (54 percent) of the 216 positions. These men hold among themselves 50 percent of the directorships of the insurance companies, 46 percent of those of the finance companies, 68 percent of the trust companies, 43 percent from the six industries, and 72 percent of the banks.[8] These 65 persons thus are a good approximation of the French-Canadian economic elite.

They divide occupationally in much the same way as does the English-Canadian economic elite (as defined by John Porter). Twenty-three (37 percent) are lawyers, 10 (16 percent) are engineers and technicians, 13 (20 percent) have commerce degrees, 4 (6 percent) have other university degrees, and 13 (20 percent) have not been to university.[9]

In 1961, of all the manufacturing firms in Quebec only thirty-nine were controlled by French Canadians. Twenty of these thirty-nine were family concerns,[10] with the result that 42 percent of the French-Canadian economic elite were scions of old and powerful families. The correct blood colour thus seems to be a requirement for securing membership in the already small French-Canadian economic elite. The inequality of opportunity and the lack of mobility for the population as a whole is again reflected in the fact that over half of this elite was educated in two schools: Collège Ste. Marie and Jean de Brébeuf.

The second elite, the Anglo-Canadian, is more important than the first: it controls larger enterprises which have greater foreign markets, and the industries it dominates are much more productive than those controlled by French Canadians. For John Porter the composition of the domestic Canadian economic elite clearly indicates that "a relatively small group of firms are responsible for a disproportionate amount of economic activity, and . . . these firms share among them a relatively small group of men who are their directors."[12] Its several hundred members and their families reside in Westmount and other exclusive districts, send their children to private schools and attend private clubs, the two most popular in Montreal being the Mount Royal with 150 representatives from the elite among its members, and the St. James with 146.[13] They also abound on the McGill Board of Governors and other equally prestigious seats of public office.*

The third elite, being the most powerful, is also the most difficult to pin down. Included in it are individuals resident in Canada or the U.S.A., with citizenship in either country (including a few British subjects), who control those corporations located in Quebec but owned by foreign interests. However, because these corporations are branch plants of larger multinational firms which are themselves interconnected with many other giant corporations and financial institutions, it is somewhat incorrect to perceive this third elite as composed of a discrete number of individuals. Instead it is better regarded as a subgroup within the American ruling class.

American controlled corporations, as demonstrated above, dominate the extractive and heavy manufacturing industries and contribute to Quebec's exports in greater measure than even Anglo-Canadian controlled firms. The facts on American control of Canadian industries are fairly well known. The most recent statistics in this regard are presented in Tables 4-1 and 4-2. These figures make it clear that the overall level of American domination is intolerably high. In addition, "foreign control in general and American control in particular is highest in those industries in which metropolitan taste-formation and technological and product innovation are crucial. These are automobiles, rubber products, chemicals, electrical products

---

* This situation has been changing slightly of late in response to the growing awareness of Quebec. Anglo-Canadian elite members are maintaining an even lower profile than usual, many of them taking up residence across the Ontario border. Their power, it goes without saying, remains in their hands.

and aircraft. All these industries primarily serve the Canadian domestic market."[14]

The huge increase in the amount of American capital in Canada has been the result of a re-investment of the economic surplus produced by Canadians. "In 1964, for instance, investment by American firms in Canada was reported at $2,557 million. Of this amount, however, only $126 million (5 percent) came from sources in the United States. Internal sources of funds amounted to $2,008 million (78 percent) – while a further $423 million (17 percent) came from Canadian financial institutions."[15] What this means is that foreign control has a built-in growth mechanism such that at a certain point, which has already been reached in Canada, the very presence and profitability of foreign controlled enterprises leads to greater foreign control merely through reinvestment. No new

TABLE 4-1

Percentage of Corporations Taxable Income Earned in Each Industrial Sector and Region Attributable to Non-Resident-Owned Companies, 1965-1968 Average.

Industrial Sectors	Maritimes	Quebec	Ontario	Prairies	B.C.	Canada
Agriculture, forestry, fishing and trapping	42.9	—	14.3	6.2	25.2	20.7
Mining	88.8	40.6	59.3	76.5	26.7	55.0
Manufacturing	59.6	60.3	70.0	60.5	44.1	63.8
Construction	9.7	12.1	19.0	23.0	42.6	20.6
Transportation, storage, communications and public utilities	16.2	44.0	20.9	19.3	12.0	22.1
Wholesale trade	17.6	32.2	39.7	38.5	30.8	35.7
Retail trade	30.4	27.2	36.3	52.2	40.5	37.4
Finance	21.8	22.3	25.6	28.3	26.7	30.6
Services	24.4	41.9	39.1	40.6	27.8	38.7

Source: *A Citizen's Guide to the Gray Report* (Toronto: New Press, 1971), pp. 31 and 32.

importation of capital is required. This fact will be taken up again in discussing the third of the contradictions – that is, historical persistence.

TABLE 4-2

Percentage of Non-Resident Ownership as Measured by

Manufacturing Industry	Assets	Sales	Profits	Taxable Income
Food and beverages	31.3	27.1	29.4	30.9
Tobacco	84.5	80.1	82.7	83.1
Rubber products	93.1	91.5	90.1	88.4
Leather products	22.0	21.4	25.2	27.3
Textiles and clothing	39.2	28.5	54.9	54.6
Wood	30.8	22.2	23.8	23.0
Furniture	18.8	15.5	20.4	23.2
Printing, publishing and allied	21.0	13.2	22.0	22.7
Paper and allied	38.9	40.7	39.8	39.0
Primary metals	55.2	51.1	62.4	64.4
Metal fabricating	46.7	45.0	64.7	62.6
Machinery	72.2	72.7	78.1	87.2
Transport equipment	87.0	90.6	89.8	88.7
Electrical products	64.0	62.7	78.0	88.1
Non-metallic mineral products	51.6	42.3	47.2	52.9
Petroleum and coal products	99.7	99.6	99.7	99.4
Chemicals and chemical products	81.3	81.1	88.9	89.1
Miscellaneous manufacturing	53.9	51.2	72.1	72.6
Total — All Manufacturing	58.1	55.0	63.4	62.4

Source: *A Citizen's Guide to the Gray Report* (Toronto: New Press, 1971), pp. 31 and 32.

Moreover, while increasing control through reinvestment does take place, it does not forestall the ability of the owning class to expropriate the bulk of the surplus back to the metropolis. Over recent years remittances to the U.S.A. (in dividends, royalties, etc.) by international corporations were twice as great as the amount of new capital which they invested outside the country. Levitt has also noted that except for the depression years of 1928-1931, American income from direct investments has exceeded the outflow of new capital for every year since 1900.[16] Between 1960 and 1967, Canadian subsidiaries and affiliates sent one billion dollars more to their parent companies in the form of profits than they received in the form of capital investment. This figure becomes two billion if royalties, licence and management fees are included.[17]

The Canadian/Quebec situation resembles the American one described in chapter one except that the most powerful element of the elite is external. What is clear, though, is that an elite of a particular complexion exists and is perpetuated and that this elite has many of the characteristics of a ruling class. The number of vital management posts that lie in the hands of a small number of men and the similarity in background, education, etc., of these men indicate this to be the case.

It is evident, then, that an external monopoly, the Anglo-Canadian and American elites, control the Quebec economy. This monopoly prevents the production of full potential economic surplus. It re-invests its economic surplus to expand its own enterprises, thereby reinforcing the monopoly structure, for new, smaller companies cannot afford to compete with it. But more importantly, it robs the society of the funds which could be used to produce social necessities such as public housing and adequate medical facilities.

These funds are acquired through the paying out of profits in the form of dividends etc.; the average rate of profit for American direct investment after taxes, in 1967 for instance, was a healthy 7.8 percent.[18] There are also, however, indirect ways. Multinational corporations can take profits at either end and many choose to take them at the level of the parent corporation. This is done usually through underpricing the raw materials shipped from the branch plant to the parent or through overpricing the machinery and other goods supplied by the parent to the branch plant. In this manner the population in the satellite is kept in the dark as to the real amount of appropriated surplus. For instance, consider the case of Proctor and Gamble, one of the companies studied by the United States Congress' Ways and Means Committee. "During the 10 year period, 1951-1961, its capital outflow from the United States was $11 million. Its income from subsidiaries over the same period was $290 million. The bulk of the income came in the form of sales of raw materials and equipment and raw products to the subsidiaries ($243 million); only $47 million was received in the form of dividends."[19]

The second contradiction of capitalism, as presented in Gunder Frank's model, describes the relationship between the satellite, which is kept under-developed (or less developed than its potential would permit), and the metropolis whose ruling class increases its profits through exploitation at home and especially in the satellites. Small indigenous industry within the satellite is eaten up by the more productive, more technologically advanced, foreign branch plants. These developments, as manifested in Quebec, were pointed out in 1961 by the Quebec Government's Conseil d'Orientation Economique (economic council) which noted "the process of the growth of enterprises which, in a climate of monopolistic competition, occurs through the takeover of small enterprises by large ones or through mergers. One consequence of this process for Quebec has been the loss of many of its firms at the point and to the extent that they attained maturity."[20]

This appropriation by the few of the economic surplus generated by the many goes on at all levels of the international monopoly capitalist system. Even within the principal world metropolis, the U.S.A., there are satellitic regions such as the Southern and Appalachian states. Also within the satellites, there are metropolitan regions which expropriate the surplus from their own hinterlands. (For example, although English Canada is an economic satellite of the U.S.A., Quebec is a satellite of English Canada.) Though the entire population of the metropolis, whether the principal one or the lesser ones, marginally benefit from their exploitative position in the world economy, it is essentially the ruling class of the dominant metropolis that gains the economic rewards. Moreover, the ruling elements within the satellites, in coalition with the dominant class of the metropolis, appropriate a disproportionate share of the satellitic nation's wealth.

The colonial pattern of domination, at its most basic, is very old. After having planted vineyards in Gaul, the Romans, alarmed by the competition with the grapes from Gaul, limited the amount of production in the colony so as to protect that of the metropolis. In India, the English cut off the fingers of

Indian weavers so that their products would not harm the British textile market. The Nazis planned an economic organization of Europe in such a way that the economy of each country would be complimentary to that of Germany.[21] The workings of the capitalist form of colonialism is somewhat more subtle.

The metropolis expropriates economic surplus from the satellites for its own growth essentially by two means, direct investment and the establishment of a branch of the American firm in Canada. The latter is often said to benefit the Canadian population by providing jobs, but looking at it on a long-term basis, even this contention is doubtful at best. The fact is that branch plant establishments always act in the interests of the home corporation. This has serious implications for both Canadian economic growth and trade policies. "If branch plants had the freedom to choose the lowest-cost suppliers, there is little doubt that they would more often opt for Canadian or non-American foreign supplies. This would be more profitable for them and, more to the point, would cut down our heavy dependence on American imports. But, because their primary responsibility is to contribute to the profit maximization of the global corporation rather than their own they can rationally purchase cost-increasing supplies from the parent."[22] Eric Kierans made the same point more bluntly: "Canada, as a major industrial nation, could produce economically thousands of items imported automatically from parent U.S. companies by their subsidiaries."[23]

Gonick notes that a significant proportion of Canada's imports from the U.S.A. are explained by the predominance of American corporations in Canada. He describes their effects on other aspects of trade. "It is no accident that the new trade relationship between Canada and the Communist countries – especially the Soviet Union and China – all occur in agriculture, one of the few major goods-producing sectors of the Canadian economy which remains under Canadian ownership."[24] Finally, in export policy, anti-trust legislation, and measures taken by the United States authorities to protect their balance of payments, "Canadian subsidiaries of United States corporations have been obliged, by American law or administrative pressures, to follow practices which are in conflict with pronounced Canadian policy; indeed, in some instances, in conflict with

Canadian law."[25] The Gray report concludes that "foreign control of domestic business affects adversely domestic control of the national economic environment . . . certain alternatives are not open to Canada . . ., the government's capacity to implement policy can be hampered by the fact that a firm is foreign controlled . . . [and] Canadian law can be more readily frustrated by firms that are international in scope."[26]

The system of capitalist development, Frank asserts, creates a metropolis/satellite division not only at the top but at various levels of the economy. In Canada this is evident in the "metropolization" of Central Canada, and especially Southern Ontario, to the detriment of other regions. It is interesting to note in this regard that 45 percent of American-controlled employment is within 100 miles of Toronto, and 64 percent is within 300 miles. By comparison, 31 percent of Canadian-controlled employment is within 100 miles of Toronto, 41 percent within 300 miles.[27] A study by professor Roy E. George showed that of the 350 foreign owned firms surveyed, only 16 percent had ever considered a site for location outside central Canada.[28] Such "regional disparities" are not historical accidents but the logical outcome of externally controlled monopoly capitalism.

Another side of the same process is cultural – the modelling of the industrial and corporate structure in the satellite on that of the metropolis, whatever the harmful effects on the former. In Quebec this is most evident in the relationship of language to hiring policies. Foreign capitalists have blocked the recruitment and mobility of Francophones in their firms by demanding that business, sometimes even at the lowest levels, be conducted in English.[29] American-controlled international corporations, such as General Motors, which normally conduct their operations in the language of the country where the different branch plants are located, refuse to accept the fact that Quebec is distinct from the rest of North America. G.M. workers at Ste. Thérèse, Quebec, are forced to speak English, even though the corporation could easily adapt to the French language. Anglo-American habits and styles of life, as well as language, are also demanded of anyone striving for top positions. Thus we found that in Montreal, Francophones constitute 60 percent of the work force but only 17 percent of management. In the rest of the province, where Anglophones are about 7 percent of the work force, they hold 80 percent of the top posts in manufacturing.*

Earlier we examined the necessity for the metropolitan American economy to maintain foreign investment. We saw that one of the tools used by the ruling class within the U.S.A. to cover up their economic objectives and to win the support of the population at large was the ideology of the Cold War. Whatever its rationalization, military power is used when necessary. Necessary to the "national interest," as defined by the dominant class and its ideologists, is world economic stability and access to investment and markets. Anything that undermines that condition presents a danger to its present hegemony. Countering, neutralizing, and containing the disturbing political and social trends thus becomes the primary objective of its foreign policy. "From the Truman Doctrine on, the suppression of insurgent movements has remained a principal goal of U.S. foreign policy. It has been the prime target of the U.S. foreign assistance program, most of the funds for which have gone for civic action teams, pacification programs, support for local police, and, above all, military aid to the local army."[30]

The United States has continually intervened in whatever form thought necessary in regions where abstract questions of internal political struggles were irrelevant to American security but threatening to American investment.[31] In some instances, such as Iran, Indonesia, Greece, and Cuba, the half-political, quasi-military C.I.A. has offered policy-makers more subtle means for attaining their goals while skirting the more vulgar military operations.[32] Of course, these interventions on the part of American forces are only for the well-being of the people of the Dominican Republic or any other country that is so honoured. The spokesmen of the American ruling class assure us that all that the less developed nations need is a mass consumption society. Technological change and the education of an entrepreneural class that can supply the energy for change are the first steps to affluence. Since the economic system that stimulates entrepreneurship is private enterprise, it is concluded that the greatest need of these less developed countries is private investment to aid the "free" sectors of their

* See Table 3-8, Chapter 3.

economy, and it is the duty of the United States to provide them with this "freedom" at any cost.

But, what we call American investment abroad is in reality foreign resources mobilized by American corporations, generating their own capital which then serves to strengthen the dominant American position rather than meet the needs of the people in the country itself. It is in fact a myth that such investment really aids the satellites. It may supply some jobs in the short term; meanwhile, it robs the society not only of the talent, will and potential unity of purpose, but also of the actual resources which could allow it to erase poverty and inequality and develop a strong economy in the interests of all its people. The United States, for example, erects trade barriers against many cheaper, freely exportable goods and commodities, and attempts to keep down prices for Third World exports. This suggests that the United States' shrinking foreign aid program is often nothing but a subsidy to its own farmers and industry rather than a gesture of concern for the world's poor. "The United States' vast expansion in its agricultural exports, and the billions of dollars of lost income to the Third World, reveals the success of the brilliant American synthesis of aid, pressure, and exclusion that is the main characteristic of its foreign economic diplomacy."[33]

At the World Conference on Trade and Development, the United States, in keeping with this policy, voted – often alone among seventy-seven countries – against such propositions as "non-interference in the internal affairs of other countries," "the sovereign right freely to trade with other countries," and "to dispose of its natural resources in the interest of the economic development and well-being of its own people."[34]

As the leader of world capitalism, the U.S.A. was only being forthright. Why be circumspect when the results are inevitable? Chile provides a good example of this. Frank reminds us that "feudal" patterns of ownership were never really important and that instead the "Chilean state and its institutions have always been part and parcel of the capitalist system in Chile and in the world and an instrument of the Bourgeoisie."[35] Whatever pious phrases may be uttered about independence, sovereignty, free trade, autonomous development and the like, the reality of Chile is evident. "The gap between the metropolis and Chile in power, wealth and income, and perhaps most important in the political, economic and technological capacity for economic development, has markedly increased over time and continues to do so. At the same time Chile . . . has become politically, economically, technologically ever more dependent on the metropolis. Not only its commerce, agriculture, and mining as in the past, but now also Chile's industry . . . and industrialists continue to become increasingly dependent on the world capitalist metropolis for finance, commercialization, capital goods, technology, design, patents, trade marks, licenses, – in short, practically everything connected with light and/or foreign-assembly 'industrial' production."[36]

The satellites' natural resources are extracted and then shipped to the metropolis to be processed and turned into finished products. These manufactured products are then packaged and re-sold to the satellites at enormous profits. Diplomatic pressure, resolutions of international organizations, fiscal arm twisting through the American-controlled World Bank and the International Monetary Fund, training and aid for expanding and modernizing police and military forces, counter-insurgency activity by the c.i.a. and, if necessary, direct military intervention, are all used by the American ruling class to maintain its advantageous position. The result of this policy is that the "rich nations are getting richer at the expense of the poor, not because history decrees it, but because the developed countries, particularly the United States, have the political power to impose terms upon the under-developed world which are profitable for the rich and impoverishing for the poor."[37]

Thus, the exploitative relationship between the metropolis and the satellite is a vicious circle: the less developed nations cannot break out of it because their economies are essentially organized in the interests of the metropolis. The Quebec Interministerial Committee to study income rates (Comité Interministèriel d'Etude sur le Régime de Rentes) described the results of the satellitic role played by Quebec.

Foreign owned firms . . . cater to the needs of the home country: they exploit local resources in line with their own interests which may well not coincide with the objectives of the Quebec economy . . . furthermore the sums that the foreign owned firms appropriate from their local operations

81

are drawn into their internal system usually according to their multinational interests. . . .

Moreover, the situation is the same for non-distributed profits and depreciation allowances which are reinvested according to simple profitability, or according to the international situation of the company or simply in response to a technological discovery which makes our own resources unattractive. Reinvestment may take place in the same sector to raise production or productivity (if the factors relating to competition are in our favour), or elsewhere in Canada, or even in foreign countries in enterprises competing with those of Quebec.[38]

Thus the second contradiction of capitalist development, like the first, is evident in Quebec; the Quebec economy has been essentially satellitic in its pattern of ownership and growth. The economic surplus generated by Quebec labour is used for expansion of the branch plant and the survival and dominance of the home office. This reinforces the monopoly structure, thereby preventing the formation of productive enterprises which could be used in the interests of the population at large. Quebec's economy is deeply trapped within the framework of international capitalist control and development and, while it does not suffer the worst ravages of that system, it is colonized nonetheless.

Such a condition is not accidental nor does it come about overnight; there is a logical historical process described by Frank as the third internal contradiction of capitalism: "the continuity and ubiquity of the structural essentials of economic development and underdevelopment throughout the expansion and development of the capitalist system at all times and places." This brings in the element of time. It says that within the framework of capitalist economic development a satellite must remain a satellite growing more rather than less subservient to and dependent upon the metropolitan economy. Certainly, this describes the history of Quebec.

"Since their origins as a people, the French Canadians have never known any regime but a colonial one."[39] Both politically and economically Quebec has served foreign interests since its beginning as a fur trading colony for France. By the 1920's a new type of colonialism prevailed: economic imperialism. The effect being that Quebec was a doubly colonized region within the Canadian colony. "Canada is a small regional economy within the metropolitan economy of the U.S.A. We have always been in the hinterland of some imperial system. Our evolution from the British system towards the American system began with the American Revolution but was not completed until the early decades of the twentieth century."[40]

According to Kari Levitt the American percentage of total foreign investment in Canada rose steadily from 15.5 percent in 1900 to 53.0 percent in 1926 to what it is now. Yet the most important real growth has been in the more recent period. In 1949, for instance, the difference between the value of assets held by Canadians abroad and those held by foreigners in Canada was $4 billion, by 1964 Canada's balance of international indebtedness had risen to $20 billion.[41] The process has continued and increased in its other manifestations as well. In Quebec the privileged ethnic and cultural group acquired more privilege; the exploited one grew more exploited. "In the last 30 years the situation has deteriorated. In 1930, Quebec residents of British descent had 3.3 percent more people in the professions, management and business than the per capita average for the population as a whole. In 1961 this group was 8.7 percent above the provincial mean."[42] The same tendency expressed in Frank's third contradiction can be seen in the actual growth of regional disparities in Canada and Quebec. Development has been painfully unequal with the residents of towns or even entire regions habitually unemployed and forced to live on state welfare payments with no hope of improvement while, as we saw, new industry flocks to the already developed and wealthy areas. At all levels and in all ways, the law of capitalist development has played itself out in the Canadian/ Quebec satellite with the effect that the rich get richer and the poor get poorer. And we saw previously where that puts Les Québecois.

This chapter has briefly attempted to analyse some of the implications resulting from foreign monopoly control of the Quebec economy within the framework of the workings of international (American-based) monopoly capital. It has been suggested that the few – the dominant class of both the metropolis and the satellite – will increase their wealth and power, while the many who labour to produce this surplus will remain relatively impoverished and powerless. It has been made clear that the ruling class of the United States is willing and prepared to forcibly maintain access to foreign markets and investment. Finally, we have seen that the permanence of the parasitic relationship between the metropolis and the colony, once it is established, is indeed frightening.

As the reader will have noted by now, we reject the notion that foreign investment, as we know it today, aids the receiving country. There is no doubt that increased employment, and the introduction of advanced technology and more efficient production methods stimulate the economy in the receiving country. But, these short-term advantages hardly outweigh the long-term disadvantages to the country in which the foreigners invest. In order to convince the colony to accept foreign investment and the "benefits" it brings, the colonizer, in effect, must reshape the culture and uproot the social solidarity which potentially exists in the historical reality of the people as a national collectivity. This "new colonialism is carried by the ideology of materialism, liberalism, and anti-nationalism. By means of these values they, the ruling classes of the metropolis and the satellites, seek to disarm the resistance of national communities to alien consumption patterns and the presence of alien power."[43]

To alter this long-term pattern only one alternative appears to be open to the underlying populace in the satellite, whatever the short-term risks involved. This is of course the socialist path to development, though one in keeping with the integrity of the Québecois as a people and borrowing from other socialist models only to the extent they are adaptable. (From what was discussed above it is quite understandable that many people on the left in Quebec today are looking to the newly-elected socialist government in Chile with great interest.) Socialism posits the needs of the great mass of the people rather than the interest of a small (foreign) elite as the basic axis of economic and social development. Recent events in Quebec as we shall see have shown that this alternative is certainly one subscribed to by significant and growing sectors of the population.

In closing, we should remind ourselves that there are different manifestations and degrees of colonialism. The fact that Americans own some enterprises in France, has little influence on French culture in comparison to, say the destruction of Mexican culture by enormous American inputs. Somewhere in between lies Quebec. When the British and then the Americans took over in Quebec, they effectively threatened to uproot the indigenous culture. They usually ignored local customs and insisted that English be the language of commerce so that Quebec would be a colony, a source of raw materials and cheap labour. Since they were essentially objects to be used, there was little effort made to respect the individual human dignity of the inhabitants or the values of their collective way of life.

The "final solution" to the resistance among the colonials is being carried out today in Viet Nam where American bombs have created vast areas resembling the desolate, lifeless craters of the moon. The Vietnamese – "the enemy" – are not people but non-people – objects – for the American invaders. The women, for instance, are presumed to have been placed there to provide sexual satisfaction for the soldiers. The raison d'être of the colonial is to serve the colonizer. Massacres, like the one at My Lai, are perhaps the horrifying ultimate form of American imperialism, the built-in contradictions of international monopoly capitalism taken to their logical conclusion.

In Part Two we shall explore the subjective relationship of colony to metropolis. It is the thoughts of the people of Quebec, their nationalism, culture, ideology and history that will be the focus of Part Two, no longer the somewhat dry statistical economic data presented above. Yet it was crucial to present these figures for they give us a picture of the objective reality of the conditions of the people of Quebec and the patterns and mechanisms by which they have developed over time. To speak of the process of decolonization we must first set out and understand the conditions and realities of colonization.

Consciousness, as expressed through the activities, actions, outpourings and utterances of individuals and groups, is the subjective side of social reality. This is not to say that the main ideas of society do not affect its social structure and formation. Quite the contrary. Much of Quebec's reality can be seen as the consequence of the spread of certain ideologies, but it is specific classes in the social structure which benefitted from these ideologies and thus transmitted them among the population. These ideologies, though, as we shall see, are ultimately grounded in the interests of certain classes in a particular concrete relationship with the basic economic and social reality. That reality, as we have tried to show, is economic imperialism.

One immediate question is the prevalent ideological justification for foreign ownersip and control. The general manner in which American-based economic imperialism is rationalized has been discussed previously; next we turn to the specific and immediate rationalization as encountered in contemporary Canada/Quebec and the theoretical questions raised by it.

Footnotes to Chapter 4

1. D. Drache, "National Consciousness," in Ian Lumsden (ed.) *Close the 49th Parallel, etc.: The Americanization of Canada* (Toronto: University of Toronto Press, 1970), p. 25.
2. C. Gonick, "Foreign Ownership and Decay," in Ian Lumsden (ed.), *op. cit.*, p. 59.
3. United Nations, *Yearbook of International Trade Statistics, 1962:* General Agreements on Tariffs and Trade, International Trade in 1962.
4. André Gunder Frank, *Capitalism and Underdevelopment in Latin America* (New York: Monthly Review Press, 1969), pp. 3-14.
5. *Ibid.*, p. 3.
6. *Ibid.*, p. 3.
7. André Raynauld, "La Propriété des Entreprises du Québec," study done for the *Royal Commission on Bilingualism and Biculturalism*, p. 99.
8. *Ibid.*, p. 200.
9. *Ibid.*, p. 202.
10. *Ibid.*, p. 216.
11. *Ibid.*, pp. 201, 202.
12. John Porter, *The Vertical Mosaic* (Toronto: University of Toronto Press, 1965), p. 23.
13. *Ibid.*, p. 304.
14. Kari Levitt, *Silent Surrender* (Toronto: Macmillan of Canada, Ltd., 1970), p. 12.
15. Kari Levitt, "Canada: Economic Dependence and Political Disintegration," *New World Quarterly*, Vol. IV, No. 2, pp. 74-77.
16. Quoted in Stanley Ryerson, "Technology, Nationalism and the Canada/Quebec 'Problematic'," *Horizons Research Letter*, January, 1970, p. 3.

17. C. Gonick, *op. cit.*, p. 65.
18. *Summary of Current Business,* October, 1968, cited in Simon Rosenbloom (unpublished manuscript), Halifax, 1970, p. 37.
19. *Ibid.,* p. 24.
20. Conseil d'orientation économique du Québec, Documents de base en vue de la planification, septembre, 1962. (Authors' translation.)
21. André d'Allemagne, *op. cit.,* p. 28.
22. C. Gonick, *op. cit.,* p. 47.
23. Quoted *Ibid.,* p. 47.
24. *Ibid.,* p. 48.
25. Kari Levitt, *Silent Surrender* (Toronto: Macmillan of Canada, Ltd., 1970), p. 116.
26. *A Citizen's Guide to the Gray Report, op. cit.,* p. 119.
27. "The Québec Liberation Movement," (mimeo) (Toronto: Hogtown Press, 1970), p. 3.
28. Simon Rosenbloom, *op. cit.,* p. 41.
29. *Report of the Royal Commission on Bilingualism and Biculturalism,* Vol. 3, p. 62.
30. Richard J. Barnet, *Intervention and Revolution* (Cleveland: The World Publishing Co., 1968), p. 9.
31. Gabriel Kolko, *The Roots of American Foreign Policy* (Boston: Beacon Press, 1969), p. xvi.
32. Gabriel Kolko, *op. cit.,* p. 29.
33. *Ibid.,* p. 68.
34. Richard J. Barnet, *op. cit.,* p. 38.
35. André Gunder Frank, *op. cit.,* p. 116.
36. *Ibid.,* p. 117.
37. Richard J. Barnet, *op. cit.,* p. 28.
38. Rapport du comité interministèriel d'étude sur le régime de rentes, Vol. II, (mai, 1964). Cited in André d'Allemagne, *Le Colonialisme du Québec* (Montréal: Editions R-B, 1966), p. 47. (Authors' translation.)
39. André d'Allemagne, *op. cit.,* p. 171. See also, Marcel Rioux, *Québec in Question* (Toronto: James Lewis and Samuel, 1971), Chapters 1, 2 and 3.
40. C. Gonick, *op. cit.,* p. 44.
41. Cited in Simon Rosenbloom, *op. cit.,* p. 1.
42. Marcel Rioux, *op. cit.,* p. 96.
43. Kari Levitt, *op. cit.,* p. 98.

CHAPTER 5

NATIONALISM
AND
INTERNATIONALISM

Class divisions in Canada then clearly exist; there is a small, relatively homogenous group of individuals at the top possessing great wealth and power. The great mass of people is divided and disorganized. It has no power and minimal wealth. The same holds true for Quebec, even more so. Quebec has greater poverty and even less effective social services than Canada as a whole. All this is clear. It is also clear that the source and nucleus of the wealth and power at the top is gradually and increasingly moving outside Canada's political boundaries, becoming foreign – mainly American. Here too the same goes for Quebec and here too it is more so, for, as we have seen, included among the foreigners are Anglo-Canadians who control corporations operating in Quebec.

In Quebec, however, the "foreignness" of the ownership class is not an abstract intellectual question, not something that requires a Gray Report or a Watkins Report to become a public question of awareness and concern. Les Québecois have always known and felt foreign domination; since the early days they have chafed under their colonial yoke. Nevertheless, it is only now that the Québecois have gained the strength and assurance to talk about and think about and plan a different kind of society, one run by the people and not by foreign capitalists. In the old days the pain and wrath of being colonized was turned inward into submission, or, when too great, channelled against scapegoats or into contentless nationalist slogans, but never allowed to directly confront the colonizers and the source of their power.*

Thus it is today that the system is hardest pressed to defend itself, to convince the people that foreign ownership and control, the domination of English money, is inevitable and therefore necessary and correct in the face of a popular movement voicing the contrary. The old Catholic ideology of submission and retreat will no longer serve this purpose; a new, more modern and far reaching one is needed not only in Quebec but elsewhere. In May 1969, the chief executives of seventy of the world's key industrial and financial institutions met in Washington, and noted that: "The volume of goods and services resulting from international investment has by-passed exports, and its present growth rate is considerably larger than that of international trade, thus making international investment the major channel of international economic relations. The international corporation is the main expression of this unprecedented phenomenon. Investment across national boundaries is largely a reflection of the development of technology, and affects every facet of the established order – financial, cultural, and political."[1]

The objective of this meeting was to discover ways "to remove some of the psychological and political barriers to the international flow of investment capital." Despite their claim that the "economic consequences of foreign direct investment are held almost universally to be beneficial," the delegates were obliged to concede that "significant obstacles of a psychological, political or economic nature exist, limiting or distorting the international investment procedure."[2] The problem was thus a psychological one. Since foreign investment and foreign control are obviously good things, people and nations who object to them must have psychological problems. What is required is educational therapy to cleanse out "narrow nationalist prejudices" replacing them with noble and suitable sentiments of internationalism and broadmindedness.

To provide educational therapy of this kind is the role of the intelligentsia – or at least the role expected of the intelligentsia by the moneyed class. The latter express their interests

* See Chapter 6, below.

directly through their actions; they expect the intelligentsia, the teachers, the experts, the social philosophers, to share those interests but to express them indirectly, ideologically – in moral theoretical terms. The educated are expected to educate the people to identify their own interests and hopes and aspirations with the interests of the economic elite; their task is to obscure class conflict and exploitation so that lower class demands remain unarticulated.

What is particularly insidious at this juncture is that the new ideology is couched in language invoking the cause of international cooperation and thus attempts to cash in on the liberal and progressive mythology and collective sentiment that has grown around this idea. This sentiment is then manipulated so as to cast those who threaten multinational capitalism, who favour national liberation, as intolerant and even racist – to use the genuine revulsion against racist brutality that has arisen since Hitler for their own purposes. To do this the intelligentsia is needed and its members have too often fallen into line, outwardly defending the causes of liberalism and progressivism but ignorant or unconcerned as to whose interest is in reality being served.

An eloquent member of the Canadian/Quebec intelligentsia is Pierre Elliott Trudeau. His intellectual abilities, French-Canadian economic elite background,[3] and of course his central political role today makes it worthwhile to consider his ideas, as expressed in his publications, in a little detail. Trudeau has viciously attacked those "harbouring narrow nationalist prejudices," while himself consistently espousing a philosophy of internationalism. Many elements of Trudeau's thinking have been humane and progressive and it would be untrue and unfair to label him simply as a mouthpiece for the business class. Nonetheless, in its essence and in the form it has taken today, his philosophy condones the role and methods of the elites – foreign and national – and precludes any method of challenging the exploitative economic system described above. It is no accident that recent historical works in Canada by George Grant, Donald Creighton and others have pinned the blame for the sellout of Canada's resources firmly on the mantle of the Liberal Party, and it is this party that made Trudeau its leader only six years after he had joined it. Somewhere there was something that made for a speedy romance and happy though rocky marriage between the iconoclastic Quebec intellectual and the middle of the road, continentalist party.

In theoretical terms another way of saying that internationalism is desirable is to say that nationalism is undesirable. This is the conclusion that follows from Trudeau's analysis of nationalism, its meaning and development and history. "Nationalism is a doctrine which claims to supply a formula for determining what section of the world's population occupying what segment of the world's surface should fall under the authority of a given state; briefly stated, the formula holds that the optimum size of the sovereign state . . . is derived from the size of the nation."[4]

In theory, the boundaries of nation-states were to be drawn by the consent of all the people who would be affected by such a decision. People would define themselves as a nation and then set up a state structure to reflect their uniqueness. Trudeau notes that such a process has not occurred, rather boundaries of states have been decided upon by a "might is right" policy. Expansionist policies, Trudeau goes on to suggest, are the result of a belief in the nation as unique and somehow superior. These irrational, emotional feelings of distinctiveness – the sum of which is what he calls "nationalism" – were transformed into a political doctrine which justified all activities because of the presumed national superiority. Such a doctrine, Trudeau argues, is necessarily conservative for it presupposes above all else allegiance to the State and its activities. Trudeau describes with distaste historical examples of the activities of states where "nationalism" had been transformed into a conservative political doctrine. For instance, "the French nation willed itself into possession of that part of Europe which spread between the Rhine, the Pyrenees, the Atlantic Ocean, and the Alps." Even worse, "there were nations who, spurning such frivolous guidelines as geography, history and language, were favoured by direct communication with the Holy Ghost; such was the privilege of the United States of America who saw the annexation of Texas and California, and eventually Canada as – in the words of O'Sullivan – 'the fulfillment of our manifest destiny to overspread the continent alloted by Providence'."[5]

Trudeau's words are true and his description apt, but a key

element is left out. What his argument ignores is that these expansionist policies were undertaken because they served the interest of the dominant social class of these nation-states. Superiority myths such as the American one called "manifest destiny" were articulated and taught to the people by the dominant class and the ideologues who served them. In the case of the U.S.A., at the bottom of the moral crusade was the push for access to raw materials and expanded markets.[6]

Among people who share similar language, customs, laws, etc., there exists as Trudeau said a "we-feeling" or ethnocentrism. This "feeling" does not simply exist by itself but on the contrary is usually incited and manipulated by the ruling class to create myths which justify their policies and gain support for them. If we compare the American involvement in Viet Nam today to the 1898 Spanish-American War, we can see that in both cases the ruling class had made war on people of different races (the Vietnamese, the Cubans, the Filipinos) attempting to win popular support through a jingoistic, and covertly racist, appeal to American duty or manifest destiny. In the case of Viet Nam, except for the earliest stages, this has been singularly unsuccessful.

What Trudeau is contending – that the "we-feeling" itself generated the military imperialism – suggests that if we scourge the earth of this type of emotionality or ethnocentrism, expansionism and militarism will end. This is simply not the case as we see in Viet Nam, and the fact that Trudeau's government has permitted Canada's economic involvement in the war dramatically illustrates the real process at work. In today's world there will remain a dominant class in the largest and most industrially advanced nations ready, willing, and able to use their coercive powers, among which is a highly developed technology of death and destruction, to promote and protect the international flow of capital.

Ignoring the realities of class interests the type of critique Trudeau offers of nationalism serves to justify economic imperialism by discrediting and demeaning the opposing position. The attack by national liberation forces on foreign investment, takeover, and domination is made to look like an emotional, racist outburst; their social, economic, and political analysis is cast as the product of a psychological disorder. Ironically, Trudeau thus is in a position identical to the ideologues of national superiority and manifest destiny he so strongly attacked.

As defender and promoter of internationalism he serves the very same interests; only their tactics have changed and their means become more subtle.

The nationalists who have borne the brunt of Trudeau's polemics have been those Québecois who in the sixties became both independentists and socialists. "Because their social thinking is to the left, because they are campaigning for secular schools, because they are open minded culturally, they think that nationalism is the path to progress. What they fail to see is that they have become reactionary politically."[7] Since nationalism is reactionary in Trudeau's eyes the nationalist left is actually on the right. In this way he can mask the class divisions within the society by associating nationalism – of the right and left – with all that is regressive, while internationalism becomes associated with all that is progressive. Yet to his growing dismay, his message is not being heeded in Quebec. He is ignored or ridiculed by intellectuals and students – the very same people whose darling he had been in the late fifties and very early sixties. They are increasingly turning into those perverse creatures, left-wing nationalists.

Left-wing nationalism, as we have seen, makes perfect sense in an economic colony such as Quebec. It is true though that no fully adequate analysis of nationalism which takes into account the class nature of society is available. Marxists, while having as yet developed no complete position on nationalism, cannot simply be said to have rejected nationalism in favour of proletarian internationalism, as is sometimes believed. The question is far more complex. Marx himself never took a stand for or against nationalism as such. He supported, for instance, Hungarian, Polish and Irish nationalism but condemned Czech and Croat nationalism.[8] In general he realized nationalism was a bourgeois ideology while the working class was international, if anything. The masses of Marx's time did resemble the illiterate, nationless, nameless Roman proletariat. The company supplied their jobs, food, housing, wives, education (if any), etc. They had little existence outside of the factory. The culture of the nation, its art, history, symbols, language, etc., were for them totally remote, the constructs of the bourgeoisie. The proletarian class was international, the situation of the English working class little different from the French, the German, etc., and Marx expected, mistakenly, that it would remain so.

Marx understood, though, that in a situation where one nation was dominated by another, the interests of the working class were at least temporarily served in the expression of nationalism. Lenin added to this an analysis of the element of capitalist expansion or imperialism, that is, that this state of national domination was inevitable in the late stages of capitalism. Therefore, except when nationalism was clearly reactionary, serving to oppress the mass of people, socialists were bound to support the national struggle of colonized people, whether civilized or uncivilized; white or black.[9] Lenin realized that capitalism was becoming more international, entering its "highest" stage – economic imperialism. Nevertheless, the proletarian struggle was still basically international even if there were national variations.

Historical events in Europe from the Russian revolution through World War II make even more fuzzy the socialist attitude toward nationalism. Stalin's 1936 Constitution guaranteed (on paper) secession rights to the nationalities of the Soviet Union. Twelve years earlier he had opposed the doctrine of proletarian internationalism declaring that the Soviet Union was the homeland of the international working class and that its survival was tantamount to all the aspirations of world socialism. In previous instances, with the exception only of Russia and Serbia, Marxist Social Democratic parties lined up solidly behind their rulers in the First World War and joined "popular fronts" with non-socialist parties after it. The national question was central to Lenin's founding of the Third Communist International at the time of the First World War and to the many subsequent splits in international socialism.

With the recent escalation of the rhetorical struggle among Marxist sects and differences among various states calling themselves "socialist," combined with the unfortunate fact that leadership of the left is still too often taken to rest with the Soviet propagandists, the "line" on nationalism has progressed little. Nevertheless, the kernel remains. For socialists, there is both left nationalism and right nationalism, both progressive and reactionary variants; one to be supported, the other opposed. Mao Tse-Tung, for instance, distinguishes between "Great Power Chauvinism" which "we should get rid of resolutely, thoroughly, wholly and completely" and national liberation which must be won. "And only by achieving national

94

liberation will it be possible for the proletariat and other working people to achieve their own emancipation. . . . In wars of national liberation patriotism is applied internationalism."[10]

Still today the phrase "the workers have no homeland" is often cited from the Communist Manifesto to support the argument that for Marx nationalism went against the interests of the workers. If one examines the context of this phrase, an opposite interpretation emerges:

> The Communists are further reproached with desiring to abolish countries and nationalities.
> The working men have no country. We cannot take from them what they have not got. Since the proletariat must first acquire political supremacy, must rise to be the leading class of the nation, must constitute itself the nation, it is, so far, itself national, though not in the bourgeois sense of the word.[11]

In this passage, Marx and Engels recognize the structural reality of the "nation" and of its dominant class. Only by taking political power can the working class become the "nation" – and in so doing transform it, and in the end transcend it. "Though not in substance, yet in form, the struggle of the proletariat with the bourgeoisie is at first a national struggle. The proletariat of each country must, of course, first of all settle matters with its own bourgeoisie."[12]

Although the common territory, language, and traditions of the nation are tied to the capitalist mode of production and thus function in the interest of the bourgeoisie, they can when transformed also belong to and serve the interests of the great majority. Evidently, many aspects of the national structure would need to be modified with a view toward the long-term obsolescence of the nation state. But, to attain its end it is essential at a certain stage that the working class gain control of the nation and its apparatus. The national territory, the national state, the national language, the national heritage, can all be national in a non-bourgeois sense, i.e. they can serve the needs of the dominated classes once the latter have ascended to power. Bourque and Laurin-Frenette elaborate on this theme with specific illustrations. For example, both the bourgeoisie and the lower classes have an interest in protecting the national language if it is threatened. But, this interest to defend and preserve the language is different for each class. This is true for all of the symbols of the nation – they are used, interpreted, and valued differently by each class within the nation; their content can be progressive or reactionary. The same symbols, they argue, have no value or significance outside of the particular class cultures in which they are incorporated.[13] While we find this assertion to be an over-statement derived from the extreme structural view of society which Bourque and Laurin-Frenette inherit from contemporary Marxists such as Althusser, it is works such as this which are reopening the "national question" to full analysis by left-wing theorists.[14] It is to this analysis that we hope to make some contribution – focusing not on the value of state power to the working class but rather on the validity and importance of the national issue and of nationalism for arousing, articulating and transmitting class consciousness in the lower classes of a colonized society.*

Marx asserts that the oppressed class will transform the society and eradicate its oppression. Yet Marx was unable to describe the process by which class consciousness develops or the forms it takes. This was inevitable because he did not have available to him, as we do today, the findings and insights of the anthropological, psychological, and sociological studies of language and culture** necessary to understand and explain the complex and varied mechanisms of consciousness. What is clear is that consciousness expresses itself in certain symbolic forms resting on the usage of language and symbolic structures. The working class cannot attain self-consciousness unless its members have available to them the components of a culture that is distinctive and is, as well, distinguished and distinguishable from the ruling culture or ideology. One type of symbol structure that can be at the base of such a culture is nationalism of the left; that is, a specific form of nationalism

---

* The debate on nationalism and class in Quebec is taken up directly in chapters 9 and 10 below.
** The fields of cultural anthropology, social psychology and related areas were either very young or not even in existence in Marx's time. One of the major thrusts of this work has been the understanding that the means, language, structure, and form by which knowledge is communicated is as important as – and related to – the content of the knowledge. McLuhan captured this fact through overstatement: the medium is the message.

can be a primary component of the expression of the collective interests of the lower classes of a state whose economy or political system is dominated by a foreign elite.

The nationless proletariat did not grow as Marx predicted. Technological innovation, imperialism and the incorporation of some reformist demands and "moderate" leaders of the trade unions into the dominant structure have seen to that. If workers in Marx's time did not have a country, they often do today. Workers in the West have gained the vote, some social security benefits, some access to education, all of which have brought them closer to the nation as an entity, though not necessarily to the ruling classes. Simultaneously the process Lenin described as imperialism has been growing and expanding (though not just as he foresaw it). The age of the corporate state and the multinational corporation has come. It is the capitalist class that is more and more international and cosmopolitan; its children are the jet-setters; its economic and social institutions traversing state boundaries as if they did not exist.

These developments, and especially the progress of the working class, have led some contemporary social thinkers to maintain that present-day social and economic realities have obscured social class divisions. Dahrendorf for instance argues that class divisions in industry no longer need coincide with class divisions in other spheres of society and that any division today is between vague competing "political classes."[15] His basic insight is correct but misplaced: given the greater complexity of modern society other cleavages are relevant – however, the international and foreign source of economic control in many societies may lead to stronger rather than weaker class divisions. The resulting ethnic or national division, for instance, may exacerbate and reinforce the socio-economic class division and provide genuine cultural content to the expression of the consciousness and collective interest of the lower classes.

During the past two decades, there has been a great proliferation of movements espousing socialist and nationalist goals, especially among the people in the "Third World," China, Algeria, Cuba, and Viet Nam are among the clearest examples of societies in which the lower classes attained consciousness at least partially via their nationalist aspirations. Yet a parallel tendency has been noted within the capitalist metropolis. One of the very few studies to examine empirically the relationship of ethnicity and class consciousness was carried out by John Leggett in a working class district of Detroit. Leggett found that in times of economic hardship, labour militancy and working class consciousness was greatest among the racial or ethnic groups that were lowest in social rank and status. Black workers were consistently most militant, Polish workers followed, etc. Class consciousness, he concluded, was strongest when stratification was associated with racial or ethnic factors.[16]

It seems, then, that modern developments allow for a possible reformulation of the Marxist view of society to account for, examine and evaluate nationalism on the left. Structural changes have tended to identify the working class with the nation – with the language and cultural particularities distinguishing the national group whose homeland is the satellite from the ruling class of the metropolis. Given the international or foreign flavour that the world of business assumes in the satellite, precisely because the owners and most of the managers and hence their perspectives are foreign, it is the working class which most authentically feels and expresses the history, aspirations and consciousness of the nation. Cultural anthropology has taught us that the expression of consciousness is symbolic and indirect – mediated through language, tradition, myth and custom. Just because the working class is unable to participate to any great extent in the increasingly Americanized social and economic life of its bourgeoisie, it is the working class of the satellite which continues to express and live the national culture.

Although there has been an upsurge of socialist forms of nationalism during the past two decades, there have been few attempts to comprehensivly analyse "nationalism" in light of the experience of these socialist movements rather than accepting the view built on the 1930 and 1940 versions. A recent study of the Arab countries by Anouar Abdel-Malek distinguishes between old-type nationalism and "le phénomène nationalitaire." The former "refers to two sorts of things: some, negative, such as the rejection of the other, the turning in on oneself, and the negation of universalism; others, more directly activist, notably frontier disputes and expansionist aims that have been at the root of European wars for four centuries. On the other hand, the "nationalitarian"* phenomenon is that in which the

---

* This word is a translation of the term used by Abdel-Malek, "le phéno-mène nationalitaire." He uses it to characterize nations fighting for independence and to distinguish these present day national liberation

struggle against the imperialist occupying power sets itself the objective – over and above the evacuation of the national territory, independence and sovereignty for the national state, and the complete uprooting in depth of the former occupying power – the reconquest of the power of decision in all domains of national life."[17]

Abdel-Malek's work is especially important bcause it is one of the first attempts to distinguish left from right forms of nationalism so that socialist nationalist movements can be clearly understood as a phenomenon totally different from "National Socialism," i.e., Naziism. Hitler's ghost, it seems, has stood in the way of the appearance of both theoretical and empirical works dealing with nationalism as it has been expressed in recent years in those underdeveloped nations where imperialism has penetrated most. However, while Abdel-Malek's work does distinguish between different sorts of nationalism by analysing the demands and goals of each, it does not deal with the actual relationship between socialist goals and nationalist convictions and strategy.

Simply put, a nation in the position of an economic colony, such as Quebec, can only retain its cultural uniqueness by ridding itself of the foreign elite. It is this elite, through their control of the satellite's economy as well as its major political parties, media and press, and cultural institutions, who force foreign consumption patterns, life styles, and language onto the masses in the satellite. Chapter one described the American ruling class' need to create middle Americans in the satellite nations, developing in them the taste to buy American goods and services. Chapter 3 described the subordinate position of French Canadians within Quebec; it was noted there that those few who have succeeded in climbing the managerial ladder in the business world have generally done so by speaking English and adopting English social patterns.

Still, the system to be implemented after the foreign elite is thrown out of the satellite depends in part upon which social class succeeds in making its goals central in the movement that gains power – the lower classes or the educated middle classes. Hence, in approaching the problem of "nationalism" it becomes imperative to closely examine the social location of those

struggles from traditional European nationalism of the past. The French phrase was initially coined by René Johannet in 1918 in his book *Le Principe des Nationalités.*

espousing the nationalism as well as those opposing it, and what they have to gain or lose. This is one of our tasks in Part II. Herein, it is proposed, is an approach to analyzing the phenomenon of nationalism in such a way as to explain the recent rise of left-wing, lower-class movements in many underdeveloped countries and to evaluate their strategies and chances of success. Such a task is of course much beyond the scope of this book, but hopefully, by using these notions to examine the social dynamic of present day Quebec, some clues and insights of a more general nature into this question on a global level will emerge and prove useful.

In conclusion, this final chapter has added to the description of (American) economic imperialism the dimension of ideology, that is, how the status quo is defended by liberal intellectuals. These latter, hiding profit and exploitation behind internationalism and brotherhood, point to how the foreign investors are "developing" the country. If the lower classes demand that their own language be used in the factory and taught in the schools, or demand working conditions or pay equal to those of their counterparts in the metropolis, or if they object to the privileges of the residents of upper-class ghettoes, they are labelled as reactionary, as expressing "racist" sentiments. Thus real grievances and legitimate class demands are too often dealt with by labelling them "nationalist."

In looking more closely at the social position of these lower classes as we have, it has become evident that the dynamics of the monopoly capitalist system ensure that a fair distribution of wealth and power among the classes cannot be accomplished without the restoration of economic control to the people in the satellite. Hence, independence, economic, political and cultural is absolutely crucial; class and national demands coincide.

Nationalism is not a monolithic doctrine or even a doctrine at all. In Quebec the espoused nationalisms range from far right to the left. It is necessary to examine the organizational structure, the tactics, and the goals of these groups as well as their historical origins in order to understand the class nature of the demands and the possibilities inherent in them.

This discussion of nationalism has completed the first part of the book. We have seen that its expression among a colonized people like the Québecois can be progressive. This kind of nationalism on the left identifies the goals of the great mass of the people – equality and justice, with national liberation – the elimination of foreign economic domination. It appeals to the nation because it is mainly the working class that today expresses and keeps alive the national culture, language and sentiment; the ownership class has been internationalized, i.e., Americanized. Hence economic and political independence is a meaningful popular need and the movement centered around it is qualitatively different from the xenophobic national chauvinism associated with right-wing governments and mentalities. Trudeau is mistaken about nationalism – there are more types than just one.

While nationalism of the left is thus a position and ideology congruent with the needs of the people of Quebec, its emergence has been long awaited and painful. To understand the origins and future of Left Nationalism we turn from economics to history – Quebec since 1930.

Footnotes to Chapter 5

1. Quoted in Stanley Ryerson, "Technology, Nationalism and the Canada/Quebec 'Problematic'," *Horizons Research Letter,* January, 1970, p. 2.
2. *Ibid.*
3. Trudeau's personal fortune is the result of an inheritance from his father who, in good Canadian fashion, sold his oil company interest to an American multinational oil corporation.
4. P. E. Trudeau, *Federalism and the French Canadians* (Toronto: The Macmillan Company of Canada, Ltd., 1968), p. 190.
5. *Ibid.,* pp. 184-85.
6. See for instance, W. A. Williams, *The Tragedy of American Diplomacy* (New York: Dell Publishing Co., Inc., 1962).
7. P. E. Trudeau, *op. cit.,* p. 168.
8. Horace Davis, *Nationalism and Socialism* (New York: Monthly Review Press, 1967), pp. 59-82.
9. See *Ibid.,* pp. 185-210.
10. *Quotations from Chairman Mao Tse-Tung* (Peking: Foreign Languages Press, 1967), pp. 176, 180.

11. Karl Marx, Frederick Engels, *Manifesto of the Communist Party* (Peking: Foreign Languages Press, 1965), pp. 54-55.
12. *Ibid.,* p. 45.
13. See Gilles Bourque, Nicole Laurin-Frenette, "Classes sociales et idéologies nationalistes au Québec 1760-1970," *Socialisme Québécois,* No. 20 (June, 1970), pp. 13-55. An English language commentary on this important paper can be found in D. Roussopoulos, "Nationalism and Social Classes in Québec," *Our Generation,* Vol. 8, No. 2, pp. 37-56.
14. An important example is the work by Nicos Poulantzas entitled: *Pouvoir Politique et Classes Sociales* (Paris: F. Maspero, 1968).
15. Ralf Dahrendorf, *Class and Class Conflict in Industrial Society* (Stanford: Stanford University Press, 1969), pp. 271-75.
16. John Leggett, *Class, Race and Labour* (New York: Oxford University Press, 1966), especially pp. 98-101 and pp. 114-18.
17. Anouar Abdel-Malek, "Sociologie de développement national: problèmes de conceptualisation," *Revue de l'Institut de Sociologie,* 1967, No. 2-3, p. 66. (Authors' translation.)

Part Two

FROM SUBMISSION
TO
SELF-CONSCIOUSNESS

CHAPTER 6

THE
THIRTIES:
AUTHORITARIANISM
AND
SELLOUT

It was during the economic crisis of the thirties. Our province was a paradise for all things reactionary, conservative (despite a regime labelled "Liberal").[1]

Part Two looks at contemporary Quebec starting from the thirties; yet in a sense it covers the entire history of Quebec. In many important ways it was the thirties that marked the culmination of Quebec history since its beginning; and the major events and new ideas that shook Quebec society after World War Two transformed a system that had remained fundamentally intact since the earliest days of the colony.

Les Québecois, as Marcel Rioux reminds us, are among the oldest, if not *the* oldest, colonized people. Quebec was settled in the early seventeenth century to serve those who ruled France. The inhabitants, "les Canayens," quickly developed a social structure and culture which reflected that colonial position. Certain aspects of life such as commerce, politics and war were closed to the participation of the inhabitants. This was the prerogative of the colonial regime.

Matters social, moral and cultural were the concerns of the inhabitants and life in the row settlements was built around preserving the traditional social patterns surrounding their activities. Central was the Church whose authority in moral and related questions was supreme. The center of the community became the parish priest who was personally responsible for the maintenance of the social structure. Thus even in this early stage the basic pattern is already in evidence. There are

105

two elite forces, one external and the other internal, each acting independently within its own domain supplemented by a process of negotiation, characterized by limited conflict, on items of joint concern. There is, however, some evidence that during the latter part of the French period this tight structure was being penetrated by a new commercial class tied to France and its colonial privileges but also beginning to identify their homeland as New France. In addition it was mainly through this class that the ideas of liberalism, rationalism and deism that were spreading in France at this time found their limited way to the colony.

Any chance that existed for a challenge to the essentially monolithic culture of the Ancien Regime lay at this point in the development of a significant French-speaking liberal commercial class. The British conquest put an end to this possibility. English and Scottish merchants and traders came to take over the commerce of the province. The working arrangement between the Church and colonial hierarchy was actually strengthened when the British assumed control of the latter. The British, sharing neither religion nor language with the people, permitted the autonomy of the clerical authority in its own sphere to be enhanced. On the other hand the Church succeeded in keeping the Canayens out of politics, commerce and any potential military action against the new rulers.

This arrangement functioned admirably for both sides until the nineteenth century. At this point a movement arose among some of the more educated of the French Canadians, professionals such as doctors, wealthier farmers, etc. (a group we will refer to as the old middle class), influenced somewhat by the triumph of American Republicanism. Its goals were democratic participation by the people in their political affairs, the liberalization of the society and the eventual independence of the Quebec state. This movement was crushed militarily by the British in 1837-38 and, afterwards, in the period up to confederation, crushed ideologically and culturally by the Church through excommunication, rigid censorship and the like.

A new class of English-speaking businessmen centered around the railroad interests had gained power in this period, especially in Montreal. It was this group that was the driving force behind confederation, which officially took place in 1867. Confederation was a minor event in Quebec. Although it provided on paper for greater political representation, its major significance was that it symbolized the transformation of the colonial control of Quebec from political to primarily economic techniques. The culture of survival ("survivance") revolving around the clerical hierarchy was not at all challenged by political change. Whatever personal, financial and status gains that could be made from it, it was understood that participation was basically just window dressing. While outwardly Quebec changed a great deal between confederation and the thirties, as rapid industrialization and urbanization occured, inwardly it remained basically static. There were certain minor changes; the Church hierarchy, once the remaining "Rouge"* elements had been suppressed, was able to incorporate the old middle class under its authority. At this point it was prepared to accept "liberalism" as defined by Wilfrid Laurier, which turned out to be basically nothing new. When popular feeling or anger rose in Quebec on one matter or another it was usually channelled into harmless forms of negative nationalist protest without concrete results. The Riel execution in 1885 followed by the emergence and disappearance of Mercier and the Parti National is an example. The ferment, during the First World War, against Ontario's educational policy and again in opposition to conscription is another. In 1926 the U.S.A. replaced Britain as the major source of foreign capital in Canada.

In this period Quebec produced an important culture in poetry, history, literature and philosophy but one which found its ideals and heroes in the past – in a romanticized portrayal of the life of the inhabitants of the seventeenth century. The nineteen twenties, which was for Quebec as for the world a period of relative prosperity, saw a great flowering of cultural expression which, if it had continued, might have given rise to new ideas to challenge the old system and the beliefs on which it rested. The depression and the resultant hardship had the effect of postponing that possibility. Quebec turned even more inwards and looked even more to the past.

During the thirties, the Church and a small elite of lay people trained by the clergy and directly under their influence

---

* The Rouge (red) tradition is one that dates back to the ideas of the 1837-38 insurrection. Its philosophy is liberal but more a combination of French and American Jacksonian liberalism as opposed to the British/Whig liberalism of Laurier.

controlled almost every non-economic aspect of French-Canadian social and cultural life. Throughout Quebec, only one view of the world was presented: the schools, the newspapers, and magazines explained the depression and analyzed its causes in much the same way, and proposed almost identical solutions. There were very few, if any, French-speaking organizations in the province which did not echo this same analysis while vainly trying to implement the God-given solutions under the direction of this elite. If an organization presenting an opposing world view somehow cropped up, it was quickly discredited and destroyed. It was virtually impossible for an opposition to develop, for no media would carry its message and all public forums for discussion were dominated by the clergy and lay people who articulated the philosophy it taught. During the latter part of the decade the Padlock Law was imposed so that any groups whose ideas were considered at all threatening were legally restrained from the use of any premises large enough for public meetings.

The depression resulted in a 44 percent decrease in provincial revenue for Quebec. The lower classes of Quebec suffered immeasurably throughout this economic crisis. In 1933, 30 percent of the province's work force was unemployed.[2] The employment that was available was little improvement over unemployment. The Royal Commission on Price Spreads in 1937 completed an investigation of many large industries. They found incredibly deplorable working conditions alongside an actual increase in the profits of these companies during the depression. At Louiseville, an American-owned textile company whose profits had increased steadily since 1929, paid female workers $9.73 for a fifty-five hour work week. The commission cited one example in which a company declared a dividend (in parts) of 80 percent, but 90 percent of its employees earned less than $10 per week. In another case, the American owners reduced wages by 10 percent and made a profit of $1,800,000.[3]

In light of these conditions we turn to the philosophy propounded by the Church and the lay intelligentsia, which together make up what we call the traditional elite, and which dominated social life and thought in Quebec during this period. The Church hierarchy found it necessary to temper its official pronouncements on social questions of the day, so as not to offend their Anglophone counterparts throughout the continent. The laymen were not so hampered and thus their statements of policy and principle often sound more extreme. It is very doubtful consequently that these two groups in fact differed on any question of significance.

The Archbishop of Montreal, Monseigneur Gauthier, saw the causes of the depression imbedded in economic liberalism. This philosophy, he said, based on immoral business practices, a materialist conception of money, and the mechanization of jobs needed by men, had the sole objective of profit making.[4] The Archbishop of Quebec deplored the system in which a worker was viewed as a production machine, devoid of human dignity or a soul, and where the company's owners ignored the worker's responsibilities to God and to his family.[5] The Church asserted that the first duty of the proprietors of industry was to pay wages which were sufficient for men to support their large families.[6] Employment of women was opposed, not on the grounds of exploitative working conditions but because the woman's role was seen as one of wife and mother exclusively.

The bishops of Quebec were always careful to distinguish between the system of capitalism, which they defended, and the abuses of the system which they hinted were the result of the greed which originated in the Protestants' liberalism and materialism. The Archbishop of Quebec described capitalism in May, 1933, as "the social system in which men contribute generally to economic activity, some with capital others with work. Such a system is neither bad nor illegitimate in itself, on the contrary, it is most in keeping with human nature and best suited to the well being and economic progress of the people."[7] The capitalist economic system is thus a necessary element of the social order but it must be correctly employed. In the words of the Bishop of Gaspé: "Capitalism plays its social role when it employs its resources in creating industry, when it gives rise to enterprises in which the workers find the opportunity to apply their mental and physical energies in work which provides them with the means of subsistence."[8]

The role of the state is to stimulate, to sanction and to orient the work of private initiative, but not to substitute for it. The vitality of professional organizations was thought to be diminished if public powers assume their tasks; furthermore state intervention to regulate the economy or to mediate poverty was viewed as the beginnings of state capitalism or socialism.

109

All forms of social insurance, of protective tariffs, of old age pensions provided by the state were harmful, for they weakened individual enterprise.[9]

The Church viewed itself and the elite which it had trained as having a duty to care for the lower classes. The privileges and comparative wealth of the elite were acknowledged and justified on the grounds that a superior class such as this was essential to protect and direct the French-Canadian flock. "Monseigneur Gauthier further explained the credo of the Church in pointing out that Catholicism, through its doctrines relating to the use of wealth, makes the rich into patrons or alms-givers for the poor; through the alm they are given the task of reestablishing the revered balance between opulence and poverty."[10]

In 1933 Monseigneur Gauthier, then Archbishop of Montreal, warned the population against the new Cooperative Commonwealth Federation. Its basically anti-elitist program which advocated state intervention, social welfare measures and centralization, opposed most of the Church's dogmatic beliefs. The Monseigneur identified the CCF with the spectre of Soviet Communism which was described as promoting violent revolution and an atheistic state. In condemning the CCF he reminded his audience that the Church emphasized the primacy of the individual and the "natural right" of private property.[11] It is clear that the Church in condemning the CCF was doing more than establishing Church dogma. Something immediate was threatening and needed to be dealt with.

In October 1933 the Catholic hierarchy published a declaration deploring the dangers of the present times as seen in the discontent and agitation following naturally from the economic crisis. "Struck by the weakening of resolve when tested by hardship," the Canadian bishops reminded Catholics that: "one, Soviet communism remains forbidden to a Catholic; two, socialism is not an efficient remedy for our ills; and three, capital is not bad in itself and wealth is not necessarily the fruit of dishonesty."[12]

The hierarchy of the Quebec Church seems to have recognized the possibility of the discontent of the lower classes turning into a clear demand for a radical change in the society. One explanation suggests that this fear forced them to become even more protective of their dominant position. In a more liberal, centralized state, France is an excellent example, the Catholic Church would lose its privileged position and much of its control over education and social welfare. The hierarchy seems to have understood the probable result if the CCF or a party with similar goals were to achieve power and fought hard to avert it.* It has commonly been assumed that the CCF failed in Quebec because of the Church's condemnation. One thing which will hopefully be demonstrated in this chapter is that it was not the official condemnation but rather the blocking of all forms of discussion, political education or even of communication of information between the party and the Quebec population which ensured the failure of the CCF and of all left-wing political action. (The English Protestant public image of the CCF did not serve to help its cause either.)

L'Ecole Sociale Populaire, a Jesuit organization, took great responsibility for disseminating the social doctrine of the Church to the people of Quebec. Its self-proclaimed task was one of "propaganda, education, and social improvement."[13] The first two, as Trudeau points out, could not lead to the latter. "Unfortunately these zealots seemed to conceive of sociology, economics and politics as deductive procedures with the help of which – starting from 'grand principles' rather than facts – an obedient people could be led toward desirable goals. Consequently this institution bears major responsibility for the fact that social thought in French Canada has been unrealistically oriented in a rationalist path narrowly bounded by clericalism, the worship of agriculture and a paternalistic attitude toward labour."[14]

Its news-agency propaganda service was described by a spokesman as follows: "Each week L'Ecole Sociale Populaire sends without charge to all the daily and weekly newspapers of Canada, . . . a newsletter for the most part dealing with communism. It contains up to date and strictly authentic news, which we send out from European agencies, about the situation in the U.S.S.R. – religious, political and economic aspects – and on communist goings on around the world."[15]

In the spring of 1933, l'Ecole Sociale Populaire opened a school to train speakers who would be "capable of spreading the social doctrine of the Church in popular activities." The

* See below Chapter 10.

people trained in this school were sent throughout the province to begin "cercles d'étude," or study groups, the purpose of which was to have the social doctrine of the Church penetrate all spheres of life in Quebec.[16]

L'Ecole Sociale Populaire also ran an information service. From 1936 to 1940, it published *l'Ordre Nouveau,* dedicated to the establishment of a corporate state in Quebec. The index shows that during this four year period, there were 64 articles on corporatism, 20 articles on trade unions, 16 articles on cooperatives, 10 articles on proprietors, 7 articles on agriculture, and 3 articles on work.[17] The publication of monthly brochures, and the organization of annual days of study in each parish were other activities carried out by l'Ecole Sociale Populaire. To foster renewed Catholic action "the school sought to contribute to the training of militants, leaders in Catholic action, through sophisticated theoretical and practical teaching: each year its director gives . . . a series of courses followed by examinations on the principles and organization of 'Action Catholique'."[18]

Each year from 1920 on, the academics within the elite of French Canada met together in "Semaines sociales" organized to study a particular problem. As described by the directors of l'Ecole Sociale Populaire, "the work of the Semaines sociales consists of studying contemporary social problems in the light of Catholic doctrine."[19]

L'Ecole Sociale Populaire was also responsible to a relatively extensive degree, for the distribution of information about the Spanish Civil War within Quebec. This war was a genuine crusade for Catholicism: "On one side the fighting man of all ideologies who partially or fully represent the old tradition and the old history of Spain; on the other side a conglomerate of fighting men whose principal objective is, more than triumph over the enemy, the destruction of all the values of our old civilization."[20]

Virulently anti-communist, anti-liberal and anti-materialist, l'Ecole Sociale Populaire proposed to solve the economic crisis of the thirties by reversing the exodus from the rural areas and colonizing the virgin lands of the province. Politically it envisaged the establishment of a corporate state as had been done by Salazar in Portugal and Dolfuss in Austria. This state would be organized hierarchically according to the social doctrine of the Church; each class performing its divinely ordained duty. The owners of industry would recognize their duty to pay wages sufficient to support large families thereby eliminating industrial conflict; the privileged and wealthy would recognize their duty to care for the aged and infirm, the widows and orphans, thus eliminating any need for state-run social welfare programs. As a whole the varied program of l'Ecole Sociale Populaire, both those parts aimed at the French-Canadian intellectual elite and those aimed directly at the masses, were relatively successful in disseminating propaganda and conducting political and social education.

The Jesuits were also responsible for initiating a review, *L'Action Française,* dedicated principally to propagating a nationalist doctrine built upon the social teachings of the Church and modelled in part on the French review of the same name edited by the rabid reactionary, Charles Maurras. *L'Action Française* was edited in the twenties by Abbé Lionel Groulx. Among other things, the existence of Anglophone schools was attacked. American economic control and cultural influences were deplored, as was the fact that Quebec had more Jews than any other province. The policies of Mussolini were applauded, with suggestions that the same reforms could be accomplished in a separate French-Canadian state.[21]

With the prosperity of the late twenties and the Pope's repudiation of its French counterpart, the review disappeared. But, the economic crisis revived it in 1932 under the name *L'Action Nationale.* The new review attacked the abuses of the capitalist system, and suggested a back-to-the-land policy to relieve the sufferings brought on by the depression. The need for bilingualism and a re-Frenchification program, were common themes as was the notion that the Jews were the cause of Quebec's ills.[22] *L'Action Nationale* strongly resented the fact that ownership and control of the province's wealth and natural resources were in the hands of foreign capitalists, while the French Canadians had become proletarianized. The only solution which all could agree upon, however, was the promotion of small businesses run by French Canadians.[23]

In 1934, when Arthur Laurendeau became editor, the need for a "chef," for someone to lead the French Canadians in the manner of the fascist dictators of Catholic Europe, became a common theme. To produce a spiritual renaissance, the French

Canadians required not a precise political plan, but the co-ordinated action of an inspired leader and elite. The editor of *L'Action Nationale* could see no virtue in democracy anywhere in the world, but for French Canadians its unsuitability was enhanced by corruption, by the violence of electoral disputes and, above all, by the absence of any "mystique nationale." Without this "mystique" democracy had made of French Canadians "vain and barren blabbermouths and bickerers."

If, for all French Canadians, democratic procedures had a quality of artificiality and remoteness, for the Action Française circle they smacked, in addition, of a materialistic pragmatism which made for extreme distaste. Many of them, not unreasonably, equated capitalism and democracy; the motives of the economic market place and the motives of the election. In each case, personal gain, lack of principle and materialistic haggling seemed to be the dominant characteristics.[24]

The traditional, right wing nationalism of *L'Action Française* and *L'Action Nationale* always held out the possibility and the hope for an independent nation and never rested content with the subordinate position of French Canadians within Quebec and Canada. It made the intellectuals of Quebec aware of the fragility of their culture, the anglicization of their language, and the changing values of the masses. To that extent it was important; however, its inability to critically look at the philosophical underpinnings of Quebec's beliefs, including its own, ensured its limited impact. Its lack of realistic solutions to aid the French Canadians to regain control of Quebec is exemplified by its focusing on the Jews for usurping the role of small businessmen which in the corporate scheme was meant for the French Canadian. When in 1937, André Laurendeau became editor of *L'Action Nationale,* he put an end to the policy of racism and adulation for European fascism which had been promoted by his father. Among the new generation of nationalists the idea of a highly structured society with the "Chef" at its head was coming into question.

La Nation, a right wing nationalist periodical staffed by academics from Laval, was begun in February, 1936, under the editorship of Paul Bouchard. Mussolini was a major hero; Hitler, the humble shepherd of the German flock in whom much good could be seen. The review was anti-democratic and anti-capitalist. It favoured corporatism and an exaggerated role for the elite in the new independent corporate state. The intensity of its anti-semitism was, within Canada, second only to that of the Nazi party. Bouchard viewed fascism as the political corollary of corporatism, and the logical extension of Abbé Groulx's philosophy.[25] In 1937, Bouchard ran against a Liberal candidate, J. M. Francoeur in a federal by-election. Wade notes the following: "It was significant of the strength of extreme nationalism that the French-Canadian federal leader [the Minister of Justice, Ernest Lapointe] felt it necessary to take part in this by-election."[26]

In November, 1936, the "Manifeste de la Jeune Génération" was published and became the program of a new nationalist youth movement, "Les Jeunes-Canada." It demanded respect for the rights of each race in Canada. It attacked the federal government for the secondary status of the French language in government publications, on paper money and in advertisements and labels. It demanded that a just share of federal civil service jobs be awarded to French Canadians. The manifesto deplored the discrimination shown by foreign capitalists in denying higher positions to French Canadians. Natural resources, it was recognized further, had to be guarded from exploitation by foreigners. Politicians were blamed for the depression and for spreading disunity within the French-Canadian nation. Les Jeunes-Canada exploited the growing anti-semitism in Montreal by emphasizing that the Jews had robbed the French Canadians of their rightful place as retailers.[27]

The Jeunes-Canada movement, which was centered around the *Quartier Latin* (student paper) at the Université de Montréal, was less reactionary and less authoritarian than the older generation, but the virulence of the anti-semitism demonstrated by this new generation was surprising. Perhaps fears of losing the few employment opportunities that did exist is a factor here. In June of 1934, members of "Les Jeunes-Canada" inspired a strike of the interns at the Hôtel Dieu Hospital in Montreal to demand the discharge of a Jewish classmate, Samuel Rabinovitch. The strike was supported by several sections of the "Société Saint-Jean Baptiste," as well as several other nationalistic Catholic organizations. Signs of "No Jews Allowed" and "Christians Only" were common throughout the province.* As

* The English Protestants, of course, were involved even more deeply if more subtly in anti-semitic discrimination.

115

late as 1939, Ste Agathe attempted to pass municipal by-laws prohibiting Jews from buying property.[28] E. C. Hughes, for one, understood the Jews as scapegoats used by the French Canadians to vent their frustrations which actually resulted from the Anglo-Saxon economic domination of Quebec. Because the Jews were principally retailers and small businessmen, their presence was very obvious, much more so than the Anglo-American capitalists who pulled the strings from behind the scene.* While true, this explanation leaves out the role of the Church's teachings in predisposing the population to anti-semitism. For the Church the Jews were the murderers of Christ; Judaism was a pagan philosophy in no way comparable to Catholicism. By further intimating that all Jews were actually Bolsheviks and atheists, the Church did nothing to dispel and rather helped to promote anti-semitism. The Church's goal lay in increased clerical power through the creation of a hierarchical corporate society composed of workers and peasants at the bottom and dominated by a petty bourgeoisie who would follow the teachings and leadership of the Church. To oppose the rampant anti-semitism would have been to ally with its liberal critics, thereby alienating its most faithful followers.

Some members of the new generation joined the camp of the virulent right wing nationalists. A group called "Les Jeunes Patriotes" published a newspaper, *L'Indépendance,* in which they called for the separation of Quebec from Canada and the creation of the state of "Laurentie." The Church's power was to be increased in this new corporate state, which would restore authority and destroy democracy and the disunifying force of political parties. The petty bourgeoisie would rule supreme; the trusts and chain stores would be liquidated. Industrialism,

---

* The Montreal Jewish community of the thirties and early forties is brilliantly captured in the work of novelist Mordecai Richler. The racism that existed between the Jews and the French Canadians was mutual. Both were struggling to gain some economic advantage while preserving their cultural identity in an Anglo-Saxon run world. The Jewish community was a center of progressive opinion and a hotbed of communist and radical sympathies in stark contrast to the conservatism of the French Canadians. However, in the post-war prosperity the Jews "made it" economically and since then have adopted for the most part the negative attitudes and perspective of the feared English with respect to the present-day development of radicalism among Les Québecois.

seen as the father of liberalism and marxism, would be cast out leaving in its place essentially a medieval state of peasants, craftsmen and small traders, governed by professional men with the clergy dominant over all. The new state would be male dominated, suppressing all women's rights. Les Jeunes Patriotes saw all the problems of Quebec in 1936 as stemming from only one source, "Jewish Liberalism."[29]

The only Québecois institution of the period anywhere near left of center is *La Relève*. *La Relève* was a political review begun by a part of the traditional elite who wished to distinguish themselves from the right wing nationalists. The medieval society was idealized, but its inapplicability to Quebec of the thirties was recognized. Their vision of the world was essentially theocentric and hiearchical but tempered by a belief in Christian humanism. The French doctrine of "personalism" led them to a belief in the primacy of the individual, and the subordination of politics to personal, moral and aesthetic considerations. Independence was seen as necessary for the growth and development of the French Canadians, and it was understood that changes had to be accomplished not by the English CCF, but by the French Canadians themselves. The right wing features of traditional nationalism were deplored, but merely vague platitudes replaced them. A constant wavering between the rightist tradition of Groulx nationalism and the French Catholic left of Maritain and Mounier was evident throughout the review. In the end, *La Relève* evolved into a literary journal. The withdrawal from politics was "as much because they quailed at the immense task of transposing their religious ethic into a political programme for Quebec as because they believed political preoccupations to be too materialistic."[30]

From this brief survey of reviews and journals, the pervasiveness of the Church's teaching among educated Francophones is evident. Even the new generation displayed attitudes not significantly different, though at times more moderate, than their parents. The monolithic ideology prevailing within Francophone Quebec was at this time impenetrable. Neither the schools, the libraries, nor the media carried information or ideas contrary to the philosophy of the Church and its elite. Thus even the intellectuals were narrowly educated, with their eyes and ears to only one outside source of information (if any) – the right wing Catholic intellectuals of France.

Almost all manner of activity in Quebec, during the thirties, was to some degree under the control of the Church. By briefly looking at some of the lay organizations which were founded by the Church, we can understand why the development of a viable opposition was impossible. Individuals require both information and a minimum of skills to begin to criticise such an all-encompassing and sophisticated ideology as that propounded by the Roman Catholic Church of Quebec and the lay elite which served its interests. Because the interests of government and the Church coincided during this era with each reinforcing the power of the other, the discontented and frustrated social classes at the bottom were prevented from acquiring either the necessary information or skills to challenge their oppressors.

"La Confédération des Travailleurs Catholiques du Canada," (c.t.c.c.) was organized by the Church and the nationalist elite who feared that French-Canadian traditions and customs were threatened by the rapid growth of international unions in Quebec.

(The reader must keep in mind when studying this chapter that international unions were present and growing in Quebec during this period. However, only now is research data on their activities being gathered and sources are few, other than fearful references here and there to their rapid growth and strength. In 1932 the c.t.c.c. had 25,000 members, 59 percent of all male union membership, which itself was only 11 percent of industrial wage earners. In 1951 the c.t.c.c. had increased to 88,000 which was then only 34 percent of trade union membership. This is because organized labour had itself increased to including one of every three Quebec workers.[31])

The c.t.c.c. was a negative response: it was anti-socialist, anti-communist, anti-international, anti-American, anti-Protestant and anti-neutral. It was this "neutrality with regard to religion" that jarred most. After all, said the Bishop of Chicoutimi, international unions "profess neutrality with regard to religion or race. Their ranks . . . are open to Catholics, to protestants and to 'free-thinkers;' to French, to English and to Jews. They pretend to ignore religious divisions."[32]

The position was worded diplomatically, appealing to both nationalist, anti-English, and anti-American sentiment when written into the c.t.c.c. constitution at the founding convention in 1921. "The C.T.C.C. believes that it is non-sensical, economically in error, and politically dangerous, as well as an abdication of national interest, to have in Canada trade unions that relate to a foreign center that shares neither our laws nor our customs nor our mentality nor even the same problems."[33]

Membership in the C.T.C.C. was limited to Roman Catholics. Each local was run by an aûmonier, a priest or chaplain whose duty it was to educate the members to be conscious of their Catholic duties in their role as trade unionists. The aûmoniers chose from among the members a select group to participate in special study sessions. The purpose of these bi-weekly study sessions, declared Abbé Fortin, was the "creation of an elite capable of combating neutralism in the trade unions and protecting the Catholic faith."[34] The aûmoniers interpreted worker legislation, describing the advantages and disadvantages. Most time was spent in the explanation of papal encyclicals and their application to the practical problems met by the union members. Democracy as well as genuine economic or political analysis was rare. "The meeting of the study group began with a prayer, followed by the reading of the minutes of the last meeting. The chaplain then chose a member from the assembly to read a passage from the encyclical. . . . The reading was followed by a period of discussion in which the members sought to interpret what they had heard read aloud. The chaplain directed the discussion and corrected the errors."[34]

This method, according to Père Archambault usually succeeded in attaining the result desired. "The study group selected in this manner proved very effective on the actions of these men. It furnished religious knowledge for their minds and made them aware trade unionists. The seclusion of the locale of the retreat was an additional factor. It strengthened, through solitary work and reflection, those beliefs already mentally learned; it fortified the will with prayer and meditation; and it made of them, by teaching the apostles' doctrine of self-sacrifice, leaders within an elite that would set the movement straight."[35]

The only economic demand viewed as legitimate for the worker, was simply that of a wage sufficient to support his family. Legal strikes were permitted only when all else had failed; sympathy strikes were immoral and thus prohibited. The worker had no access to technical information to aid him in understanding the system of which he found himself a victim.

He was prevented from developing skills of argument and of public speaking by the authoritarian role of the chaplain. The idea of the owner as a man with a different role to play in the social order was propounded. The idea of class conflict was violently repudiated, as was the notion of a collectivist economy. Pontifical teachings were used to justify the right of private property.

A unionist's catechism was published, containing thirty-nine questions and answers. The first hour of each union meeting was devoted to the memorization of this catechism. Among the major articles of faith were the following:

> . . . the fundamental rights of workers include the right of freedom of conscience with respect to life, to moral surroundings, to the rest prescribed by God, to a salary adequate for a family as well as the right to organize into an association. . . .
>
> He [the unionist] must preserve his life and his health. He also has duties towards his soul, that is to say his moral duties: to observe the commandments of God and the Church. . . .
>
> . . . a Catholic cannot allow neutral unions because the latter consider all the problems of work as economic so that moral considerations do not enter into the solutions to these problems. They are guided only by self interest which does not always coincide with justice. . . .
>
> The Catholic worker must choose a national trade union if he wants to restore the corporate society, if he does not want to allow Canadian workers to be dominated by foreign leaders, and if he does not wish to risk the political danger of Canadian working men abandoned to being led in a foreign direction.[36]

The c.t.c.c. and other organizations launched by the traditional elite were meant as solutions to the practical problems of the day. They were also corporate structures, meant to train individuals in Catholic ways of doing things and to lay the foundation for a corporate state where each class and professional body would occupy a position in keeping with its moral place and duty. The prevalent paternalism and elitism, the ignorance of social and economic realities, the belief in hierarchical authority, and the dependence on the pontifical teachings to solve day to day problems are echoed in the structures and professed objectives of these organizations.

The movement of "caisses populaires", credit unions, was begun at the turn of the century. Organized on a parish basis, they were meant to teach the virtue of savings and to provide low interest loans to members. But they provided a more important service. In 1932, the provincial government passed a law, at the urging of the Fédération des Caisses, that all investments must be made within Canada, in the forms of loans to municipalities, to school boards, for the building of churches, cemeteries, etc. In this way the parish priest exercised a good deal of influence on the decisions made.[37] To join the local branch an individual had to swear, "I am a French Canadian and a practising Catholic."

During the summer of 1923, the Church began a co-operative in an attempt to relieve the poverty of the Gaspé fishermen, but the lack of technical knowledge and experience in business led to its failure.[38] A farmers' co-op was established on l'île d'Orléans because "to make the island into one big family is only partially possible. It is possible only among the farmers, the poultry farmers, and the gardeners whose interests do not concretely oppose the ideal which is proposed to them."[39] Although suffering many of the same problems as the fishermen's co-operative, the one on l'île d'Orléans faced another. L'Ordre Jacques Cartier, a right wing secret organization of the petite bourgeoisie and professionals, infiltrated and had its members become directors of the farmers' co-op.*

Every Catholic parish usually had a Catholic action committee composed of all married men over thirty. The function of such groups was the discussion of papal teachings and the Church's position on relevant social and ethical questions. The Catholic action committee of Saint Charles de Limoilou was initiated when the priest chose three men whom he tutored in Catholic doctrine for a number of months. A series of Catholic action meetings were then organized, out of which the permanent Catholic Action Committee of Saint Charles de Limoilou was formed. Père Albert, the parish priest, made the nominations: "Before going any further, my dear friends, I suggest that we proceed to the election of officers who will be

* See chapter 7 below.

called to direct the Catholic action movement. I submit the names of J. Sylvio Roy, as president, David Brown, as treasurer, and Roméo Guimont, as secretary, since all three have studied the principles of Catholic action for several months."[40]

In November of 1929, Adrien Arcand, a journalist who had been fired from *La Presse* for organizing a union, began the fascist review, *Le Goglu.* It talked of the necessity for returning-to-the-land, an always popular theme. "Our farmers must remain on the land and town-dwellers must help conquer the country. Each French Canadian that is capable of it must prepare himself for a return to the land, to that healthy and natural life that strengthens the fortitude of races."[41] *Le Goglu* joined the struggle against the trusts and called for the nationalization of the hydro-electric companies. Foreign exploiters were viewed as having robbed Quebec of its natural resources.

The nationalism of *Le Goglu* was almost indistinguishable from that of *La Nation, L'Action Nationale* under the editorship of Arthur Laurendeau, or from that taught by Groulx and his disciples in schools throughout the province. "The hour cannot be delayed to call our race to manifest itself in its own ideal, reign in the province, cradle of its fathers, in all its liberty and all the breadth of its power. Everyone according to his means must help in the preparation of this French-Canadian mission over their native land – Québec."[42] A national saviour, a "chef," would accomplish this mission by establishing a corporate state.

'L'Ordre Patriotique des Goglus' was founded along with the review. It was a para-military, hierarchical, authoritarian movement dedicated to "general purification, the conservation of our Latin character, our customs and traditions, and to the defense of our rights and privileges."[43]

In 1934, "le Parti National Social Chrétien" was formed primarily by old Goglus. Arcand wrote *The Key to the Mystery,* a violently anti-semitic pamphlet, which the Nazi party translated and distributed throughout Germany. The family, the natural hierarchy and the basis of fascism in nationalism and Christianity were common themes for speeches and articles. The party seemed to indulge principally in educating its members and lobbying with both federal and provincial members of parliament. Citizenship was to be granted only to Christians; the Jews were to have no rights to their newly acquired schools in Quebec, and Canada should press for increased imperialistic effort through the Commonwealth.

In 1937 the American Nazi leader finally persuaded Arcand to form a Canadian Nazi party and Arcand became its leader. However, the Nazi party's policies of internationalism and pan-Canadianism were not popular in Quebec. Consequently the party remained on the fringes of political developments in the province.

The Church never condemned Arcand and his followers. Monseigneur Gauthier went only as far as to warn the people that Naziism had many contradictory positions which needed to be clarified. The anti-semitism of the movement was never mentioned. The attacks on fascism in Quebec were seen as diversions from the real threat – communism. Monseigneur Gauthier noted that "we must understand the attitude of hundreds of young people who engage in physical exercise and quasi-military training, and who wish to be in the center of action, if one day or another, we are faced with the same threat. . . . It is more important to know if the reasoning of our young people doesn't contain some truth in it, and if our weakness, our indecisive attitudes do not add up to helping the cause of communism."[44]

The actual membership of the Goglus, the Parti National Social Chrétien or the Nazi Party is hard to establish. Arcand says Le Parti National Social Chrétien had 12,000-16,000 members in Quebec before the war. In May, 1940, a rally in Montreal was attended by 10,000 people. It should be noted that Arcand had ties with the Conservative Party. He himself maintains that R. B. Bennett offered him the position of Minister of Labour if he could win a seat in the 1935 election.

This movement is important in understanding this era of Quebec's history. The fact that the traditional elite condoned such activities, and even suggested that attacks upon the fascist movements were diversionary tactics used by communist sympathizers is significant. The close correspondence between the analysis and solutions proposed by Arcand and those of the traditional elite explains why there was no thought of condemnation.

The Church and traditional elite promoted their authoritarian policies and ideas by attempting to integrate them into the daily lives of the Québecois in ways and through organizations that we have described and many others. Because the ideology espoused by this elite saw no role for the French Canadian in big business, it condoned the activities of the ruling Liberal Party, whose economic program seems to have been little more than selling Quebec to foreign investors at a cheap price. Foreign capitalists were encouraged by the government's minimum of restrictions and control over such matters as public utility rates, corporate financing and the sale of securities. Grants of land, tax exemptions and other concessions further promoted the exploitation of raw materials. An increase in taxes would paralyze progress and hinder initiative. Social welfare legislation was to be avoided as it increased taxes, as well as destroying the individual's sense of responsibility and initiative. Groups and individuals seeking guarantees for adequate wages, proper working conditions and the right to collective bargaining and union organizing were opposed as threats to economic stability.[45] Taschereau, the liberal leader, "regarded the prosperity of the large enterprises as the primary source of general well-being."[46]

Taschereau and the Liberal party were not alone in their beliefs. In Quebec City a movement of citizens attempted to force the city government to municipalize electric services within its limits. This was quite understandable considering that residents of Quebec City paid electric rates three times as high as the citizens of Hamilton and five times as high as those of Ottawa, two cities of comparable size. To such a suggestion the Montreal *Gazette* said: "Is a city to be allowed to become a competitor after private enterprise has sunk millions of investors' money? The capital of the province should be as safe a spot as the world boasts for the individual wanting to place money."[47]

Taschereau bewailed the fate of the three thousand stockholders of the Quebec Power Company, pointing out that one of the largest owners was the Church itself.[48] The movement for municipalization was soon smashed. The citizens of Montreal came upon another strategy in an attempt to demand government regulation of the power companies. They jumped the meters by tapping the wires and mains. Hundreds of prosecutions by the Montreal Light, Heat and Power Company and subsequent jail sentences packed the courts and publicized conditions that prevailed in working class Montreal.[49]

In the spring of 1933, an immigrant named Zynchuck was

shot by a policeman apparently for no reason.* The Protestant Ministerial Association, the Montreal Women's Clubs, the Delorimier Liberal Reform Club were among the groups demanding an inquiry.[50] Taschereau refused to institute such an inquiry and stated: "Foreigners who are not satisfied to breath the air of Quebec have but to depart to other lands."[51] The next day in the legislature he paid homage to the Montreal police. In a speech to the Police and Fire Chiefs' Association of Quebec, the premier declared: "When public bodies condemn the police and side with aliens, then I say they are wrong. . . . I have no hesitation in telling you that the arms placed in the hands of the police are to be used for the protection of life and property. . . . The grilling system has its advantages. When you read that after a sixteen-hour grilling the police were able to get some information in an abduction case, I think those who have done the grilling will say it is a useful way of obtaining information. . . . I even wonder if the man found with a revolver in his hand about to commit a crime should not get life imprisonment."[52]

The editors of *Canadian Forum* aptly summed up the Quebec situation under the Taschereau regime: "cases of police brutality and of callous disregard for the rights of the citizen have multiplied to such an alarming extent in the Province of Quebec recently that the shooting of the unfortunate Zynchuck by a policeman is only one incident among many. It is becoming increasingly clear that Quebec, with the open connivance and approval of the Government of that province, is openly becoming a center of Fascist infection and of the blackest kind of reaction."[53]

* It is incidents like the campaign to pack the courts with people arrested for jumping the wires to their electric meters, and a demonstration attended by 10,000 people to demand an inquiry into the "Zynchuck affair" that suggest there is an unwritten history of Quebec. Because the media were so closely controlled by those in power and for the many other reasons herein discussed as responsible for the isolation of Francophone Quebec, the existence, strength, or activities of protest movements is concealed. However, from the circumstantial evidence obtained, it would seem as if a very low level protest movement demanding better working and living conditions did exist. It seems to have had little if any political sophistication, and was aimed at demanding increased social welfare measures from the provincial government.

Onésime Gagnon, a young Conservative MLA and later Lieutenant-Governor was still not pleased: "time had come to stop the swing to the left, the wrong road, and begin a swing towards Fascism, the right road."[54] Taschereau demonstrated the same sentiments when he asked the Young Liberal Club of Quebec City to consider "whether democracy had not gone too far. Whether Mussolini was not sometimes right."[55]

This was the party supported by almost all English Quebecers, and deeply tied to those at the top. This was the party the English had helped keep in power in the mid-thirties. The Liberals met an opponent too strong for them – the Church. It seems as if the innumerable directorates held by Taschereau and his cabinet members on the boards of large banks and companies with operations in Quebec, alienated the Church. The Church felt that the Liberals were now too tightly connected with the English corporate world and thus not sensitive enough to the demands of the Church. For this error in judging power, Taschereau and his party paid dearly.

In fact, of course, the Liberals had been rather cosy with English-speaking business. Lomer Gouin, for instance, Taschereau's predecessor in Quebec, admitted readily to being on the board of directors of the Bank of Montreal, the Royal Trust and other powerful corporations. These practices, we know, neither began nor ended with him, but in the relative boom years of the twenties the moral authorities of the Church could afford to close one eye to these goings on. Not so in the depressed thirties with its seething resentment and frustrations.

In 1933, the Jesuits of L'Ecole Sociale Populaire wrote "Le Programme de restauration sociale." This was an interpretation and programme for the practical application of the papal encyclicals, *Rerum Novarum* and *Quadragesimo Anno* to the problems of Quebec. Le Programme became the basis of the platform for a break-away faction of the Liberal Party, "L'Action Libérale Nationale" (ALN). The Liberal party was seen as a corrupt tool of the Anglo-Saxon business establishment. Influential independent MLA's such as Albert Rioux, the president of the Catholic Farmers Union and René Chalout, a director of *L'Action Nationale,* became ALN candidates. Paul Bouchard, editor of *La Nation,* organized a coalition containing Les Jeunesses Patriotes, Les Jeunes Canada, Les Jeunesses

126

liberale-nationale, and some labour groups to work for him in the election of 1936.

The program of L'Action Libérale Nationale was heart-warming to the Church and lay elite. The rural way of life was idealized. Low credit rates, subsidies for some farm markets, assistance in marketing, the development of small and medium-sized industry to complement farm activity and destroy the "milk trust" were proposed. Co-operatives were to be organized to efficiently compete with and curb the power of large foreign enterprises; to promote rural colonization, roads, schools and churches were to be built in yet unpopulated areas.

Workers were to be guaranteed adequate wages and working conditions. Health insurance, pensions for needy mothers and the aged, and slum clearance programs were described. By "every possible means" the electric, paper, coal, gasoline, and bread trusts were to be destroyed. Conflicts of interest would be ended by prohibiting cabinet ministers from sitting on boards of directors of companies holding government contracts. The upper house was to be abolished.[56] These more progressive elements of the ALN program, however, were never to be implemented.

L'Action Libérale Nationale entered into a coalition with the dormant and ineffective Provincial Conservative Party. The money, political techniques and practical knowledge for the new party, the Union Nationale (UN), would be supplied by the Conservatives; popular support, as well as new men and ideas were to be contributed by the Action Libérale Nationale. For the election of 1935 the UN fielded candidates in all constituencies, winning 42 of 90 seats. Taschereau and the Liberals had used all manner of corruption, from stealing ballot boxes to beginning public works projects in crucial areas just months before the election and stopping work on them the day after the election, and still just barely sneaked through.

According to the agreement of the coalition, Duplessis, as leader of the Conservative party, was to lead the UN, while Paul Gouin, the leader of L'Action Libérale Nationale, along with his colleagues, were to form the majority of the cabinet.* Duplessis was a shrewd and skillful politician. He immediately

* As opposition party the UN could have only one leader – and that was Duplessis.

forced the re-opening of the Public Accounts Committee and raked the Liberal party over the coals for their mishandling of public funds. Taschereau was forced to resign and the new leader, Godbout called an election.

During this short period, it had become evident to the initial group of dissident Liberals who had formed the Action Libérale Nationale that Duplessis was not very different from their former leader. He quickly took control of the UN and, when parliament was dissolved in 1936, Paul Gouin resigned almost without notice. Duplessis fought the 1936 elections by stirring up nationalist feeling and appealing to the small businessmen and farmers. The corruption of the Liberal party having been exposed, Duplessis was easily voted into power winning 76 of 90 seats.

Duplessis' economic policy was essentially the same as that of Taschereau, although neither he nor his cabinet ministers ever became as outwardly integrated into the Anglo-capitalist elite. Rural inhabitants benefited from UN policies such as easier systems of credit, roads through rural areas, and the opening of new areas for settlement. In fact, Duplessis carried out almost all of the immediate agrarian reforms suggested in the "Programme de restauration sociale." The Church had been rewarded for its support of the new party.

Duplessis had no more respect for fair electoral practices than had Taschereau. He seems to have shared many of his predecessor's views with regard to the police, to opposition, and to democracy itself. Duplessis was different from Taschereau, in that he did not want to make it as an equal with the English corporate elite. He wanted this group to do its job of developing the province and providing jobs, while paying due respect to the power of the Premier. Similarly, Duplessis saw the Church as having specific functions, such as education, caring for orphans, the aged, the blind, etc. From the Church too, he sought respect for his power.

Duplessis' policies and programmes were those of a right-wing nationalist. To what extent he actually believed in the social doctrine preached by the Church, or the extent to which he simply manipulated it so as to stay in power, is hard to determine due to his inscrutable and secretive nature. There is little doubt that the Church and traditional elite collaborated with Duplessis on the virulent anti-communist campaign which he soon launched. This campaign resulted in a repressive atmosphere in which no opposition to the government or Church was free from being labelled communist. One was either for the status quo or a communist, atheist revolutionary.

In March, 1937, the infamous Padlock Law came into existence. It provided for the padlocking of all premises used for "communist" purposes or wherein communist literature was found. The definition of "communism" was deliberately vague and never clearly specified by the government, police, or law courts. For example, a Japanese boycott parade organized by the Quebec C.C.F. and the League for Peace and Democracy was stopped by the "Red Squad." Professor R. P. Y. Scott of the United Church Theological College was to have addressed a meeting on "The Peril of Fascism in Quebec." The meeting was cancelled as the proprietors of the building where it was to be held were warned that it would be padlocked. When another building large enough to hold the meeting was found, its proprietors were similarly threatened.[57] Were the authorities confusing communism with Protestantism? The padlock marked the limits of Catholic toleration and there was indeed room for such confusion. As Cardinal Villeneuve put it in January, 1938: "Freedom of speech and the press, freedom of worship, freedom of teaching: liberties true, decent and precious when they are used in free matters and within the limits of the moral good, beyond which they are abuses, weaknesses and destructive principles . . . there are perhaps . . . strangers to our faith . . . listening to me . . . I tolerate you . . . I tolerate you so that you will tolerate me. I tolerate you . . . so that you may admire at once the splendour of my religion and the delicacy of my charity. . . . I tolerate you in order to have your collaboration in the common good, and when such collaboration stops, *when you preach corrosive doctrines and spread everywhere poisoned seeds, then I can no longer tolerate you.* Such, gentlemen, is Catholic liberalism."[58]

With the definition of communism left sufficiently vague so as to apply to almost any philosophy other than right-wing Catholicism, Duplessis proceeded to use the Padlock Law against any form of opposition to his regime. "Illegal arrest, if arrest it can be called when the whole proceeding takes place without charge laid, is one technique of 'enforcing the Padlock Act' without too much painful publicity. . . . Another delicate method of reaching the same objective is to get the landlord to evict any tenant who has incurred the displeasure of the Attorney-General (Duplessis) by threatening the landlord with a padlock order."[59]

Archbishop Gauthier voiced the dominant feeling in the Church hierarchy in his public reaction to such activities: "Prohibition . . . in . . . Montreal of meetings of the Communist Party, and throughout the province the seizure . . . of the evil literature which it spreads. God be praised! We have been very slow to protect ourselves, but at last the public authorities . . . have had the courage to take measures of a pressing necessity. . . . Note the . . . disguises with which Communism covers itself: . . . the campaigns against Fascism, the saving of democratic institutions, freedom of speech and meeting. . . ."[60]

Thus, with the moral support of the Church, Duplessis was able to wage an all-out war against any and all opposition. Policemen, rather than judges or Justices of the Peace, issued warrants. Homes were raided and ransacked to teach people lessons. The home of John MacCormac, Montreal correspondent for the *New York Times,* was broken into and ransacked. Duplessis had publicly complained bitterly about his articles on Quebec. The machinery of the state was available and used to plug up leaks in the information network – to keep "subversive" ideas and unwelcome facts out of the minds of les Québecois.

But if government machinery was not sufficiently sensitive to the demands of doctrinal subtleties, the Church had its own methods of suppression. In 1936, three members of the Spanish Republican cabinet came to Montreal on a speaking tour. When the organizers refused to cancel the rally to be addressed by the Spaniards, and when the padlock proved unavailable, the streets were simply flooded with marching school children and university students carrying rebel flags. Chaos reigned and traffic was completely halted; the police stood by. The speakers were unable to address the meeting. The next day Duplessis solemnly congratulated the students. "I want to make it known just how proud I felt. . . . These students in the pride of those principles of their forefathers that made the epic story of Canada, have honoured it with an act of great piety."[61]

Duplessis demonstrated his faith and also eliminated opposition criticism through direct censorship. In 1938 alone the police seized 54,369 papers, 39,317 reviews and books, 23,602

circulars, 15,000 assorted pamphlets and 4,900 buttons and badges.[62] As Quebec is surrounded only by English-speaking neighbours, this censorship was most effective. The school system, even the universities, was closed to all but Catholic doctrine, and its socio-political corollary, right-wing corporatism. For example, the Calendar of the University of Ottawa in 1936 made it known that all letters receivd or sent by students could be opened and read by the Rector.[63] The Calendar of the University of Montreal stated boldly that the authorities would take all due care to prevent the students from falling into the errors of "liberalism, materialism, and modernism."

Opposition to Duplessis and his allies seemed fruitless. Ernest Lapointe, the federal Justice Minister, refused to refer the Padlock Law to the Supreme Court, noting that all opposition to it came from English Canadians. It was easy for supporters of the regime to attribute opposition to the law to racism on the part of the English-speaking left-liberals of the c.c.f., the Civil Liberties Union, and other such organizations and thus gain support for the law and the regime. The English-speaking ownership class in Quebec was not threatened by Padlock and other forms of censorship and repression. Quite the contrary; smugly, and with the old proper racist touch, the *Montreal Star* spoke in the defense of Duplessisme: "This province is not only the most firmly democratic community on the continent but there is probably more individual freedom in Quebec than anywhere else between the Rio Grande and the Arctic Circle. . . . The Padlock Law . . . is . . . not the English way. . . . Of course we who live here know that it means nothing whatever to the liberties of practically all our people. It is just a Latin way of doing what the English would do, but differently."[64]

Summing up, we have described the intelligentsia that was predominant in Quebec during the thirties; how it was linked to the Roman Catholic hierarchy and consequently put forth a right wing ideology based on Catholic dogma. Because of the language barrier around Quebec and with the co-operation of the provincial government, this intelligentsia wielded almost exclusive control over the flow of ideas and information within the Francophone community of the province. The anger and frustrations of the depression were recognized and great care was taken to channel them in a "constructive" direction – that of building a corporate hierarchical, theocentric state of Quebec. The widespread belief that only the elite were to be educated, and the paternalistic attitude maintained at even the lowest levels of the clergy, left the masses helpless in the face of this impenetrable monolith of ideas and power. When the Taschereau government seemed too publicly responsive to Anglo-corporate interests, to suit the Church ideologues it was put out of office. The new premier, for the moment, satisfied the intelligentsia and the Church.

During all this, Quebec was continuing to industrialize. Anglo-Canadian and American capitalists invested heavily in Quebec to exploit its natural resources, but also to reap the benefit of lucrative tax concessions, cheap land leases, and minimum government control. Perhaps most important of all, the new companies appreciated the comparative passivity of the Quebec work force and the repressive labour legislation which allowed them to pay exceptionally low wages with little fear of strikes. The intelligentsia and the Church supported these activities. Accepting the fact that Anglo-Saxons and not French Canadians were destined to be industrialists, they demanded nothing more than that the workers be paid wages sufficient to support their families and respect for Church holidays and customs. In return, through the C.T.C.C., they would convince the trade unionists of the good faith of the capitalists and use their power and moral authority to block the organizing attempts of the international unions. The government found foreign investment a painless way of providing a few jobs and money to keep the machinery going. It did little to offend the investors.

Addressing ourselves directly to a central question of this book, we can begin to outline the reasons why left-wing nationalism *did not* develop in Quebec during the thirties. The first factor which seems to be important is the relationship of the Quebec lower classes to the foreign economic elite. As this chapter has suggested, the economic elite found it unnecessary to convince the population of the justness of either its presence in Quebec, or its activities. The traditional elite, viewing the world of big business as the exclusive domain of the materialistic Protestants, built an almost impenetrable ideological shield between the masses of Québecois and the foreign economic elite. Because of their almost complete control over the flow of information and ideas within Quebec, and the help of the state when necessary, the ideology of the traditional elites remained virtually unchallenged among les Québecois throughout the nineteen-thirties.

The economic elite found it unnecessary, in most cases, to deal directly with industrial conflict. The traditional elite controlled the Catholic trade union; in it they taught that the owner and the workers' interests were not in conflict, but rather that each merely had a different role to play in industrial development. The immorality and illegitimacy of strike action except in the most extreme cases was driven home; furthermore, it was common practice for owners to work through local leaders of the traditional elite, usually the local curé or the mayor, and count on their help at moments of conflict. Thus, "economic stability" was maintained. It was unnecessary for the economic elite to go to the trouble of educating the society to the desirable benefits of consumer capitalism (a rather difficult task during the depression). The politicians with their generous laissez-faire economic policies, and the Church intellectuals with their ideology which justified the poverty and powerlessness of the Francophone masses,* guaranteed the maintenance of large profits and continued economic hegemony for the Anglo-American elite.

None of the above should be taken to imply that there was no militant labour activity at all in this period. As we said before, there is an unwritten history of Quebec in the thirties. One recent work that brings light to a small part of that unwritten past is *Dans le Sommeil de Nos Os* by Evelyn Dumas. Retelling in detail the events of five of the major strikes in Quebec in the thirties and early forties, Dumas' narrative clarifies certain points for us. First, non-Francophone workers especially immigrants and international unions rather than the C.T.C.C., were disproportionately involved in strikes of the period. Second, the primary goal of the C.T.C.C., in many instances, was to discredit the international unions rather than

* Lest we be misunderstood, our attack is *not* directed on the Church's analysis of society nor its program for the corporate state *per se*. In its noblest interpretation this doctrine includes many positive elements, social solidarity, collective responsibility, respect for nature, etc. It is its ideological function in Quebec of this period that is here depicted and deplored.

133

aid the cause of the workers. The international unions were seen as a greater enemy than the owning class, especially in the forties when militancy increased. In the thirties the average had been less than 25 strikes per year. In the early forties it was near 100.

Finally, it cannot be concluded that French-Canadian workers were totally apathetic to working class goals though it is clear that their degree of militancy was low. What can be said is that French-Canadian workers, or their locals, who went on strike faced the constant knowledge that they were totally isolated from the community – that the truth about their actions would be hidden from their fellows under tales of communist subversion. They know that as long as their struggle remained localized Duplessis would be able to use his police goons in the service of the employers without opposition. And so he did.

It was basically in limited areas such as textiles in Montreal that the international unions were able to make headway against the padlock. On the whole, the workers in the thirties had not been able to build any force to oppose the power at the top; slowly and imperceptively, nevertheless, the understanding was growing that the power at the top had to be opposed.

The monolithic ideology which reigned throughout Quebec identified the ethnic and cultural distinctiveness of the lower classes as the cause and legitimation of their socio-economic position. French Canadians were not destined to be wealthy capitalists. All discontent was carefully channelled by the traditional elites away from the true oppressors and, when useful, focused upon two scapegoats – the communists and the Jews. But, herein lies the contradiction within this elite's position. Why was it legitimate for the English to have material wealth at the expense of the French Canadians? The Church did not approve of the capitalists' ideology; they frequently spoke of its non-Christian, evil character. Yet, they forced their own people to accept its legitimacy and tried to eradicate those elements in the society which struggled against it. The reaction of the people of Quebec, apart from a small number of zealots, is quite interesting. The ideology was accepted, not believed; its tenets and commands submitted to not joyously received. Underneath, the people were aware of its contradictions and futility; yet, it was all they had and so as true colonials, they submitted for a time.*

Thus, the coincidence of interests among the economic, the political and the traditional elites during the thirties reinforced the power of each within their own sphere, rendering them un-challengeable.†† As long as the alliance remained firm, no opposing group or viewpoint could gain prominence. Its par-tially contradictory basis meant, however, that sooner or later a crack would show and decline would set in.

The thirties had seen the Ancien Régime in all its force, repeating a pattern that was centuries old. Military and political colonization was replaced by a predominantly economic form, but the alliance of internal and external elite went on as before. Opposition forces from the outside, the CCF, the Communist Party, the international unions, were fought and excluded. Potential internal opposition was neutralized. The Action Libérale Nationale was co-opted – its progressive platform and leadership cut away and its support channelled into the reac-tionary quasi-nationalism of the traditional elite and the Union Nationale. This was not the first time this happened, nor the last time it would be attempted.

* It has been possible to statistically represent the state of Quebec's economy and to use historical events and the speeches of leaders to describe the elite of the thirties. Yet no similar method lends itself to an analysis of the feelings of "plain ordinary people" during this period. It is these feelings that are crucial to consciousness and change and thus to our own analysis. Nevertheless, we are able to assert something about the feelings of everyday people through a sifting of some of the very excellent and important literature to come out of French Canada during the ideological thaw of the fifties and sixties. This literature is typically in the form of quasi-autobiogra-phical novels, intensely personal, attempting to explain what it meant to grow up in Quebec under the old order. One of the important themes running through this literature is the importance of the woman as mother and center of the family maintaining the established rules and moral precepts, not out of conviction but out of resignation, stubbornly defending that little that was permitted to be Québecois against any external influence. The reader is referred to the novels of Gabrielle Roy, Marie-Claire Blais, Yves Thériault, Claire Martin, and Claude Jasmin, among others.

†† The political elite has not been treated separately, but as a part of either or both of the economic and traditional elites. Thus, the change of government in 1936 was understood to be a shift of the relationship between the latter two elites.

Footnotes to Chapter 6

1. Gérard Dion, "La Doctrine Sociale de L'Eglise dans le Québec," *Perspectives Sociales,* 1962-1963, p. 17. (Authors' translation.)
2. Réal Caux, "Le Parti National Social Chrétien," M.A. Thesis, Laval University, 1958, p. 6.
3. Cited in P. E. Trudeau (ed.), *La Grève de l'Amiante.* (Montréal: Editions Cité Libre, 1956), p. 79.
4. Jean Hulliger, *L'Enseignement Social d'Evêques Canadiens de 1891-1950* (Montréal: Editions Fides, 1958), p. 175.
5. *Ibid.,* p. 176.
6. *Ibid.,* p. 251.
7. *Ibid.,* p. 245. (Authors' translation.)
8. *Ibid.,* (Authors' translation.)
9. *Ibid.,* p. 262.
10. *Ibid.,* p. 243. (Authors' translation.)
11. *Ibid.,* pp. 192-95.
12. *Ibid.,* p. 172. (Authors' translation.)
13. W. Saint Pierre, "le Fondateur," *L'Ecole Sociale Populaire,* No. 269-270, 1936, p. 3.
14. P. E. Trudeau, *op. cit.,* p. 41. (Authors' translation.)
15. R. P. Archambault, S.J., "Les Trois phases de l'Ecole Sociale Populaire," *l'Ecole Sociale Populaire,* No. 269-270, 1936, p. 45.
16. J. B. Desrosiers, "L'Ecole Normale de Vaudreuil," *l'Ecole Sociale Populaire,* No. 269-270, 1936, p. 38. See also *Ibid.,* p. 35.
17. P. E. Trudeau, *op. cit.,* p. 42.
18. R. P. Archambault, *op. cit.,* p. 46.
19. *Ibid.,* p. 55.
20. "La Verité sur L'Espagne," *L'Ecole Sociale Populaire,* Mars, 1937, p. 4.
21. See Mason Wade, *The French Canadians* (Toronto: Macmillan of Canada Co., Ltd., 1968), pp. 867-90.
22. *Ibid.,* p. 903.
23. Herbert Quinn, *The Union Nationale* (Toronto: University of Toronto Press, 1963), p. 38.
24. Michael Oliver, "The Social and Political Ideas of French Canadian Nationalists, 1920-1945," Ph.D. Thesis, McGill University, 1956, pp. 130-32.
25. *Ibid.,* pp. 207-12.
26. Mason Wade, *op. cit.,* p. 909.
27. *Ibid.,* pp. 901, 902. See also, Michael Oliver, *op. cit.,* pp. 181, 182.

28. Michael Oliver, *op. cit.*, p. 181-82.
29. See 'Quebecer,' (Frank Scott), "French Canadian National-ism," *Canadian Forum*, March, 1936, p. 12.
30. Michael Oliver, *op. cit.*, pp. 155-80. See also Jacques Pelletier, "La Relève: une idéologie des années 1930," M.A. Thesis, Laval University, 1969, pp. 107-12.
31. Herbert Quinn, *op. cit.*, p. 205.
32. Jean Hulliger, *op. cit.*, p. 120. (Authors' translation.)
33. *Ibid.*, p. 125. (Authors' translation.)
34. Gilles Laflamme, "L'Education Syndicale à la Confédération des Syndicats Nationaux," M.A. Thesis, Laval University, 1968, p. 30.
35. *Ibid.*, p. 20.
36. *Ibid.*, p. 39-40.
37. "Les Caisses Populaires," *L'Ecole Sociale Populaire*, No. 271, 1936, p. 22.
38. Louis Bérubé, "Une Victime de l'Age de Fer," M.A. Thesis, Laval University, 1948-1949, pp. 4-20.
39. Gilles Croteau, "Etablissement et Intégration de l'Institution Co-opérative à L'île d'Orléans," M.A. Thesis, Laval University, 1952, p. 98.
40. Gaston Cholette, "Le Comité d'Action Catholique de Saint-Charles de Limoilou," Licence, Laval University, 1943, p. 24. (Authors' translation.)
41. *Le Goglu*, 19 juin, 1931, quoted in Réal Caux, *op. cit.*, p. 24. (Authors' translation.)
42. *Le Goglu*, 30 janvier, 1931, quoted in Réal Caux, *op. cit.*, p. 24.
43. *Ibid.*, p. 40. (Authors' translation.)
44. Quoted in *Ibid.*, pp. 67-68. (Authors' translation.)
45. See Herbert Quinn, *op. cit.*, pp. 30-34.
46. Quoted in *Ibid.*, p. 31.
47. Quoted in *Canadian Forum*, March, 1932, p. 205.
48. *Ibid.*
49. Quebecer (Frank Scott), *op. cit.*, p. 11.
50. *Ibid.*, p. 12.
51. Quoted in E. A. Forsey, "Politics in Quebec," *Canadian Forum*, June, 1933, p. 326.
52. Quoted in *Ibid.*
53. *Canadian Forum*, June, 1933, p. 323.
54. Quoted in E. A. Forsey, *op. cit.*, p. 326.
55. Quoted in *Ibid.*
56. Herbert Quinn, *op. cit.*, Chapter IV.
57. Eugene Forsey, "Under the Padlock," *Canadian Forum*, May, 1938, pp. 41, 43.

58. Quoted in *Ibid.* (Authors' emphasis.)
59. Eugene Forsey, "Duplessis Marches On!" *Canadian Forum,* January, 1939, p. 298.
60. Quoted in Eugene Forsey, "Under the Padlock," *op. cit.,* p. 42.
61. Quoted in Frank Scott, "Quebec Fascists Show their Hand," *Canadian Forum,* December, 1936, p. 8. (Authors' translation.)
62. E. A. Forsey, "The Padlock – New Style," *Canadian Forum,* March, 1939, p. 362.
63. Quebecer (Frank Scott), *op. cit.,* p. 13.
64. *Montreal Star,* February 17, 1938, quoted in *Canadian Forum,* April, 1938.

CHAPTER 7

THE
DECLINE
OF THE
OLD
ORDER

The forties and fifties were a time of significant change in the attitudes of many of the people of Quebec. However, because a political climate of repression prevailed, these attitude changes for the most part did not become manifest until after the victory of the provincial Liberal party in 1960. In this period there arose a new group of intellectuals who had somehow managed to escape the indoctrination of the previous generation. Some were educated in Europe and influenced by liberal Catholicism and other progressive currents. Others were learning critical social science, where doctrine was subjected to the test of fact rather than vice versa, in the U.S. or English Canada or at the "traitorous" social science faculty at Laval under Dominican Père Georges-Henri Lévesque. This group's aim was to replace the old ideology with modern Western thought. Liberal democracy instead of corporatism was the proposed solution to all problems, whether economic or social.

The philosophy of this new intelligentsia was rooted in a violent reaction to the right-wing nationalism of the traditional elites, and in the pan-Canadianism of Laurier and his Francophone descendants in the Federal Liberal party. This latter tradition manifested itself in the "Union Démocratique," and the "Institut Démocratique" founded by Liberal party members and supporters in 1943 to group men "cherishing freedom of thought, believing in science, and having large views on the questions of races and nationalities."[1] T. D. Bouchard, one of the founders of the Institut Démocratique, contrasted the old type of personality with the men of the Institut: the former were "men who have faith only in the rules established by the partisans of ancient traditions and antique theories." This new breed are men "who have the spirit of research, who believe in evolution towards perfection, and who do not fear to experiment with reforms in all spheres of intellectual, economic and social activity. . . . These are the two opposed poles of the magnetic field of human society."[2] It is interesting to note here the similarity of these ideas with notions put forth by Laurier in his speech in 1877 as he attempted to legitimize the Liberal party and neutralize the Church's violent opposition to it. Laurier argued that liberalism and conservatism were philosophical attributes of human nature. By birth an individual was said to have either the charm of habit or the charm of novelty. The latter was the force of change, an innate temperamental characteristic of some men.[3]

Even within the group who formed L'Institut Démocratique, and who were the forerunners of the new intelligentsia, the antagonism toward all forms of nationalism can be seen. The traditional elite was condemned for breeding racial hatred by blaming the English for Quebec's ills. The Institut Démocratique sought to end Quebec's isolation by developing public spirit and advancing the arts, letters and sciences. Education was to be improved to give youth a broader outlook. Radio, newspapers, lectures and contests would be used to popularize its democratic ideas.[4]

The notions of progress, liberalism and democracy were not well accepted in the early forties. André Laurendeau denounced the Institute as the "Institut Plutocratique," in a radio broadcast.[5] T. D. Bouchard was fired as head of Hydro-Québec by the Liberal Premier, Godbout; and his assertion in the Senate that the Church both supported the right wing "L'Ordre Jacques Cartier" (see below) and sowed the seeds of national disunity by teaching history so as to venerate the French Canadians and make evil doers of the English brought loud opposition from Cardinal Villeneuve.[6] After Abbé Maheux published a series of CBC broadcasts in 1942-43, which attempted to refute the historical interpretations which lay at the base of the anti-English and anti-confederation feelings in Quebec, he was denied the rectorship at Laval for which he had been slated. He was virtually isolated within his own university, by his own people. Still, Abbé Maheux succeeded in forming an academic axis between Laval and the University of Toronto which brought together the liberal writers and scholars of English and French Canada.[7] *Le Devoir* protested against the distribution of Maheux's broadcasts in pamphlet form to all classical college students, and accused the Wartime Information Board of distributing biased literature at the expense of the taxpayer.[8] The power of the traditional elites may have been gradually weakening, but these few more-liberally oriented individuals were hardly much of a match at this stage for an elite whose power had been unchallenged for so long.

Nevertheless the ideology of the new intellectuals gained converts and exposure in Quebec through the forties and fifties and became a concrete and threatening alternative to the right-wing nationalism of the traditional elite. Benefitting from a wider education than that acquired by any other generation, members of the new elite were equipped with skills and technical knowledge such as economics, political science and sociology, which allowed them to analyse their own society in a way formerly done only by foreigners. Though most establishment positions were closed to them, they were able to place themselves in newly developing positions of influence, such as in the trade unions and the media, from where they could attempt to redirect Quebec.

In 1950, individuals from this group founded a review, *Cité Libre*. This journal disseminated their ideas among the new generation of university students, radical elements of the clergy, and the more educated elements of the society at large. *Cité Libre* proclaimed itself to be a journal for the young who had experienced a world very different from that of their parents. It set out to develop a coherent philosophy of humanism, to break the traditional dogma, and to eradicate the nationalism of the old elites.[9] The review analysed all aspects of Quebec society: religious, economic and political. The relations of the Church and state, and the role of the laity in the Church were questioned. Loud opposition was voiced to the Church's intolerance of other religions and cultures. A more equitable distribution of wealth, and the regulation of the capitalist economy were proposed as necessary responsibilities of government. Yet no full statement of the kind of political program envisioned by its editors ever appeared. The writers of *Cité*

Libre attempted to formulate a positive political philosophy, but in the end it became but a rallying point for anyone who opposed Duplessis and the traditional elite regardless of their position vis-a-vis the specific policy proposals aired in *Cité Libre*.

Marcel Rioux sums up the contribution of *Cité Libre* as follows: "if one closely examines the issues of *Cité Libre* . . . one notes that this was really a review of protest – against Duplessis, the clergy, the system of education and many other subjects – but it never developed the positive aspects of its ideology in a systematic way. From its beginning in 1950, until early 1960, it fought the 'ideology of conservation'; from 1960 it began to counter the thrusts of the new ideology. . . . If one could schematize the thoughts of the principal spokesman of this [*Cité Libre*] ideology, it does not seem that they questioned the fundamental postulate of the "ideology of conservation," the understanding that Quebec forms a culture, that is, an ethnic group that possesses certain characteristics – language, religion, and traditions which distinguish it from other ethnic groups of Canada and the North American continent. If Quebec is retarded in relation to other ethnic groups it is because of its elites who have led it in the ways of conservatism, nationalism, chauvinism and messianism. For them, this ethnic group must now acquire a more open culture· and ideology and integrate itself into Canadian society."[10]

The initial thrust of this new elite was a renunciation of the temporal powers of the Church. Education and social welfare were viewed as responsibilities of the provincial and federal governments. The traditional elite quickly retorted, branding the young upstarts anti-clerical and their ideas communistic.

Many policies of the C.C.F. which aimed at regulating big business and increasing welfare programmes were praised in the pages of *Cité Libre*. The necessity for political education was thought to be most important, for only when the population understood its rights and the responsibilities of governments, could elected representatives be forced to respond to the wishes of their constituents on pain of not being re-elected. This new intelligentsia argued that because the traditional elite had taught the people to use the British system of democracy *only* as a means to protect their identity and culture, and because this traditional elite had condoned all manner of political corruption, the people of Quebec lacked democratic convictions. Proceeding from this assumption, this new elite looked to English Canada as a model liberal democracy. "It is no exaggeration to say that because of Quebec's history and its intellectual and political climate, only one reasonably clear model of an alternate society suggested itself to the critics: the model of the other North American societies. What most of them wanted was a liberal democracy for Quebec, like that of Washington or Ottawa. Some of them were influenced by currents of thought in Europe, France especially – as expressed in the review *Esprit,* for example – but the majority looked consciously or unconsciously, to the Ottawa model. In this period, some professors and students of the Laval social sciences faculty were open supporters of Ottawa."[11]

Given the widely varying backgrounds of the individuals and groups that joined forces against the regime, and the strength and power of the enemy they faced, the group's intellectual spokesmen in *Cité Libre* were never able to agree on the goals of society they wished to construct. Thus, when in 1960 the enemy was vanquished, the group soon divided and its social and political analysis became increasingly irrelevant.

From our own vantage point the contribution of the intellectual opposition of the forties and fifties appears relatively insignificant. It did not, after all, have much effect on the actual historical events of the period, even if it did change people's attitude toward them. Viewed in the light of its time, however, this change in attitude was crucial for it opened the way to new movements, new organizations and a new positive philosophy for Quebec, which emerged in the sixties and transcended the essentially negative doctrines of *Cité Libre*. To understand how one monolithic ideological barrier – the construction of which culminated in the thirties – was penetrated, we must look more closely at this period of the forties and fifties, at historical events and structural developments.

With the memory of the 1917 conscription crisis still vivid during the late thirties, the people of Quebec feared the Second World War in a different way than English-speaking Canadians. They feared that the federal government would again force them to leave the only way of life they knew, to risk their lives in an English-speaking army fighting in a war which in no way involved them. In the autumn of 1939 when Canada declared war, a poll was taken in the constituency of Argenteuil. The results are probably not unrepresentative of the province as a whole. Fifteen percent of the eligible voters were in favour of Canadian involvement and conscription to the last dollar and the last man; 65 percent favoured co-operation within Canada's means and resources, preferably by an extension of credits, gifts of provisions and foodstuffs and the manufacturing of planes and munitions; and 30 percent favoured complete isolation.[12]

As Canadian participation of one sort or another became inevitable, the four federal cabinet ministers from Quebec made a promise to the people of their province. Ernest Lapointe publicly declared that he and his cabinet colleagues would resign before they would allow the Mackenzie King government to implement conscription. The strength of the sentiments against conscription can be roughly gauged by the results of the provincial election in the fall of 1939. Lapointe had threatened that he and his cabinet colleagues would resign immediately if their war policy was not supported by electing a Liberal provincial government. The resignations, it was suggested, would almost inevitably mean conscription. Sure enough, Godbout and the Liberals defeated Duplessis. There was in this same period another block of French-Canadian members of parliament, led by Ligouri Lacombe, who felt that any policy other than neutrality was too high a price to pay for national unity. Before war was declared they presented a petition signed by thousands of French Canadians demanding that the federal government not commit Canada to participation in any foreign wars.[13]

When Hitler occupied Danzig, Duplessis' chief organ, *L'Illustration Nouvelle,* maintained that the German dictator did not want war. Rather big business and the international news agencies were responsible for propagating this war monger image of Hitler in their own interests.[14] At about the same time, the editor of *L'Action Catholique* argued that Germany and Italy, the have-not nations, were not wrong in complaining of their needs, since the wealth of the world was unjustly distributed. However, Mussolini and Hitler were blamed for their violation of treaties and their attempts to plunder weaker nations.[15]

After Hitler invaded Poland, the French-Canadian press in general viewed Britain's war against Germany as legitimate.

No word of protest was raised, for instance, at the arrest of Adrien Arcand in 1940. Nevertheless, Canadian neutrality or limited participation were the only policies they found acceptable. *L'Action Catholique* went so far as to warn the populace that Russia was still their most dangerous enemy.[16] Once Canada's role had been delineated by the Federal government, the press merely insisted upon moderate participation and the maintenance of Canada's interests above those of Britain. All of the nationalist newspapers bitterly accepted participation, except for *Le Devoir* which continued to voice opposition and assailed the mounting costs of the war.[17] *L'Action Nationale* pointed to American isolationism as a fine example for Canada to follow in her foreign policy. The basic point was that since Canadians were divided on the issue, it should be left up to the individual to decide for himself.[18]

The general attitude of French Canadians was that they would be quite willing to defend Canada if her territory was threatened, but that it was foolish for Canada to expend such great sums of money and resources, which in the long run meant very little to the allied cause. The fall of France caused relatively little stir among the populace of Quebec, with the elites arguing for and against the virtues of Vichy. *L'Action Catholique* and *Le Devoir* both openly displayed sympathy for Pétain.

In the spring of 1942 the federal government announced it would hold a plebiscite to inquire whether the Canadian population would agree to conscription if the government deemed it necessary at some point in the future. The "Ligue pour la Défense du Canada" headed by Jean Drapeau, actively campaigned within Quebec for a "no" vote. Practically every non-Liberal organ in the province called for a negative vote. Despite a massive propaganda campaign by the federal government, Quebec voted 72 percent "no" while English-Canada voted 80 percent "yes." The final blow to Quebec came when Mackenzie King interpreted these results to mean that his government had been released from its earlier promise not to implement conscription. Such an interpretation is hard to justify given that the promise was made in the first place to the Francophones of Quebec.

In October, 1942, the Ligue pour la Défense du Canada took political form in the "Bloc Populaire Canadien" with Maxime

Raymond as its head and André Laurendeau as secretary-general. The Bloc exploited the widespread feeling in Quebec that Canada was undertaking too great a commitment overseas. It never hesitated to point to attacks upon the French Canadians as slackers, traitors and fascists by their English-speaking countryman.[19] The Bloc was essentially composed of former Action Libérale Nationale leaders like Hamel, Chaloult and Gouin, and a following composed of many readers of *L'Action Nationale* now that André Laurendeau as editor had purged its racist and fascist tendencies. The description of its program as reported by Paul Gouin emphasizes its similarity to policies of the traditional elites: "On the provincial field the Bloc should work for a French State: the absolute control of our land, our natural resources, our economy and our educational system; a French state which will be the loyal application of the whole B.N.A. Act, in letter and spirit, which a young compatriot has summed up in a happy and very just formula: 'Autonomous provinces in a free country'." Echoing Abbé Groulx's celebrated dictum of 1937 and the platform of the Action Libérale Nationale two years earlier, he went on:

> This French state is due us, and we shall have it. The proposed Laurentian state should have a pro-French-Canadian and an anti-trust policy. It should nationalize outright the production of electricity, gas, mines, and chemical fertilizer. It should strictly control the insurance companies and the textile, forest, distilling, refining and tobacco industries. It should replace the coal, milk, farm implement, butchering and cold storage, fishing and chain store trusts by co-operatives. It should establish a provincial bank to head the system of credit unions. Agriculture should be aided and the industrial workers given an equal share of the profits of industry, while corporatism should be applied to correct the evils of capitalism. The family should be protected by workmen's compensation: insurance against sickness, unemployment, old age and death; family allowances; strict regulation of the labour of women and children; and aid to young couples.[20]

The Bloc grew in strength. In the two federal by-elections of September, 1943, one Bloc candidate won and another was just beaten out by the Communist candidate. A Canadian Institute of Public Opinion Poll at about this same time indicated that the Bloc was now supported by thirty-three percent of the Quebec electorate.[21] Anti-Liberal feeling was fully exploited by the Bloc: conscription and the regulations requiring employers to report defaulters, the internment of Camillien Houde, the replacement of French-Canadian workers by English-Canadian ones at the Defence Industries plant at Sainte-Thérèse, the huge profits of the Aluminum Company, the statement that all Quebecers should learn English by Edouard Simard, head of Marine and Sorel Industries whose profits had sky-rocketed due to the war; the campaign in favour of a single Canadian history text, the immigration into Quebec of Jewish and British refugees, and the enormous sums of money and other gifts being given to Britain – all of these incidents seem to have increased the sentiment that they, the French Canadians, were being used by the Anglo-Saxons with little respect for their own wishes.

In an attempt to reduce the violent anti-semitism of the often over-enthusiastic youthful supporters, André Laurendeau brought Henri Bourassa out of retirement to speak on behalf of the Bloc. However, although Bourassa deplored the anti-semitism of the youth, his sympathies with European fascism emphasized the Bloc's fundamental similarities with the goals of the traditional elite of the thirties. Speaking in Montreal in November, 1942, Bourassa stated: "Are there any Christian nations left? There remain Portugal, Spain since the restoration of Franco, France under the regime of Pétain. And, I would add, Italy under the reign of Mussolini."[22]

When Hamel, Chalout and Gouin split from the Bloc because they felt the new leader, Lacroix, opposed their anti-big-business policies, they seem to have taken with them many right-wing nationalists. On the whole, it seems to have been mainly the young, educated, middle-class who supported it. André Laurendeau became both editor of the newspaper, Le Bloc, and provincial leader disclaiming all rumours of an alliance with Duplessis. Disappointingly, neither the provincial election of 1944 nor the federal election of the following year proved successful for the Bloc. Yet in the latter it polled one-seventh of the total votes cast in Quebec.

The Church grew alienated from the people during this crisis. It continually supported the federal government's policies with respect to military participation. Church spokesmen in fact often participated in recruitment rallies. From their pulpits the clergy preached the necessity for registering as dictated by the National Resources Mobilization Act. Once conscription had been implemented, full compliance with the law was urged. The Church showed little concern and no support for the large numbers of draft dodgers hidden in Northern Quebec.

This same alienation between the Church and the people had occurred during the conscription crisis of 1917. But, the consensus among the elites in the period that followed at least outwardly healed the wound. This time, however, the rise of the new intellectuals, the growing division between elements of the Church and the Duplessis government's increasing corruption and anti-labour stance, and, finally and consequently, the mounting evidence of a split within the ranks of the Church itself on the question of industrial conflict and the rights of workers changed all this. At the end of the war, attention was shifted from the national question and the issue of conscription to the social question and trade union demands; and the divisions sharpened.

The forties were marked by violent conflict among the three labour centrals in Quebec: the Fédération Provincial du Travail, (F.P.T.), which was composed of international and national unions affiliated with the Congrès des métiers et du Travail (T.L.C.) and the A.F.L.; the Congrès Canadien du Travail (C.C.T.), a federation of industrial unions (C.I.O.); and the Confédération des Travailleurs Catholiques du Canada (C.T.C.C.). One reason the international trade union centrals, the F.P.T. and the C.C.T., attempted to organize Quebec workers was to protect their members in English Canada and the United States by achieving similar pay rates everywhere on the continent.[23] Their organizers saw the clergy as a reactionary force which had effectively destroyed the solidarity of the working class by keeping the Quebec workers under their thumbs. The clergy were, correctly, accused of collaborating with the owners and with the government.

At this time, many larger international companies often recognized the benefits of dealing with the C.T.C.C. rather than a more powerful international union. By giving in to initial demands for a recognition of French-Canadian particularity and paying wages which in Quebec were high but were below the average for the continent, they often succeeded in obtaining the loyalty of their workers. This type of benevolent paternalism was shown, for example, by the Aluminum Company of Canada at Arvida. By simply giving in to the inexpensive, nationalist demands of the clergy and the C.T.C.C., this company was able to keep out the international unions and pay its workers less than its employees in English Canada or in the U.S.A. But, other enterprises with less perceptive owners preferred to deal with the international syndicates. These Anglo-Saxon entrepreneurs felt less baffled by Anglo-Saxon-run trade unions than by the "irrational" attitudes of the French-Canadian Roman Catholic clergy.

It was the companies who made contracts with the C.T.C.C. that usually benefited. When the F.P.T. began an organizing campaign at the Aluminum Company of Canada, the local clergy and the Jesuit Père Genest fought against it vigorously. When the F.P.T.'s organizer was a Jew, he was denounced for being so; when he was replaced by an Irish Catholic, "foreign Catholics" were denounced from the pulpit. C.T.C.C. affiliated unions served more often than not simply as company unions. At the Dominion Textile plant at Magog, for instance, the chaplain received a company pension after having successfully broken up a C.I.O. organizational campaign.[24]

The traditional elite campaigned vigorously against the international unions. At its annual convention in 1944, C.T.C.C. President, Alfred Charpentier, described the A.F.L. as the worst enemy of the C.T.C.C. – an enemy who was not afraid to use any means to attain its end. At this same meeting, Bishop Douville of Saint Hyacinthe warned that support for international unions threatened French-Canadian interests: "American labour unions, to which certain Quebec workers are affiliated, will logically protect their own before taking care of your welfare. The situation in Quebec must be unique in labour annals with labour groups here awaiting orders and directives from foreign leaders."[25] The Bishop urged simultaneous development of workers' and employers' syndicates "as a prelude to the economic corporatism which we consider essential to the future of labour and employers as well."[26]

At about this same time, Msgr. Parent, the auxiliary Bishop of Rimouski, addressed the National Federation of the Wood Industry: "Have nothing to do with neutral unions, albeit they may have made gains in the great cities. Communism glides in their shadow like a snake. It attempts to fish in troubled waters and tries to turn the workers against the employers, as occurred in the last tramway strike in Montreal. Such unions stir up the workers against the employers, against religion, and against the clergy."[27] But the clergy's campaign was not simply a collection of speeches. Often the wives of working men would be warned by their priest that he would deprive them of the sacraments if their husbands joined international unions.[28] Increased labour militancy in the early forties had brought a strong response from the traditional elite. It seemed as if nothing had changed in Quebec.

When Duplessis returned to power in 1944, it was soon apparent that his antipathy towards organized labour had not mellowed during his years in the opposition. Quinn describes the U.N.'s policies: "the government often did nothing to compel employers to negotiate with a certified union. Although company-dominated unions were illegal, the Labour Relations Board certified a sizeable number every year. Many trade union leaders who had been dismissed by their employers for trying to organize the workers found it almost impossible to get remedial action by the Board. Certification of unions was sometimes withdrawn without any other justification than the claim of the employers that such unions no longer represented a majority of the employees. Applications for certification were frequently held up in the Department of Labour for months, a delay which provided the employers with plenty of opportunity to intimidate or bribe employees into leaving the union. Government boards of arbitration set up to settle a dispute might take a year or more to make their report. Meanwhile no strike could be called."[29]

But, when the session of the legislative assembly opened in 1949, it was evident that Duplessis wanted even more stringent methods to suppress growing labour union activity. Bill Five, which was to establish a comprehensive labour code, was so reactionary and unjust in its proposed treatment of the working man, that the warring labour federations formed a common front to oppose it. Even the Church hierarchy publicly voiced its opposition declaring several aspects of the code contrary to social justice.[30] Duplessis was forced to withdraw the bill, although he subsequently enacted it through piece-meal legislation. The early success of the common labour front resulted in a feeling of solidarity among the union membership – a sentiment until this moment unknown in Quebec. Alfred Charpentier, old-liner par excellence, was replaced at the head of the C.T.C.C. at this time by Gérard Picard. Picard, a man open to new ideas, brought with him a new group of officials – some trained by Lévesque at Laval.

It was in this atmosphere that the illegal strike of the C.T.C.C. against the Johns-Manville Company broke out at Asbestos. The position of the union was stated by the confederation secretary, Jean Marchand: "The workers are not opposed to arbitration, but everyday it is being proven to them that when it is applied to them the outcome is almost always unfavourable. Arbitration has become a weapon in the hands of the employers to use against the worker."[31] Strike action was the only recourse. Duplessis' first reaction was to send in the provincial police and publicly insult the C.T.C.C. leaders.

The solidarity among the labour unions which followed their successful campaign against Bill Five grew as the asbestos strike proceeded. Unions affiliated with the C.T.C.C. sent chartered bus loads of members to demonstrate their support to the workers of Asbestos. With them they brought money to help feed and pay rent for the strikers and their families. By the end of the strike these donations, plus funds from the C.T.C.C. treasury, amounted to $300,000.[32] Trade unions affiliated with the C.C.T. gave $7,700 and the F.P.T., $6,500. Two A.F.L. leaders from Johns-Manville Companies in New Jersey came to Asbestos to demonstrate their sympathy with the cause of the miners. They assured the C.T.C.C. that the slow-downs in their factories, resulting from the strike, would be accepted as necessary to win the just struggle of the asbestos workers.[33] Even the newspapers of the Association of Catholic Trade Unionists in the U.S.A. commented on the strike and wished the workers well in their struggle.[34]

As the strike wore on, as police brutality, instructed judges and the complete support for the company by the Duplessis regime became evident, an even more significant development took place. Some elements of the Church shattered all expectations by siding with the workers. Archbishop Charbonneau of Montreal declared in a sermon at Notre-Dame-de-Montréal: "The working class is the victim of a conspiracy which wishes to crush it, and when there is a conspiracy to crush the working class, it is the duty of the Church to intervene."

"We wish social peace, but we do not wish the crushing of the working class. We are more attached to man than to capital. This is why the clergy has decided to intervene. It wishes that justice and charity be respected, and it desires that more attention cease to be paid to financial interests than to the human factor."[35] Archbishop Maurice Roy of Quebec, and Bishops Philippe Desranleau of Sherbrooke and Arthur Douville of Saint-Hyacinthe, though more reservedly, also publicly supported the strikers and authorized collections at the church doors after mass in aid of the asbestos workers and their families. But, not all of the Church hierarchy was so inclined. For example, a group of Laval students who had planned to visit the strikers at Asbestos were forbidden from making the trip on pain of expulsion.[36] Yet the concept of a Church that was pro-worker had been raised. When the unwritten history of Quebec is finally compiled we will find no doubt many isolated examples of worker-priests, among the dock workers and fishermen for instance, but now for the first time the hierarchy was caught up in this question and henceforth isolation would not come as easily.

The asbestos strikers never really won their cause. The strike was eventually settled but the local union leaders suffered severe legal penalties and loss of employment. However, the strike had profound effects upon French-Canadian society. "The asbestos strike was also a strike for the recognition of trade unions within the French-Canadian community. Since the war the trade union movement tried to define its place within French Canada: the stage was set. Previously, autonomous trade-unionism had been accepted in the French-Canadian milieu on the condition that it did not introduce social goals different from those of the society as a whole. But during the war, the Catholic trade union movement had increased in size and a change in its objectives occurred. The members of the C.T.C.C. adopted the goals of modern trade-unionism and resolutely sought the achievement of the economic objectives which were expressed at the end of the war . . . French Canada was to undergo a sociological transformation of the same sort known by other modern democratic countries. The working class, for so long deep in the shadows, had acquired freedom of action and official status."[37]

The new intelligentsia was beginning to effect changes in Quebec. The social science graduates from Laval, like Jean

Marchand, had succeeded in fundamentally transforming the C.T.C.C. As early as 1943, the chaplains were stripped of their formal power within the unions. The new orientation of the C.T.C.C. was described by Boisvert: "The C.T.C.C. had to recognize the fact that the capitalist world, through the inhuman structures that it constructs, weighs with all the weight of a machine on the human person; that the proper role of trade-unionism is precisely to liberate the people and to put the machine at their service; and that only then can man again assume little by little the human figure. The society that will then be formed will genuinely be worthy of its name."[38]

Working-class consciousness and solidarity had begun to develop and spread among the French-Canadian working masses. Signs of division were increasing within and among the elites. The ability of the latter to localize all economic strife and thus use repression without fear of public opposition was no more; union solidarity, the rift within the Church and the spread of a liberal attitude towards journalism in the news media saw to that. Duplessis, aided by ultra-conservative Jesuits led by Bishop Courchesne of Rimouski, succeeded in gaining temporary revenge by having Monseigneur Charbonneau removed as Archbishop of Montreal. On being sent to administer a small parish in Victoria, British Columbia, the priest stated: "I have been smashed and hurled to the Pacific Coast . . . It came to me as a bolt out of a blue sky."[39] The reactionary forces were still on top but their power was being seriously challenged for the first time since the Rebellions of 1837.

By 1957, the C.T.C.C. had grown to 90,000 members as compared to the C.C.T. with 45,000 and the F.P.T. with 130,000. The latter had made a pact with the Duplessis' regime claiming that in this way it gained more benefits for its workers, but as Boisvert documents, this claim is completely unsubstantiated. The F.P.T., echoing the right-wing tendencies of the A.F.L. which reached its peak during the McCarthyite hysteria, shattered the solidarity which had grown up around the asbestos strike by passing a resolution at its 1952 convention denouncing the revolutionary mentality of the C.T.C.C.[40] A few months later the F.P.T. and C.C.T. amalgamated to form the F.T.Q. (Fédération de Travailleurs du Québec), imitating the 1954 merger of their American parents to form the AFL-CIO and the 1956 merger of their Canadian parent bodies setting up the C.L.C.

A significant step in the development of class consciousness was the strike of a union affiliated with the C.T.C.C. against a traditional French-Canadian department store. "The strike at Dupuis Frères, perhaps more than any other, showed the trade-union consciousness of the people of the C.T.C.C. . . . Trade union consciousness had to be, in effect, excellent for a Catholic and almost entirely French-Canadian central, defying prejudice, pseudo-traditions and a stagnant and ritualized public opinion, to engage in a particularly aggressive action against a company considered by all, and in particular by those who mattered, as a national institution. This strike put things in their place. The C.T.C.C. broke with the way of thinking of all those who, according to the words of Michel Chartrand, "defended the French language by starving those who spoke it." It was, in this case, to denounce this opium of the people, this peculiar patriotism very common at the time and practised most notably by the 'Union Nationale' and the provincial government, which consisted of using verbal, hypocritical nationalism to mock the betrayal, the misappropriation of public funds, the exploitation of people, and a complete indifference towards their economic and intellectual needs."[41]

Thus, a split had occurred within the Church itself and between elements of the traditional elite and the Duplessis regime over the latter's labour policy. There was no longer an insurmountable barrier to all thinking and activity opposed to right wing Catholicism and laissez-faire capitalism. Civil rights and a liberal notion of social justice were coming to be seen as necessary by at least some segments of the population. The working class was becoming conscious that its socio-economic position was the result of power relationships in the society rather than the result of divinely proclaimed racial destiny. By the time of the strike at Dupuis Frères it was clear that the new intelligentsia had changed the C.T.C.C. to the extent that it was willing to treat employers —whether French-Canadian or Anglo-Saxon — simply on the basis of their policies towards their employees. The C.T.C.C. was no longer a tool of the traditional elite, but instead a militant labour union struggling for internal democracy and social justice for its members.

Another issue which weakened the power and influence of the traditional elite and its ally, the government, was that of political corruption. The clergy were divided among themselves, and Duplessis was infuriated at the pamphlet published by two priests, Fathers Dion and O'Neil, entitled *L'Immoralité Politique dans la Province de Québec.* "Certain activities," they observed, "such as buying votes, the violation of the electoral law, threats of reprisals for those who did not support the 'good party,' the false sermons, false personal allegations, the bribing of election officers, seem to have become normal aspects of our social life at election time. Some urban areas have seen examples of the use of violence that would make the most fervent anarchists jealous."[42] Duplessis' use of the mass media to misinform the voters and censor information also came under their attack. "Modern methods for the diffusion of ideas permit the construction of immense collective lies, the unceasing repetition of false slogans by newspapers, radio and television to the point that the man on the street becomes incapable of resisting and ready to accept that 'which became truth.' This technique . . . has now become a part of our election customs. The lie manipulates the complexes, the fears, of the popular soul to distort the ideas of opponents, to destroy people's reputations. . . . "[43]

Dion and O'Neil attacked the traditional elite and the Duplessis regime for suggesting that governmental social security programmes meant the state was becoming Marxist and that the promotion of health insurance was sabotaging the religious communities. Finally, they ridiculed the notion, propagated by the traditional elite and Duplessis, that giving food to the hungry in underdeveloped countries was an approval and encouragement for communism. The Church was accused of using anti-communist propaganda to mask fascist sympathies. Communism was simply a scapegoat introduced by those in power to justify the failure to implement liberal reforms, and to maintain their power and privilege intact.

Hence the philosophy of the new intelligentsia gained support from some elements within the Church. The traditional elite and Duplessis had dealt with the new C.T.C.C. leaders and the writers of the review *Cité Libre* by branding them as communists. But now members of the clergy had rendered this tactic ineffective.

Another source of conflict between the Church and the Duplessis regime was the latter's attempts to take over control of the universities, heretofore the exclusive domain of the Church. After having Archbishop Charbonneau, who was Chancellor of the Université de Montréal, shipped off to British Columbia, the

Union Nationale was unhampered in its administration of the university.[44] In the early fifties Duplessis struggled hard to wrench Laval away from the clergy. With rising costs due to the very rapid growth of Laval and an enormous increase in the number of lay teachers, the Church found it more and more difficult to financially support the old university. Duplessis recognized that he had the money so badly needed at Laval and used this as a lever to ensure the obeisance of the university personnel. For example, two Laval scientists campaigned for electric furnaces for the processing of Ungava iron in the province; the two professors were told by the Union Nationale to end their campaign immediately. To prevent the possibility of any further slips like this one, the government sought to administer Laval itself.[45]

Duplessis wanted Georges-Henri Lévesque fired, for his social science faculty often criticized the tactics and policies of the Union Nationale and it educated those who led the opposition to Duplessis. When Laval began a huge fund-raising campaign, the government pledged four million dollars and gave the rector two million on the opening night of the campaign. The rector was quietly informed that the other two million would follow as soon as Lévesque was fired.[46]

In the spring of 1950, Lévesque addressed the Congress of Industrial Relations where he warned the gathering of workers and employers again of "letting anti-Communism become a soporific, or a mere tom-tom for election campaigns. We will never establish social justice by mere speeches. . . . Only positive acts of reform in the social and economic structure of our society can save us from the dictatorship of the proletariat. . . . The true anti-Communists are those who build the new society with justice and love."[47] This speech was interpreted as an attack on Duplessis and Lévesque was reprimanded by the university's rector.

Lévesque believed that it was necessary for the Church to identify itself with social reform by working in rural co-operatives and labour unions. This belief was premised on Pope Pius XI's conclusion that, "The great scandal of the nineteenth century was that the Church lost the working class."[48] Lévesque further outraged the Union Nationale by accepting a position as a commissioner on the Massey Commission which the provincial government had refused to recognize on the grounds that culture as a part of education, came under provincial jurisdiction.

"You could reduce Lévesque's position to three general principles," wrote Blair Fraser, "a belief in intellectual freedom; a desire for social reform; and an all-Canadian as distinct from a parochial patriotism."[49] The social science faculty was highly respected in academic circles, hiring professors on the basis of intellectual capabilities rather than doctrinaire orthodoxy. Although Lévesque received the support of his own Dominican order, the more conservative Jesuits, who predominated in the hierarchy of the Quebec Church, quietly but intensely opposed him. In 1945, Lévesque wrote a pamphlet in which he argued that co-operatives could be non-confessional and open to non-Roman Catholics without being "neutral" in the technical sense as condemned by the Pope. Archbishop Charbonneau and other liberal churchmen who worked with the co-operative movement and the unions supported Lévesque's position; but, a group of Jesuits referred the pamphlet to Rome in an attempt to have it rebuked by the Pope who eventually took no action in the matter.[50]

Thus it was not only the opposition of Duplessis with whom the reformist elements in the Church had to contend. Their opposition within the Church and traditional elite cannot be discounted; nor was much of it overt. The counter-reformist movement was still strong and expressed itself in some of the forms described in the chapter on the thirties. Also, another secret society entered the fray.

Since 1928, a right-wing organization dedicated to the establishment of a separate, corporate state in Quebec, and composed of members of the French-Canadian middle class, was organizing and propagandizing under cover in Quebec. The organization was first publicly exposed by Jean Charles Harvey in his *Le Jour* in November, 1941, in a series of articles entitled "Le Klu Klux Klan du Canada-français." On June 21, 1944, as noted above, T. D. Bouchard in a speech in the Senate denounced the support given to this undemocratic, clandestine organization by the Church hierachy and the political elite. Then in 1963, a former member wrote all he knew about "L'Ordre Jacque Cartier" (O.J.C.) in *Magazine Macleans*.[51] By using only facts upon which the three sources are in agreement, we can get some idea of the influence which should be attributed to the O.J.C.

L'Ordre Jacques Cartier was organized hierarchically so that each member knew the identity of only the other members of his cell. The head of each cell served as liaison with the per-

TABLE 7-1

Spheres of Influence (Infiltration) of the O.J.C.

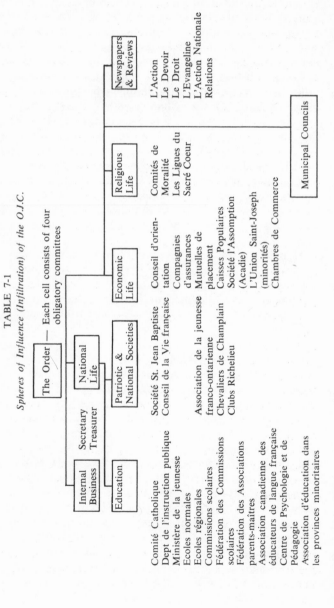

The Order — Each cell consists of four obligatory committees

Internal Business	Secretary Treasurer	National Life

Education	Patriotic & National Societies	Economic Life	Religious Life	Newspapers & Reviews
Comité Catholique	Société St. Jean Baptiste	Conseil d'orien-tation	Comités de Moralité	L'Action
Dept de l'instruction publique	Conseil de la Vie française	Compagnies d'assurances	Les Ligues du Sacré Coeur	Le Devoir
Ministère de la jeunesse		Mutuelles de placement		Le Droit
Ecoles normales	Association de la jeunesse franco-ontarienne	Caisses Populaires		L'Evangeline
Ecoles régionales		Société l'Assomption (Acadie)		L'Action Nationale
Commissions scolaires	Chevaliers de Champlain	L'Union Saint-Joseph (minorités)		Relations
Fédération des Commissions scolaires	Clubs Richelieu	Chambres de Commerce		
Fédération des Associations parents-maîtres				
Association canadienne des éducateurs de langue française				
Centre de Psychologie et de Pédagogie				
Association d'éducation dans les provinces minoritaires				

Municipal Councils

158

manent regional committee so that "each cell . . . is led by a Grand commander . . . elected by the members of the cell, assisted by a dozen officers with sometimes pretentious titles (Great Knight, Great Standard-Bearer . . . , etc.) and assisted by a chaplain (usually the curé of the parish) named by the regional chaplain, who issues religious and moral directives."[52] A person was invited to become a member only after all present members agreed and then an initiation ceremony was held. This was presided over by the chaplain and the member was put through water and fire tortures and other rites to affirm his eternal loyalty to the order. Only middle class men in positions of influence were asked to become members. All meetings of the O.J.C. were secret as was their newspaper *L'Emérillon,* and all commands contained therein. In May of 1957 *L'Emérillon* justified the order's structure: "the order was hierarchically organized, established according to the principle of authority rather than according to essentially democratic rules. . . . The authority surrounds itself with advisors who are as trustworthy as they are prudent (for example Father Louis Lachance, O.P.) so that the orders, if given, are always inspired by the greatest wisdom. . . . The system of authority . . . suits the sensitivity of Latin people or descendents of Latins. . . . Our society must be organized like an army where decisions are taken at the highest rank."[53]

The strategy of the O.J.C. seems to have been to infiltrate all the important decision-making bodies in the province and all possible sources of public influence (see Table 7-1), to achieve their ends. All programs for re-Frenchifying Quebec were vigorously supported as was the campaign for bilingualism of federal government publications and the civil service. In the thirties the movement "Achat-chez-nous," buy at home, was initiated by the O.J.C. It was aimed at destroying the Jewish retail merchants who had sprung up throughout the province, returning small business to the French-Canadian domain where it belonged. All together, the O.J.C. seems to have differed very little from the traditional elite in the thirties in its view of society and strategies for change.

There seems to be a fair amount of evidence that the O.J.C. was quite successful. A graduate student at Laval in studying the farmers co-operative on L'Ille d'Orléans was informed by a number of old members that it had been taken over by the

O.J.C.[54]. In an article written by Charles Gagnon, he reminisces about being asked to join the youth study group run by the O.J.C. when he was studying to become a priest.[55] Many people in Quebec admit to the existence of the O.J.C. and to the fact that it significantly influenced the right-wing political parties and organizations in the province. In 1941, Harvey said the O.J.C. had 11,000 members; in 1956, *L'Emérillon* is quoted by Dubé as recognizing 30,000 members. Even the former figure is significant given the class nature of its membership and its stringent recruitment policy.

Hence, the traditional elite was still powerful by the late fifties. But, it was split. It was challenged from within its own ranks. Younger clergy were more liberal, democratic and supportive of the ideas of the separation of church and state. The new intelligentsia refused to fall into line: it fought the reactionary forces by attempting to educate the masses in a more realistic manner about the way in which their society was structured. And, for all its organization, secretiveness, and success at infiltration, the O.J.C., along with other elements of the traditional elite, was unable to slow the tide of social change in the direction of a secular liberal society that followed the death of the "chef" in 1959.

An important reason for this has been attended to previously. The Church and traditional elite had lost its stranglehold control over all the modes of expression and communication – that is, the media. No longer could labour strife, the expression of dissenting views, or the exposure of corruption at the top be localized, kept within tight geographical bounds. The new journalists and intellectuals had found ways of socializing the conflict – nationalizing it. No longer could opposition of any form be suppressed as a "private matter." Instead, conflict became public, matters for popular consideration.

The Asbestos strike became vital in the changing role of some elements of the press. Once Church leaders became involved the press had to enter and the result on the latter is well described by the then editor of C.T.C.C.'s *Le Travail,* Gérard Pelletier. "Until the conflict of 1949, the majority of our newspapers treated industrial conflicts as so many non-descript events, foreign to the social context of French Canada. . . . Briefly, workers' actions were not recognized on the editorial page, little care was taken to examine the profound causes of a strike, or to evaluate the objectives. Rather it was all denounced as a subversive act or it was not mentioned. Very rarely could one read an article of serious opinion devoted to a strike. . . . By its breadth, its duration, its style and the particular character of its objectives, this conflict (at Asbestos) forced everyone, even the minor papers of the province, to take part. For the first time, the attitude of polite indifference became impossible. . . . For the first time they were involved with a social problem, no longer in theory, detached, but concretely and with terrible immediacy."[56]

Le Devoir was the only paper to cover the strike in detail from beginning to end. Independent in the sense that it was tied to no financial interests and to no political party, *Le Devoir* created a precedent in Quebec by devoting innumerable stories, editorials and comments to the asbestos strike, "not only did this newspaper take up the cause of the striking workers, but it conducted a systematic campaign in their favour during the entire duration of the conflict. It would be easy to show that its information was always fuller, more detailed and more up to date than that of other newspapers."[57] Still it was not alone. Both *La Presse,* a Montreal daily, and *Le Standard* covered the strike in a very professional manner. The different points of view of the unions, the company, the municipal councillors, the curé, and the provincial police were all documented.

On the other hand Duplessis' papers, mostly notably the *Montréal Matin, Le Clairon,* and the *Gazette,* made no comment on the strike until two months after its outbreak. At that time, the illegality of the strike was stressed and the honesty of the c.t.c.c. leaders was questioned. There was never any attempt to understand the cause of the strike. While these papers presented the government's side of the conflict, the Liberal papers, especially *Le Canada,* spent their time attacking the Union Nationale for its incompetence in settling the strike. The Church papers demonstrated both sympathy and prudence in their approach to the strike. Pelletier summarizes the position taken by *L'Action Catholique.* "Despite the cautious style and the infinite prudence demonstrated . . . despite the long silence . . . 'Action Catholique' maintained, in opposition to the government, that an 'illegal' strike does not deny the right of the strikers to demand 'certain' assurances before returning to work. There is nothing in it, of course, that might compromise public order, still those who know the usual practices of 'Action' and of its Editor-In-Chief find their outlook astonishing."[58]

The reporting by *Le Devoir, La Presse,* and *Le Standard* allowed the asbestos strike to be discussed among the public with some knowledge of the "facts" at their disposal. The government's policy was seriously challenged openly in the media and by other than opposition party organs. This new phenomenon of freedom of the press and professional journalism provided a forum for discussion of ideas opposed to those of the traditional and political elites. It provided a forum for the ideas of the new intellectuals and aided the penetration of the ideological barrier that had been constructed.*

Technological developments contributed as well. The discovery of television and the wide expansion of radio made room for inventive young broadcasters and journalists. Especially Radio Canada (the CBC) because of its relative immunity to reprisals on the part of Duplessis and the elite due to its status as a federal Crown Corporation, should be mentioned in this regard. The monolithic idea network was being replaced by a pluralist one.

The labour unions, liberal churchmen, and new generation of liberal university graduates formed a common front in the late fifties to oppose Duplessis. The new intelligentsia were the strategists of the movement and their ideology became the banner under which the common front organized. But, as was pointed out earlier, no political philosophy was accepted by all members of the common front – just an agreement to get rid of Duplessis and introduce a system where freedom of speech, of the press, and more liberal educational institutions would provide the atmosphere for further politicization of the population.

Towards the end of 1956, the new intelligentsia attempted to bring together all the activists and intellectuals who opposed

* The ignominious role of the English-language press, especially in Quebec, in distorting and refusing to mention many of the issues when their philosophy, unlike that of say *Le Devoir,* was ostensibly liberal and progressive, should be noted. It is unfortunate that many of those new intellectuals who blamed the traditional elites for the status of the French Canadians did not learn from the response of the English papers just exactly where the basis of the oppression lay and which interests were being served. Perhaps they might have then seen the need to redirect some of their energies.

Duplessis to begin a campaign of political education which would result in the defeat of the Union Nationale in the 1960 election. A letter, inviting these individuals to a meeting to be chaired by Jacques Perrault and Pierre Trudeau, enunciated the following points: the state was controlled by a small number of people; the recent collusion between the Union Nationale and the federal Liberal party has bolstered this oligarchy; until the present many had protested their disfavour with the Duplessis regime by not participating, but non-participation in a democracy means consent; the anti-democratic laws, the injustices of the electoral map, the reprisals taken against opponents of the regime must all be attacked. The proposed topics for discussion at this meeting were the nationalization of resources, social reforms to increase the quality of education and the amount of social security, and ways to democratize the political structures of Quebec.

Le Rassemblement, a group which grew out of this meeting, was a conglomeration of union officials, c.c.f. members, reformers within the Liberal party, socialists from sects like the Quebec Fabian Society, the Ligue d'action Socialiste and others. The group remained formally constituted for only about a year and a half, but its ranks brought together the individuals who led the struggle which in 1960 finally overthrew the Union Nationale regime. Few members of the Rassemblement supported the *Cité Libre* group, really the core of the new intelligentsia, in the struggle to have Quebec's political structures modelled on those of English Canada. But there was little time for detailed discussion of what would come after Duplessis was gone. Repression was so severe that many of them were forced to leave Quebec to find employment, for the Union Nationale would brook no opposition. Ideological discussion was laid aside as a luxury which could not be afforded until a less oppressive political regime had been instituted.

The editorials of *Cité Libre* which enunciated the doctrines of the most politically active and articulate element of the new intelligentsia blamed the province's underdevelopment on the myth preached for so long by the traditional elites. If only the people would rid themselves of this old fashioned doctrine and adopt the principles of classical liberal .thought, all would be well. But in the end it was a system of almost laissez-faire capitalism and its practitioners which exploited the people of

Quebec, and only secondly a mythology believed by the elites. What the *Cité Libre* group failed to understand was that an attack on this mythology, or in Marxist terms on the super-structure, did not constitute, in itself, an attack on the roots of the problem. Certainly the myths had to be shattered and the complicity of the traditional elites exposed for all to see; but, one cannot end there.* The social and economic structure that had produced this elite division had to be changed – perhaps uprooted. Unfortunately this could not be accomplished through polemical magazine articles.

In spite of themselves the new intelligentsia helped unleash a popular movement whose commitment and goals far transcended those of their philosophical mentors. But this movement was not directed at ideas but at social realities, it sought not to change the thoughts of Les Québecois as much as their lives. And, to the dismay of the *Cité Libre* group, it began slowly at first and then at an accelerating rate, to attack the socio-economic basis of Quebec – its colonial status. But the solution was neither to be found in the "survivance" of an ephemeral nationalism as had been believed in the thirties and previously, nor in the "rattrapage" (catching up) advocated by the thinkers of the fifties.

* The young Hegelians of the early nineteenth century believed that by exploding the myths of reactionary Germany they would bring about a liberal democracy. This parable written by Marx to explain the the hollowness of their cries is equally applicable to the notions of the *Cité Libre* group:

"Once upon a time an honest fellow had the idea that men were drowned in water only because they were possessed with the idea of gravity. If they were to knock this idea out of their heads, say by stating it to be a superstition, a religious idea, they would be sublimely proof against any danger from water. His whole life long he fought against the illusion of gravity, of whose harmful results all statistics brought him new and manifold evidence. This honest fellow was the type of the new revolutionary philosophers in Germany."

Karl Marx, Preface to *The German Ideology*.

Footnotes to Chapter 7

1. Quoted in Mason Wade, *The French Canadians* (Toronto: Macmillan Company of Canada, Ltd., 1968), p. 964.
2. Quoted in *Ibid.*, p. 964.
3. O. D. Skelton, *Life and Letters of Sir Wilfred Laurier* (Toronto: McClelland and Stewart, Ltd., 1965), pp. 42-45.
4. Mason Wade, *op. cit.*
5. *Ibid.*, p. 965.
6. *Ibid.*, pp. 996-1008.
7. *Ibid.*, p. 955.
8. *Ibid.*
9. Louis Savard, "Cité Libre et l'idéologie monolithique du vingtième siècle au Canada français," M.A. Thesis, Laval University, 1958, p. 18.
10. Marcel Rioux, "Sur l'évolution des idéologies au Québec," *Revue de l'Institut de Sociologie*, 1968, No. 1, p. 118. (Authors' translation.)
11. Marcel Rioux, *Quebec in Question, op. cit.*, p. 71.
12. Reported in Mason Wade, *op. cit.*, p. 921.
13. *Ibid.*, p. 919.
14. *Ibid.*, p. 918.
15. *Ibid.*, p. 917.
16. *Ibid.*, p. 922.
17. *Ibid.*, p. 928.
18. *Ibid.*
19. *Ibid.*, p. 953-54.
20. *Ibid.*, p. 958.
21. Reported in *Ibid.*, p. 980.
22. Quoted in Stanley B. Ryerson, *French Canada* (Toronto: Progress Books, 1943), p. 197.
23. Mason Wade, *op. cit.*, p. 969.
24. *Ibid.*, p. 976.
25. Quoted in *Ibid.*, p. 979.
26. Quoted in *Ibid.*
27. Quoted in *Ibid.*, p. 1019.
28. Reginald Boisvert, "La Grève et le Mouvement Ouvrier," in P. E. Trudeau (ed.), *La Grève de l'Amiante* (Montréal: Editions Cité Libre, 1956), p. 362.
29. Herbert Quinn, *The Union Nationale* (Toronto: University of Toronto Press, 1963), pp. 91-92.
30. *Ibid.*, p. 93.
31. Quoted in Reginald Boisvert, *op. cit.*, p. 348. (Authors' translation.)
32. *Ibid.*, p. 352.

33. *Ibid.*, p. 353.
34. *Ibid.*, p. 355.
35. Quoted in Mason Wade, *op. cit.*, p. 1109.
36. Gérard Pelletier, "La Grève et la Presse," in P. E. Trudeau, (ed.), *op. cit.*, p. 286.
37. J. C. Falardeau, quoted in Gilles Beausoleil, "Histoire de la Grève à Asbestos," in P. E. Trudeau, (ed.), pp. 209-10. (Authors' translation.)
38. Reginald Boisvert, *op. cit.*, p. 359. (Authors' translation.)
39. Quoted in "Mgr. Charbonneau et l'opinion publique dans l'Eglise," *Cité Libre*, janvier-février, 1960, p. 3.
40. Reginald Boisvert, *op. cit.*, p. 363.
41. Paul Bélanger, "Mutations du Syndicalisme Québecois," *Recherches Sociographiques*, Vol. 9, No. 3, 1963, p. 271.
42. Gérard Dion et Louis O'Neil, *Le Chrétien et les Elections* (Montréal: Editions de l'homme, 1956), p. 16. (Authors' translation.)
43. *Ibid.*, p. 114.
44. Roger Lemelin, "The Silent Struggle at Laval," *Maclean's Magazine*, August 1, 1952, p. 11.
45. *Ibid.*, p. 36.
46. Blair Fraser, "The Fight Over Father Lévesque," *Maclean's Magazine*, July 1, 1950, p. 52.
47. Quoted in *ibid*.
48. *Ibid*.
49. *Ibid.*, p. 54.
50. *Ibid.*, p. 53.
51. Charles Henri Dubé, "La Verité sur l'Ordre de Jacques-Cartier," *Magazine Macleans*, mai, 1963, pp. 23, 24, 72-74.
52. Quoted in *Ibid.*, p. 72. (Authors' translation.)
53. Quoted in *Ibid.*, p. 72. (Authors' translation.)
54. Gilles Crotcau, "Etablissement et Intégration de l'Institution Co-opérative à L'île d'Orléans," M.A. Thesis, Laval University, 1952.
55. Charles Gagnon, "Je Venais de loin quand j'arrivai à Montreal en septembre 1960," *Magazine Macleans*, juillet, 1970, p. 34.
56. Gerard Pelletier, *op. cit.*, p. 278-79.
57. Quoted in *ibid.*, p. 283.
58. Quoted in *ibid.*, p. 300.

CHAPTER 8

THE
FLOODGATES
ARE
OPENED

The story of the "Quiet Revolution" does not require retelling in detail. The Lesage victory which followed a short period of housecleaning by Paul Sauvé, Duplessis' successor, and then Sauvé's untimely death, signalled the arrival of a new era. The intellectuals, technocrats and would-be reformers who had advocated "rattrapage" as opposed to "survivance" and had therefore been on the defensive in Quebec or in exile in Ottawa came out onto the stage. There was a sense that suddenly all barriers were removed, everything was now possible; energies would be directed positively – toward building Quebec – rather than pent up or used only to defend its past and myths.

In this period, which might roughly be dated from 1960 to 1966, Quebec built up an infrastructure of a modern capitalist society. It trained a bureaucracy able to administer a modern state and it set up an educational system suitable for such a state. The government began to take a positive role in regulating the economy and several state enterprises were set up – the most notable being the nationalization of electric power under Hydro-Québec. Even union activity was recognized as legitimate, even desirable, and ranks, particularly of the c.t.c.c. (now cntu), soared.

The culture and atmosphere of Quebec changed dramatically as well. Censorship of films, books, plays, etc., which had been oppressively, absurdly heavy, almost disappeared entirely; Quebec began to produce a relevant and consciously Québecois art and music of its own. Speaking French became something to be proud of and encouraged rather than something to be ashamed of or at best defensively clung to. Since everything was now legitimate, journalists and commentators found themselves in the extraordinary position of being able to tell the truth and provide honest assessments. *La Presse,* the old staid family newspaper, became, under Gérard Pelletier, a vibrant and open voice of the new Quebec. The slogan of the provincial Liberals, "Maîtres Chez Nous" took on a mainly cultural meaning which for a time seemed to unite all classes of Quebecers. It spoke of a common liberation from the weight of the past, a common present in the sharing of a genuine and increasingly rich cultural expression, and a common future built on the collective explora- tion and assessment of all possibilities and the implementation of those which best served the needs of all the people. In sum, all was possible.

The intellectuals of "rattrapage" were pleased though a little taken aback at the rapidity of events and strength of feelings. Somehow, they must have realized, they had outlived their purpose. *Cité Libre* faded into the background as if outgrown by its readers. And underneath all this, nationalism, rather than having been soundly vanquished and expelled forever, was rearing its head; a new nationalism very different from that known by French Canadians over the past centuries.

Even the ruling Liberals in Quebec began to interpret Maîtres Chez Nous in ways that smacked of political nationalism. They demanded, as outlined by their constitutional thinker Paul Gérin-Lajoie, a "special status" for Quebec; Quebec was not to be a province within confederation like all the others. Lesage went to Ottawa with concrete demands for increased jurisdiction in taxation, social welfare, and foreign and cultural policy. The Provincial Liberals went so far as to set up their own party organization fully independent from the Federal Liberals. By setting themselves against the Ottawa government in these ways, the Liberals, not unconsciously, helped fan the flames of the dreaded nationalism. In the spring of 1964, René Lévesque, the most outspoken nationalist in Lesage's cabinet, endorsed an associate state relationship between Quebec and the rest of Canada.

There are two reasons for this singular turn of events. The first is administrative: Quebec found it simply did not have the power to institute nor the revenue sources to pay for many of the integral reforms of the Quiet Revolution, and its leaders did not like the idea of having to get Ottawa's approval and perhaps revisions on many of these programs. Second, and in the long run more crucial, the quasi-nationalism of Lesage springs out of the basic weakness and contradictions inherent in the Quiet Revolution.

While the reforms of the period were genuine and did transform Quebec society, they operated only at the middle level. The basic pattern of economic control, investment, and development was, except for a few adjustments, basically left untouched. Foreign interests were dominant and indeed many of the reforms were designed to encourage even further foreign takeover by providing the owning class with a modern economic infrastructure. As such there was a definite limit on the changes which the architects of the Quiet Revolution could accomplish, beyond which meant attacking the basic economic system root and branch. For the Liberals, being as always, a party supporting and supported by big business, such as possibility was dismissed out of hand.

Thus the Liberals found themselves building up expectations and hopes they could not possibly allow to be fulfilled. What if the intellectual and political freedom of expression took form in a movement for defining "maîtres chez nous" in economic and therefore socialist terms? Ottawa was a more suitable villain, and given their own anger at the Ottawa government for its refusal to make the kind of constitutional concessions desired, the resentment was already there. So, following the path so well laid out by Duplessis, the ruling Liberals developed a sort of pseudo-nationalism, railing against Ottawa as the cause of the failures and unfulfilled hopes of the Quiet Revolution.

The intellectuals and activists who had worked together to defeat Duplessis became active in various spheres of Quebec during this period. Some, like LaPorte and Lévesque, went into the Lesage cabinet; others took various administrative posts in the new government. Here they were influenced by and some took leadership in the pseudo-nationalism of the government. Only the *Cité Libre* group members such as Trudeau and Pelletier seemed determined to fight off the virus at all costs and, as we know, by the mid-sixties when the disease seemed to be reaching near epidemic proportions they went to Ottawa to fight it from a distance and on more quarantine grounds.

169

The socialists within the group, at least most of the French-Canadian socialists, also very quickly moved in the nationalist direction – though making it clear that their new nationalism bore little resemblance to the reactionary and ephemeral form they had fought under Duplessis. By briefly examining the evolution of the Quebec wing of the New Party (NDP) from 1960-65, the initial alliance of nationalism and the principles of social democracy can be seen. Among the founders of the New Party were a small group of Francophone Québecois, both intellectuals and labour union leaders, most of whom had actively worked to overthrow the Union Nationale, and a group of English-speaking intellectuals, predominately McGill faculty and longtime CCF members. Because of the position taken by the CLC in 1961, the QFL officially supported the New Party. But, because of this labour federation's tacit collusion with the Duplessis regime during the fifties many public commentators questioned the sincerity of their newly espoused progressivism.[1] Inside the Confederation of National Trade Unions, CNTU, (Confédération des Syndicats Nationaux, CSN), a number of leading activists, Pierre Vadeboncoeur, Gérard Picard, and Jean Robert Ouellet, openly supported the New Party.[2]

In the fall of 1960 a Conference of French-Canadian intellectuals on the New Party was presided over by Marcel Rioux. The speech delivered there by Vadeboncoeur was perhaps the first public declaration of the need for a Francophone left-wing movement. "The left must not participate in the work of the Liberal party but must organize itself politically and ideologically. It must work out its fundamental critique, sharpen its thinking, and integrate itself into the national milieu in which it must act and in so doing develop its political strategies."[3] The importance of Vadeboncoeur's proposal lies in its demand for Liberals and "la gauche" to split; all Quebec intellectuals to the left of the government must identify themselves concretely as an opposition force.

During the summer of 1961, some New Party intellectuals began a move to orient their party to a position of sympathy with the underlying grievances expressed in the early separatist movement. In a letter published in *Le Devoir* on the sixth of June, leading Francophone New Party members stated: "We believe that Canada is formed of two nations: the English-Canadian nation and the French-Canadian nation. The British

North America Act implies the respect of the rights of each: it was the product of a pact between the two nations that constitute Canada."[4] At the New Party convention in August, Michel Chartrand moved to delete all references to one nation in the party's platform and sought the acceptance of the two nation theory. Eugene Forsey led the opposition with an impassioned plea against Chartrand. To the surprise of most Quebecers including the editors of *La Presse* and *Le Devoir* the two-nation philosophy was accepted. Both Pelletier and Laurendeau were impressed by the influence of the Quebec delegation and the position it had taken at the convention.[5]

The next step was the founding of the provincial party, but growing divisions paralyzed efforts in this direction. By the end of 1961, two incompatible groups had emerged; a nationalist group demanding a separate party and a federalist group wanting a provincial NDP consistent with the policy of the federal party. The first group was composed of intellectuals and trade unionists such as Rioux, Vadeboncoeur, Chartrand and J. Y. Morin: all were Francophone. The federalist group led by McGill professors Michael Oliver and Charles Taylor, included all the active Anglophones.

In his study of the NDP for the Royal Commission on Bilingualism and Biculturalism, Sherwood points to three incidents which he documents as having encouraged the nationalists to press forward with their demands for a separate party. Tommy Douglas had been accused of unjust treatment of the Roman Catholic minority while he was premier of Saskatchewan. Certain he had nothing to fear, the new NDP federal leader invited journalists to investigate his accusers' claims. Having taken up this invitation, *Le Devoir* of November 15, 1961 concluded that, "the accusations against Prime Minister Douglas were justified."[6] The declaration of Douglas Fisher, a leading NDP member, on the "contributions" of French Canadians to Canadian culture (see chapter ten), led *Le Devoir* and others to seek his expulsion from NDP ranks. Then in January of 1962, NDP leader Douglas made a speech in Toronto which was interpreted by Francophone Quebec as a rejection of the two nation theory. The press commented prolifically on each of these incidents and their implications for the role of the Quebec party, never failing to note a statement by an NDP stalwart which failed to support the two nation concept. In this way it was made public that

171

NDP Anglophones too often shared attitudes typical of English Canada – attitudes which the nationalist faction saw as barriers to co-operation between a federal (predominately English) party and a provincial (Francophone) party. They also realized that unless the NDP eradicated the old "Anglais" image of the CCF it had little chance for electoral support within the Francophone community. Oliver, Taylor, Picard and Romeo Mathieu became the buffers, trying to ease relations between the federal party and the Quebec wing.

Both the nationalist and the federalist factions were surprised at the party's failure to gain support in Quebec in the 1962 federal election. The nationalist group maintained that the failure was due to party policy, while the federalist group blamed it on a lack of organization and the election strategy. The Provisional Council was completely paralyzed by the split and little was being done to set up a Quebec NDP. The nationalists began to gain control of the party bureaucracy. Lebel, the provincial organizer was firmly on their side, as was most of the staff although the new president, Fernand Daoust, was, as yet, undecided. By the early months of 1963 the English intellectuals who led the federalist faction understood that they could no longer grant all the demands of the nationalists; they were now fighting from a defensive position.

Not only the press, but also the students got into this philosophical fight. During the 1962-63 session of the model parliament at Université de Montréal the NDP formed the government.[7] Its first pronouncement demanded a separate party for Quebec. After some delay the nationalists in the party responded. The outcome was the formation of the Parti Socialiste du Québec (PSQ) which was to contest provincial elections with the Quebec wing of the NDP handling federal elections. Two separate parties were thus established. The split between the nationalists and federalists had been paralleled by a split between English and French social democrats. From this point on Anglophones on the left as well as the establishment became separated from the Francophone left by a growing rift over national independence.

The PSQ fell apart within a year. It takes more than ideologues to form and direct a political party. It was only in March of 1965 that the NDP finally founded a provincial party, but its tame social democracy brought back few PSQ adherents.

The development (or lack of it) of the Quebec NDP is

important not for the public support it aroused, which was minimal, but as an indication of the ideological growth of left-wing leaders and thinkers, many of whom play crucial roles in other organizations in the years to follow. Apart from the advanced but isolated nationalism of the PSQ and the pseudo-nationalism of the Liberals, the most important political organization to take form was in the R.I.N. (Rassemblement pour L'Indépendance Nationale) and its various factions. An important source of support for this essentially centrist movement came from elements within the "new middle class."

The very rapid development of bureaucracies in urban centers became the structural basis for what the new home-grown Francophone social scientists called the "new middle class." Between 1950 and 1960 the percentage of the population between the ages of 5 and 24 years attending school rose from 53 to 62. Attendance in grades nine to twelve more than doubled and beyond grade twelve it increased by more than 50 percent.[8] The "new middle class" was university or technically educated but its "newness" was most noticeable in its lack of role models. Never before had such a class existed within Francophone Quebec society. This new class confronted the reality of the social structure of Quebec, and the power of the Anglo-corporate elite. They perceived this elite as a barrier to their own mobility, for executive and management positions in the business world of Quebec had for centuries been an English prerogative. The data presented in chapter four demonstrate that their perceptions of blocked mobility were not incorrect, nor were their sentiments that little would change quickly. Many among them perceived but refused to accept the limitations of the Liberal Quiet Revolution.

Thus, representatives of the "new middle class" proposed a technocratically managed independent state for Quebec to solve their own, personally felt, dilemma. "The most important group to propose the new nationalism is surely that of the technicians, engineers, economists, sociologists, etc. that constitute the new technocracy of the public and private sectors."[9] "It is likely that the technicians ideal doesn't necessarily entail a classless society, but surely one where class divisions are dulled and where conflicts are settled through reason and science. Though they may be less paternalist than their predecessors, the technicians see no less a privileged position for themselves in the new society."[10]

173

The political philosophy of this new group reflected their desire to secure their advantageous position in the class structure. They wanted to re-organize Quebec society so as to increase their power. This would necessitate eliminating political ties with Canada, thereby discrediting the old elites and in the process bringing about a liberal democracy – or a meritocracy – in which they would be the new governing class. As early as 1964, Guindon attempted to discover the reasons for the growth of nationalism predominantely among the "new middle class." "Why has the new French-Canadian middle class become virulently nationalist and, to an important extent separatist? . . . Separatist leaders as well as their rank and file are to be found among the better-educated, younger, professional and semi-professional, salaried, white collar ranks . . . The nature of separatist grievances also underlies its class bias. Separatist discontent, in the final analysis, boils down to protest against real or imagined restricted occupational mobility. The objects of separatist indictment are the promotion practices of the federally operated bureaucracies, of Crown and private corporations."[11]

In the spring of 1965, Charles Taylor wrote to the same effect, except that he – in a prophecy he probably wishes had not been fulfilled – saw a possible further development: "I have maintained that the new nationalism, . . . is mainly a middle-class phenomenon, largely the creation of what I have called the intelligentsia, that its roots are to be found partly in the situation of this class, competing for promotion and careers in a modern economy which is in origin and stamp largely Anglo-Saxon. . . . Nationalism has little intrinsic appeal to classes lower in the social order, worker or peasants; it appeals only when it is linked with the solution of deeply felt economic ills. . . . This has not happened yet in Quebec although there are signs that it might. If it does then Quebec will accede to independence in a short space of time."[12]

Taylor's reluctant forecast has, as we shall see, turned out to be correct. The radicalization we see today of the working class toward a nationalism of the left far stronger and more committed than the one expressed by the new middle class makes clear that on a fundamental point the new middle-class theorists were mistaken. They pointed to a visible phenomenon not understanding that it might point to something far deeper beneath the surface. Could it not be that aside from their class interests, new middle class individuals, more educated and self-assured than their lower class compatriots, also articulated a growing lower class sentiment that only later would find expression in genuine working class forms. As early as 1963 the *Maclean's* poll revealed workers to be slightly above the average in support of separatism.* In addition, the new middle class theorists chose to ignore the left nationalism of the PSQ intellectuals because of their paltry numbers and organizational setbacks; thus failing to see the influence these individuals were likely to have in various spheres – labour unions, the media and education. Finally the theorists neglected to note the increasing importance of the trade unions, especially the CNTU, in bringing together in its ranks elements of the new middle class and the traditional working class. This will be explored in detail below. Having set the context of the nationalism of the new middle class, in the early sixties we return to its chief political organ, the RIN.

A study of the RIN, carried out by Barker, *et al.* during the winter of 1964-65 for the Royal Commission on Bilingualism and Biculturalism,[13] examined a sample comprised of seven executive members, five regional committee members, two regional leaders, and two influential members. All were Francophone males who had been raised as Roman Catholics. Six said they were agnostics. The ages ranged from 32 to 48 years. Ten of the sixteen had been to a classical college; only one had not completed secondary school. Eleven of the sixteen had a university degree, although thirteen had attended university. Three were businessmen, three were journalists, five were in the civil service, two were lawyers, two were public relations specialists. Eight of the sixteen had a high degree of contact with English Canadians, an excellent knowledge of English and had spent at least one year in English Canada. In other words the group was a middle class one.[14] In 1964 the RIN carried out a study of its 6,000 members. Their average age was 31 years; 41.7 percent of the members were between 20 and 29 years old. Only 10 percent were women. Fifty percent were residents of Montreal. The membership was composed predominantly of professionals.[15]

* The figures were 13 percent overall and 16 percent among blue collar workers in favour of separation. See below, this chapter.

The RIN was founded in September, 1960. Its first convention was held in Montreal in November and about five hundred persons attended and elected Marcel Chaput president. Because it was the first of the new wave of separatist organizations, the RIN attracted separatists of many political persuasions. Few had a coherent, well articulated political position, but all felt the need for an independent Quebec.

By 1962, right and left wing factions of the party emerged and a split occurred over a resolution that the RIN become a political party. Chaput led the more conservative group in favour of the motion and when it was defeated he founded and became a leader of the new "Parti républicain du Québec." Guy Pouliot was elected president of a badly shaken RIN, whose political philosophy was gradually crystallizing and moving left of center. Not only an independent Quebec, but one with increased welfare measures, protection of individual civil liberties, and extensive economic planning was envisioned by the RIN membership.[16]

The RIN was democratically organized and concerned that all members participate in decision making. Student members had their own university groups with guaranteed representation on regional and central councils. The group at Université de Montréal grew from 10 members in 1960 to 150 in 1965. During the winters of 1963-64 and 1964-65 RIN members were elected to the students' council (AGEUM) and to the editorial board of *Quartier Latin*. It was an RIN member who prepared AGEUM's brief to the constitutional committee of the Legislative Assembly and another who authored the AGEUM draft protesting the Queen's visit. Clearly there was significant support for the new organization within the university community.[17]

Between 1962 and 1965, a more clearly defined social democratic philosophy emerged in the program of the RIN. At the congress held in the spring of 1963 the membership voted in favour of becoming a political party. The "Parti républicain du Québec" was dissolved and many returned to the RIN. But Chaput's group had lost their influence and their conservatism was no longer reflected in RIN policy. However, at the spring congress the following year, the right-left split manifested itself again in the presidential election. Pouliot was supported by a more conservative, non-Montreal and staunchly Roman Catholic group, reminiscent of the old nationalists of the thirties.

They labelled the opposition candidate Pierre Bourgault, social-ist and anti-clerical, failing to understand that among at least some sectors of the Quebec population these adjectives no longer were synonymous with sin and evil. Bourgault was elected president and the right split to form another separatist organization, "le Regroupement National" (RN).[18]

The RIN is probably best known for its street activities. Although these demonstrations were few in number, they were nevertheless important, first because they initiated a decade of mass actions of "Québecois, dans les rues;" and secondly because they provoked a brutal over-reaction on the part of the authorities which made independence an issue on which all had to take sides. The Queen's visit in the fall of 1964 presented an opportunity to dramatize Quebec's desire to be independent of the British crown. A large demonstration in Quebec City and a small turnout of Québecois at the processions to view "their Queen" lead to powerful anti-French-Canadian feelings in the English-Canadian press. In 1965, a Honey Dew shop was the scene of a sit-in as it had only English advertisements in its windows. The next day signs in French appeared.[19]

In the 1966 provincial election the RIN received 5.5 percent of the votes; the RN received almost 3 percent. Impressive in themselves, these votes had the effect of ensuring the defeat of the Liberal Government. With its unexpected electoral defeat the Liberals began a period of retrenchment which culminated two years later when Lévesque, "probably the most powerful minister in the Lesage government," was forced to resign for his indépendantiste views. Canadian nationalist, Eric Kierans, successfully led the move supported by the party's English contingent and its old guard. Lévesque became leader of "le Mouvement Souveraineté-Association" which was joined by the RN to form the Parti Québecois (PQ) in 1968. Soon Bourgault led all but the extreme left of the RIN (which became the FLP, Front de Libération Populaire) into the PQ. The Parti Québé-cois now united almost all indépendantistes behind a left-center program. It demanded an independent Quebec and proposed policies in all other fields similar to those of the NDP. Popular participation at all levels, local, regional, central, was en-couraged. The PQ became a reasonably democratic as well as vibrant focus of the new nationalism.

Yet in our discussion of the new nationalism among political

177

groups in Quebec we cannot overlook the right-wing elements that remained. As the demands for social legislation and changes in the social structure of Quebec became more widespread and manifested themselves in the legislative program of the Liberal party in the early sixties, a resurgence of right-wing nationalism was apparent among members of the traditional elite. These people, growing more irrelevant as the technological society emerged, clutched at separatism in an effort to reassert their diminishing power. These elements were represented by organizations like the St. Jean Baptiste Society. Included among them are a few small financiers representing indigenous capital which is locally rather than internationally centered and in fact threatened by multinational capitalism. These people have a lot to gain economically if Quebec becomes independent, for essentially they are the only French Canadians with large amounts of liquid capital. On the other hand, their sympathy for a program of changing property relations and economic redistribution is rather lacking.

As early as 1957, "L'Alliance Laurentienne" (AL) was formed to work towards the establishment of a sovereign Quebec state of Laurentia. Recruitment concentrated upon militant nationalists within the Saint Jean Baptiste Society, L'Action Nationale, followers of the late Abbé Groulx and students and intellectuals of the right. By transforming the elite, a Christian social order was to be established. It was the Church that would define the characteristics of the republic, of Christian corporatism, Christian interventionism and the rights of Christian nationalities. By 1963, L'Alliance Laurentienne disappeared, but the Regroupement National (RN) took much the same political position and represented the same class of people. The RN declared itself to be a separatist organization in the tradition of those of the thirties, and emphasized the point by appointing the aging René Chalout vice-president. The RN was less conspicuously tied to right-wing Catholic doctrine than the AL but its manifesto hardly strayed from basic Church dogma. "The RN regards the family as the basic unit of Quebec society. . . . Family values must not be lost in the changes of the twentieth century. These basic values are intimately linked to the national life of French Canada."[20] The only significant way the RN wanted Quebec to change was to be politically independent of Canada. The Liberal government of Jean Lesage was opposed for it was "socialistic."

178

A study of the RN's roughly one hundred members in 1965 showed them to be Roman Catholic, Francophone males about 35 to 40 years of age. They were predominately members of the older middle and upper classes and the lay elite: lawyers, doctors, teachers and owners of businesses, residing in Quebec City.[21] Thus such party themes as "Too much welfare could bring a lazy and unproductive society"[22] are understandable in terms of the class in whose interests the RN sought separation. It is undoubtedly many of these same elements who, finding the PQ too "gauchiste," returned to the fold of the Union Nationale and constitute the main element within its nationalist wing.

During this entire period the UN skated carefully on the nationalist question. Desperately trying to stave off extinction during the Quiet Revolution, the remnants of Duplessis' organization went from being more nationalist than the liberals to more federalist and back, trying to cash in on popular feelings. Because of the rurally-weighted electoral system, the vote of the RIN, the disaffection of many people with the uncertainties of the reforms of the Quiet Revolution, and the skillful leadership of Daniel Johnson, the UN was victorious in 1966. Elected unexpectedly on essentially a protest vote, it took power with no program and no philosophy. Johnson, however, proved quite competent in seizing the opportunity – leaving intact the reforms and bureaucratic machinery that had been instituted during the previous five years, and, in a manner much more adept than Lesage, maintaining the attack on Ottawa as the source of Quebec's ills. "Egalité ou Indépendance" was the new slogan – a clear escalation over "Maîtres Chez Nous."

When the Liberals became resolutely federalist after their election defeat, the UN became the sole official pseudo-nationalist party. The disparate elements within it that Johnson had so well contained broke into open conflict after his death in 1968, and it was soon clear that the pseudo-nationalism of his successor, J. J. Bertrand, placated neither the nationalists nor the anti-nationalists within his ranks. By this time, however, the debate had become for the most part academic for the 1970 election results made clear just how irrelevant the party was to the new Quebec.

The extreme right was still around in this period, its solid foundation maintained in various places such as the Jesuit order. In it, the "most extreme members, and the ones the

179

liberals fear most, are adherents to a lay movement called Cité Catholique, which is of French origin and just now rearing its head in Quebec. This movement is not unlike the John Birch Society in the U.S.A. It rigidly opposes all change. It holds as its principal enemies communism and what it calls laicism. In Cité Catholique terms, laicism is any school of thought that would reduce the clergy's role in anything, and Cité Catholique sees laiciste plots everywhere."[23]

L'Ordre Jacques Cartier seems to have to some extent continued its activities within the UN and different municipal governments and school commissions. That it was still supported by the Church hierarchy, is said to be demonstrated by the presence of Cardinal Léger at an initiation ritual in Montreal in May, 1962.[24]

Yet, mobilized and organized as they were, the forces of reactionary nationalism played at best a defensive role. The goals of the popular movements for Quebec independence have been consistently left of center and continually moving in that direction. Unlike in the thirties, the nationalist movement has repulsed all attempts to channel it into a racist and past-oriented direction. Even the language issue, as we shall see, has been pressed for the most part on egalitarian and progressive rather than on racist lines. The right is not dead, and its ideology still appeals to certain groups such as sections of the non-metropolitan middle-class that are confused and frightened by the rapidity of change. Still it seems that history has passed it by: once the stops are pulled on a repressive society it is most difficult to put them back. Having glimpsed the light, les Québecois are not about to be led back into the darkness.

The growth of nationalism and of radicalism was not limited to primarily political bodies. Its traces can be found in virtually all the expanding spheres of society. Quebec, like elsewhere, was the scene of an important and impressive process of radicalization among its student and youth population. As in English Canada the movement began with slogans and marches of "Ban the Bomb" in the early sixties. Soon the opponent became not only nuclear war but exploitation as symbolized by American imperialism in Viet Nam.

The civil rights movement brought with it not only new tactics and strategies but also led students to draw parallels between the status of the blacks in the U.S.A. and that of the

French in Canada. As the black movement increased in militancy with an understanding of cultural colonialism, so did the left-nationalist movement, and by 1968 these movements recognized each other as fighting the same enemy to achieve similar goals. The growth of the American anti-war movement led to much discussion of "imperialism" and the Third World. The invasions of the Bay of Pigs and the Dominican Republic and continued escalation of the war in Viet Nam in many ways verified the rhetoric of the student radicals.

Among all this ferment it became clear that imperialism was not only something "out there," that in more subtle ways it was at the base of the social and economic structure of Quebec itself. The students were beginning to confront the condition of their own society, to escape the ivory tower that had so long moulded their thoughts and kept them isolated. And this very process of opening themselves to the community, of making contact with labour unions and citizens groups, was itself a radicalizing process. Unlike in the United States, and English Canada to some extent, the students were neither isolated from nor taken as opposed to, the articulated interests and demands of the working class. In Quebec the radicalization of the students paralleled a radicalization that took place in the unions and among significant sectors of the population.   Students and young intellectuals became participants and they have provided one important source of expertise and leadership.

The university campuses in the early sixties became highly politicized. Quebec students, as early as 1964, founded the Union Générale des Etudiants du Québec (UGEQ) and split from the national organization, the Canadian Union of Students (CUS). UGEQ quickly became a left-nationalist organization demanding free education, student participation in the administration of the university and a separate Quebec. By supporting different striking unions and sending "animateurs" to use their skills to organize people in poverty areas, UGEQ encouraged students to integrate themselves into the society and form coalitions with Quebec's progressive elements.

At its 1966 Congress, for instance, UGEQ's guest speaker, Marcel Pepin, was the new President of the CNTU; and he seconded the call for a strong student-worker alliance. (Imagine, if you will, George Meany keynoting an SDS convention.)

Edward Corbett described the political atmosphere at the

Université de Montréal. "Socialism and independence have been *Quartier Latin* goals for several years. Its editorial team was forced out of office in the fall of 1965 for pushing its views too vigorously, but the new editors pledged only to be more adroit in disseminating the same themes. The AGEUM has been pressing for a student trade union, free tuition, and a student share in control of the university."[25]

By the end of the decade UGEQ had disappeared, having served its purpose. Student activism, however, recurred with renewed and even increased militancy, against McGill, against Bill 63 and in a series of strikes that swept the junior colleges (CEGEP's) in 1968. By the end of the decade, in Quebec as elsewhere, the scene of radical activity had (temporarily) left the campus. The university had been transformed in the process and so had the thinking of the young people of Quebec. "The facts have already established, beyond a shadow of a doubt, that the majority of young Québecois are won to the cause of Quebec Independence . . . Even young workers outside of the educational system are becoming more and more open to the indépendantiste options. The proof is so strong that it can be genuinely argued that as a group Quebec youth favours independence."[26] The last important period of student militancy was in the fall of 1968 with the ten-day occupation of the CEGEP's* and· the student support for the actions of the MLT (Taxi Liberation Movement against Murray Hill). The culmination was the McGill Français demonstration in March 1969.

Quebec's youth has to some extent learned and incorporated the "counter cultural" or life-style revolution of their American counterparts.† The political and economic struggle has been opened to questions of human and women's liberation – of freeing one's life-style from the false needs created by consumer-oriented capitalism. And this "New Left" orientation is a vital input to the wider movement to prevent it going the way of the North American "Old Left" – toward hypocrisy and co-optation.

The most militant of the students were undoubtedly readers

* (Collège enseignement général et professionnel.)

---

† Some of this "counter-cultural" sentiment can be seen in several issues of the magazine, *Quartier Latin* (Winter 1970-71), and in the current population publication, *Main Mise*.

of the Marxist nationalist review *Parti Pris,* first published in the fall of 1963. The individuals composing the original collective which began the review were young and university educated. Their views on the necessity for Quebec's independence had evolved from an initially traditional Marxist philosophy. Of the 3,500 readers in 1963, 60 percent were university students, 20 to 30 percent were professionals, civil servants or intellectuals, while 10 percent were workers.[27] As for its political position, "the doctrine that moves the group is socialism, laicism is but an aspect and independence only a step. . . . At *Parti Pris* the national question is accorded a weight equal to the class issue – in the sense that one nation can dominate another in the same way because its structural reality is almost equal to that of a class."[28]

In an important essay entitled "From Damnation to Liberty," poet Paul Chamberlain described the French Canadians: "The condition of the minority is essentially an alienating one. The minoritarian being is a divided one: he wants at the same time to be his own man, preserve his specificity, and participate as an equal partner in the creation of a society the character of which is determined exclusively by the majority."[29] The analysis owes much to the work of Third-World revolutionary theorist, Franz Fanon. "From several viewpoints the revolutionary ideologies of Fanon [from *The Wretched of the Earth*] and Chamberlain . . . are similar. However, it is with regard to the basic theories and overall conceptual framework that the parallels are most striking."[30]

The revolution and the process of de-colonization will result in the creation of the "new socialist man." One can see in these words the influence of another personnage, Che Guevara. Chamberlain continues: "Socialism constitutes on the whole a political theory and practice, methods and techniques which provide knowledge for the triumph of the popular classes over the exploiting minority and the accomplishment of a society planned by the people and serving their needs . . . Here are the values of the national liberation struggle: power, health and freedom. In a word, humanity."[31]

The manifesto of the fall of 1964 also heralded the magazine's "New Left" orientation. "The socialism which we must build will be neither Russian nor Chinese nor Cuban, it must be and can only be Québecois. Marxism-Leninism, as we practice it, is not a catechism but above all a method of analysis and work which we must make use of in Quebec."[32]

Parti Pris was aimed at the intellectuals and students who would help organize the revolutionary workers' party and it was the driving force behind the setting up of the MLP. *Parti Pris* saw its responsibility in the creation and continued education of this vanguard who would then educate and politicize the lower classes. A few years ahead of its time, *Parti Pris* was quite important, setting before its readers the goal of liberation as opposed to the idea of "rattrapage" now being voiced more and more stridently in the pages of *Cité Libre*.

When the students and progressive intellectuals for the most part left the campus in the late sixties to work for the movement in trade unions, community organizing, political parties, etc., they went armed with a relatively sophisticated knowledge of the effects of foreign-controlled capitalism on Quebec society.

The sixties, especially from '65 on, were characterized by an ever-increasing movement for social change and an ever growing popular impatience with the status quo. A social historian is needed to capture these events in all their dimension and breadth in Quebec; but in many respects the pattern was similar to what was happening in many parts of the world. People at the bottom refused to be exploited and manipulated any longer: whether the issue was housing, pollution, consumer protection, welfare rights – citizens and community groups sprung up to fight them. In Quebec, Comités des Citoyens, Comités des Ouviers, Comités d'Actions Populaires, cooperative movements like the Caisses d'Economie, etc., were among the forms these activities took. Former students were training themselves to aid in this action as "animateurs sociales" and set up political education groups ("Comités de Formation Politique") to aid the members and leaders of the various organizations to understand the actual system they were struggling against.

The artistic and cultural community too changed greatly in this period. Not only did Quebec produce a lasting and important genuinely Québecois art and music but many of the top artists, filmmakers, playwrights, musicians, consciously contributed to the growing political cause. In this way Quebec was unlike the United States and English Canada, where the lack of unity and clear political perspective meant that a great part of the energy of the sixties was dissipated and neutralized. In Quebec the presence of a growing movement and a clear cause seemed to bring together the activities of the various spheres.

Finally, this period was characterized by the actions of a small group, or rather several small groups, generally taking the name *Front de Libération du Québec* (FLQ) which through their actions succeeded in bringing the message of Quebec's colonization home to many people and in having the "Question of Quebec" raised not only in Canada but abroad. The FLQ was founded in 1963, and in that year claimed responsibility for innumerable bombings and attempted bombings of symbols of the federal powers – armories, mail boxes, RCMP offices, etc. It reappeared several times in the next eight years. Its espoused aim was to awaken the Québecois to their colonial status within Canadian confederation. Organized into cells, the members seemed to have been predominantly young workers and students who knew little about revolution or politics except romantic rhetoric. In the chapter to follow we shall see how the FLQ reached its zenith of popular support and political sophistication and the (temporary?) end of its usefulness in the Cross-Laporte kidnappings of 1970.

Still, the most important and unexpected locus of left-nationalism that developed in the sixties has not yet been covered. We are referring of course to the trade unions. Before looking at their actions and policies we shall briefly set out the organization and structure of the key federations.

The two principal confederations of labour in Quebec throughout the sixties are the Confederation of National Trade Unions, CNTU (Confédération des Syndicats Nationaux, CSN) and the Quebec Federation of Labour, QFL (Fédération des Travailleurs du Québec, FTQ), the latter a provincial federation of the Canadian Labour Congress, CLC. There are approximately 750,000 organized workers in Quebec, of these approximately 230,000 belonged to CNTU,* approximately 210,000 to the QFL. Of the remaining 300,000 some are in international unions affiliated with the CLC or only with the AFL-CIO, while some are totally independent.

* These figures refer to the membership roles before the split in June, 1971, which led to the formation of the Federation of Free Trade Unions (Confédération des Syndicats Démocratiques).

In the last twenty years the CNTU has been attracting young university educated Québecois to its permanent staff. In 1960, the union deconfessionalized, and in 1961 Jean Marchand became president, succeeded by Marcel Pepin in 1965. The CSN prides itself on its decentralization and horizontal distribution of power. Important to this is the twofold organizational pattern where each local is a member of a federation, set up along industrial lines (e.g. hospital services, construction, printing and media) and of a regional council set up along geographical criteria (e.g. Montreal Central Council, Quebec Central Council . . .). The congress, composed of over 1,500 delegates from the locals, meets every two years and constitutes the ruling body. The elected bureaucracy consists of: (1) executive (five members); (2) the bureau confédéral (the five executives, one representative from each federation and representatives from the largest regional councils); and (3) the conseil confédéral (representatives from the 21 regional councils, the bureau confédéral and the 13 federations). The Conseil Confédéral is the supreme body between conventions.

The QFL is much more a coalition of powerful and independent unions. It is thus a much less structured organization, with a smaller budget; it receives only 8¢ per affiliated member per month while the CSN receives $1.63.[33] The limits of the authority of the QFL under the CLC are also unclear. Under its president the QFL has sixteen vice-presidents* to try to accommodate the extremely powerful federations within it. All of the decisions of the biennial congress must be ratified by the CLC, while the unions are required to have them ratified by their own internationals first. Nevertheless variation exists among the component unions. The United Steelworkers of America, for example, has a great tradition of autonomy and militancy in its Canadian regions dating back to its CIO origins and the great strike against Noranda Copper mines in Murdochville in 1957.

The CNTU is particularly decentralized in its organization and financial structure. It leaves a great deal of autonomy and power over expenditure with the local. This increases the mobility of any union local because it can switch union affiliation without financial difficulty. In addition, the remaining money goes in far greater proportion to the confederation itself rather than to the

* This number has since been reduced to 6.

federation – so that greater solidarity of action is possible. This combination of centralized resources and decentralized decision-making power makes the CNTU extremely democratic by any standards. The QFL, on the other hand, by leaving much effective power and money in the hands of the affiliated international unions works less effectively, and somewhat less democratically as well.

Paul Bélanger points out how this difference applies to the collective bargaining process itself. In the CSN "it's the local executive that chooses the negotiator . . . the decision to strike requires approval neither from the federation nor the con-federation."[34] In the international unions the choice of a nego-tiator is often made in the higher echelons, also, ". . . the charters of the international unions often provide that this [strike] decision be approved by the international president."[35]

It is no wonder then that since the asbestos strike changes and developments in the CNTU should reflect similar changes and developments in the people of Quebec as a whole. Hence it is to the CNTU that we should look for indications as well as leadership of the process of radicalization of Quebec's working class.

During the Quiet Revolution relations between the CNTU and the Liberal government were quite cordial. The trade union movement, like other modern sectors of society, was able suddenly to step out of the shadows and reveal itself in full view of the society, to express what it saw as the demands and interests of its workers without fear or stigma. It was understood that one of the features of a modern society was a large, successful and moderate labour movement. Hence the policies of the government actually facilitated the spread of trade unionism. Many individuals joined unions and many new locals were certified. Quebec was catching up with the rest of North America to make up for years lost under Duplessis in the best tradition of "rattrapage." Everyone was pleased.

The CNTU in particular benefited from the policies of the Liberal administration; CNTU president, Jean Marchand, was known as a close collaborator and confidant of Jean Lesage. When the Quebec public employees were given the right to form bargaining unions in 1964, the law provided only for affiliation with trade unions without political party affiliations. Because of the CLC's and hence QFL's verbal endorsement of the NDP the effect of the law was to exclude the SCFP (CUPE), one of the more militant national affiliates of the CLC and QFL, and ensured that Quebec public employees joined the CNTU. In these ways, the CNTU grew from 80,000 to 230,000 between 1960 and 1970. This growth was particularly marked in the public sector and among "middle class" elements. Thus the present membership of the CNTU is over half public and para-public employees with a not insignificant representation of teachers, office workers, engineers and technicians.

The CNTU and trade unions affiliated with other organizations began to intensify their demands for fair working conditions. At the outset the actions were relatively tame – aimed at some of the most oppressive industries and firms – with some minor successes. By the mid-sixties the struggle had begun to intensify and Quebec was characterized by many militant strikes, lock-outs, etc. The CNTU, particularly, began to take a more and

TABLE 8-1

| | Number of Work Days Lost in Strikes | | |
	1964	1965	1966
Quebec	401,710	606,820	1,926,890
Ontario	714,080	1,340,720	1,356,130
Canada	1,580,550	2,349,870	5,178,170
% of total workdays	.11	.17	.34

Percentage of Quebec strike-lockouts involving CNTU affiliated unions (in man-days and not including federal jurisdiction) 50 or more workers or more than 250 man-days:

$$1964 \quad \frac{164,520}{400,000} = 41.1\%$$

$$1965 \quad \frac{316,890}{606,820} = 52.0\%$$

$$1966 \quad \frac{1,370,000}{1,927,000} = 71.1\%$$

1966 includes 555,590 in Dominion Textiles and 433,410 in Quebec Government service.

In 1966 Quebec had only 137 strikes compared to 297 in Ontario, but they were generally of a much greater duration.

Sources: *Labour Organization in Canada,* Federal Department of Labour, 1955-67.

more decisive role in these actions. Both these facts are documented in Table 8-1. The promises and rhetoric of the Quiet Revolution were wearing thin when faced with the reality of the socio-economic status of the French-Canadian workers. Among the many important strikes of this period, one that stands out symbolically is that against Seven-Up. Because of its American ownership, its location in the wealthy English suburb of Town of Mount Royal and its particularly bad working conditions and anti-union policies, Seven-Up became a target for the whole union movement and served to help educate the workers to the economic realities of their society.

In certain areas the groundwork for later political action was laid in this period. For instance, out of the CNTU came the Caisses d'Economie, credit unions for the people, which would serve the interests of the members and invest in socially useful projects – rather than integrating themselves into international capitalism like the Caisses Populaires Desjardins.

In the mid-sixties the right winger Provost was replaced by the moderate Louis Laberge at the QFL and Jean Marchand went to Ottawa. The militancy continued to rise more or less unabated, and this period marked the appearance of a more clearly political orientation – especially as concerned the National Question and the related question of language.

It was previously noted that the *Maclean's* Poll in 1963 revealed that 16 percent of blue collar workers were separatists. Also, the RIN received some support among workers in the 1966 elections. Nevertheless, what is true is that organized labour, as such, until 1965-66, showed little evidence of "nationalist" feeling.[36] The turning point here may very well have been the departure of Jean Marchand for Ottawa in 1965.

In 1966, a joint memorandum was issued by the QFL, CNTU and UCC (Union des Cultivateurs Catholiques, the Catholic Farmers' Union) to the constitutional committee of the national assembly. While not advocating separatism, it did evidently voice certain nationalist aspirations: "Quebec should embark upon an immense linguistic effort . . . to make the French language once again the current one . . . in the area of work. . . . At the provincial level the only official language should be the language of the majority."[37]

In this period, the QFL began a continuing challenge within the CLC for more power. At the 1966 CLC convention in

Winnipeg the QFL delegates raised the subject of greater autonomy. The result was that the QFL lost the principle, i.e. its right to negotiate with the other Quebec Federations, but won the point in that the results of its past negotiations with the CNTU were ratified by the CLC.

At this same convention, the issue of a "Special Status" for the QFL was central and the entire Quebec delegation chose the more nationalist Gérard Rancourt over official candidate Roméo Mathieu for Vice-President. By 1969 this process had reached a stage where the QFL unanimously readmitted a union, the teamsters, which the CLC had expelled years before, contrary to Article 8 of its constitution which reads: "The QFL can affiliate no union struck with expulsion . . . by the CLC."

Finally the 1969 congress passed a motion to the effect that Quebec was unique, a nation, and that, therefore, independent action for the QFL was essential. It called for a total restructuring of the CLC-QFL system, recognizing this fact both in principle and in finances. This congress, too, passed a motion from the floor binding the QFL to seeking joint action and eventual unification with the CNTU, CEQ (Corporation des Enseignants du Québec, Quebec Teacher's Corporation), and the UCC, an idea which then seemed quite far off, but which recent events have turned into a not too distant possibility.

One of the sources of the change in the QFL was its participation in a fierce and sometimes bitter rivalry with the CNTU for members. Noting the success of the CNTU's nationalist appeal, the QFL, in spite of the wishes of some of its leaders, was forced to follow. In the next chapter we shall see how the in-fighting that had for so long held back the trade union movement has been replaced recently by a new spirit of cooperation and unity.

As for the CNTU, the necessity for rethinking the entire role of trade-unionism and for a thorough analysis of its goals in light of the economic and social structure soon became evident. "Ideological" questions, which had been banished by the new "rattrapage" thinkers, were now being brought back, sometimes by the ex-students and intellectuals who had found staff positions with the CNTU. But, the ideological questions were no longer the ones of faith and tradition: real answers were needed to the objective conditions of Quebec's workers and the ideas of national liberation and anti-imperialism were among the issues being raised. For instance, Marcel Pepin, in his address to the 1966 CNTU congress attacked the American Government for its role in the Viet Nam war.[38]

During the winter of 1967-68, the CNTU organized a public campaign to demonstrate the necessity of government controls to restrict the exploitation of Quebec's natural resources by American owned firms. Where monopolies existed in areas of natural resources, the union recommended nationalization.[39] In 1968, the official statement of the Congress quoted *Monthly Review* in condemning the role of the CIA as an instrument of American imperialism in Latin America. It further noted, "Quebec, like Canada, is a satellite of American imperialism."

If we must choose a symbolic date for the end of the period of "rattrapage," of the Quiet Revolution, and of "cooperative" federalism, it would be around 1968. By that time the PQ had been organized into the first real indépendantiste political challenge. The 1968 convention of the CNTU, in retrospect, becomes significant as well. It initiated the "second front," the idea that trade union objectives could not be achieved simply at the negotiating table but required political and social involvement, in local elections, through the setting up of cooperatives, etc. It suggested the need to work in common fronts with other progressive forces to combat unemployment and poverty and to fight manipulative finance companies and other social parasites. The adoption of the second front opened an entire new area of concern to the trade union movement: if a totally new means to achieve its objectives was accepted, it was inevitable that the actual content of those objectives was soon to come into question. Below the surface in this period was the national issue – with a growing grass roots support for "indépendantisme." This issue surfaced first in relation to the language question, and we shall discuss it early in chapter nine, but there is every indication that indépendantiste feeling was steadily growing in this period. For instance, a poll conducted by the *Toronto Telegram* during 1969, not exactly a PQ mouthpiece, revealed among other things that 32 percent of Quebecers were solidly in favour of independence and 38 percent thought it inevitable.[40] All indications are that the working class as well as youth, etc. are over-represented in these 32 percent.

From our vantage point today, we can make out the significant weaknesses at the base of the Quiet Revolution. While it opened the world of ideas to all possibilities, it limited changes in structure to those which meant catching up with the rest of North America. Those spheres of society which had been held back under the older order were permitted to expand and grow. The schools, the media, the arts, all experienced a renaissance and soon became the locus for the spread and discussion of the new ideas. The changes, though fundamental in relation to the old order, did not at any point challenge the underlying economic structure of Quebec. And when some intellectuals and writers were no longer content to rail against Ottawa and devise even more complex constitutional schemata, but instead chose to attack the economic system head on; and when these new ideas began to receive attention and consideration among the students and trade unionists – then the authorities decided that things had simply gone too far.

"Law and order" came back into style. The new strong-man of the Liberal cabinet was the square-jawed neolithic Claude Wagner. René Lévesque, former darling, was out. Pierre Vallières and Charles Gagnon, two intellectuals who had supported the FLQ, were thrown into jail and kept there for several years (new charges being laid every time the old ones were thrown out of court). The FLQ became a term used to justify repression. Every bomb thrown became an excuse for ever increased police surveillance and harassment. Radio Canada was soon to begin to crack down on indépendantiste views with censorship and dismissals.

Yet the forces that had been unleashed could not be so easily restrained. Trudeau and his friends went to Ottawa and called on their ex-colleagues to engage only in "functional politics"; but fewer and fewer were listening. The idea that there had to be a genuine economic and cultural liberation to be combined with political liberation was spreading. Activities in the various sectors, among the students, in the arts and media, in community groups and trade unions, seemed to coalesce and gave the sense of a growing movement. As activity increased in frequency and grew in popular support one chant was coming to be heard more and more: "Ce n'est qu'un début; continuons le combat."

Footnotes to Chapter 8

1. D. H. Sherwood, "The NDP and French Canada, 1961-1965," Study done for the Royal Commission on Bilingulism and Biculturalism, p. 48.
2. *Ibid.,* p. 42.
3. Quoted in *Ibid.,* p. 42.
4. Quoted in *Ibid.,* p. 55. (Authors' translation.)
5. *Ibid.,* p. 68-73.
6. Quoted in *Ibid.,* p. 81. (Authors' translation.)
7. *Ibid.,* p. 118.
8. Jacques Brazeau, "Quebec's Emerging Middle Class," in Marcel Rioux and Yves Martin (eds.), *French Canadian Society* (Toronto: McClelland and Stewart, Ltd., 1964), p. 325.
9. Gérald Fortin, "Le Nationalisme Canadien-Français et les Classes Sociales," *Revue d'Histoire de l'Amérique Française,* Vol. XXII, No. 4, Mars, 1969, p. 532. (Authors' translation.)
10. Gérald Fortin, "Transformations des Structures du Pouvoir," in "Le Pouvoir dans la Société Canadienne-Française," *Recherches Sociographiques,* 1966, p. 93. (Authors' translation.)
11. Hubert Guidon, "Social Unrest, Social Class and Quebec's Bureaucratic Revolution," in Hugh G. Thorburn, *Party Politics in Canada* (Scarborough: Prentice-Hall of Canada, Ltd., 1967), p. 185.
12. Charles Taylor, "Nationalism and the Political Intelligentsia," *Queen's Quarterly,* Spring, 1965, LXXII, No. 1, pp. 167-68.
13. G. Barker, A. Lévesque, G. Dozois, G. A. Vachon, "Les Idées Politiques des Canadiens-Français – Four Nationalist Movements," Study done for the Royal Commission on Biligualism and Biculturalism.
14. *Ibid.,* Part II, p. 65.
15. *Ibid.,* Part II, p. 75.
16. See *Ibid.,* Part II, pp. 7-9.
17. See *Ibid.,* Part II, pp. 44-49.
18. See *Ibid.,* Part II, pp. 90-91.
19. *Ibid.,* Part II, pp. 90-99.
20. Quoted in *Ibid.,* Part II, p. 127.
21. *Ibid.,* pp. 149-50.
22. *Ibid.,* p. 132.
23. Peter Gzowski, "The Cardinal and his Church in a Year of Conflict," *Maclean's Magazine,* July 14, 1962, p. 15.
24. Charles Henri Dubé, "La Verité sur l'Ordre Jacques-Cartier," *Magazine Macleans,* May, 1963, p. 23.

25. Edward M. Corbett, *Quebec Confronts Canada* (Baltimore: The Johns Hopkins Press, 1967), p. 81.
26. Jacques Lazure, *La Jeunesse du Québec en Révolution* (Montréal: Les Presses de l'Université de Québec, 1970), pp. 23-24. (Authors' translation.)
27. G. Barker, A. Lévesque, G. Dozois, G. A. Vachon, *op cit.,* Part II, p. 171.
28. *Ibid.,* pp. 184-85. (Authors' translation.)
29. Quoted in *Ibid.,* p. 195. (Authors' translation.)
30. *Ibid.,* p. 212. (Authors' translation.)
31. Quoted in *Ibid.,* pp. 208 and 210. (Authors' translation.)
32. Quoted in *Ibid.,* p. 218. (Authors' translation.)
33. J. Crispo, *International Unionism* (Toronto: McGraw-Hill, 1967), p. 49.
34. Paul Bélanger, *et al.,* "La Rivalité Intersyndicale au Québec," *Recherches Sociographiques,* Vol. X, No. 1, Janvier-Avril, 1969, p. 55. (Authors' translation.)
35. *Ibid.*
36. A. Verdoodt, "FTQ: Objectifs-Projectifs" (unpublished text), International Centre for Research on Bilingualism, Laval University.
37. Quoted in *Ibid.* (Authors' translation.)
38. Marcel Pepin, "A Society for Man," in *Moral Report of the National President of the Confederation of National Trade Unions,* 1966 Convention, p. 252.
39. Gaetan Lavertu, "La Participation de la Confédération des Syndicats Nationaux aux Affaires Internationales," M.A. Thesis, Laval University, 1968, pp. 42-43.
40. Cited in R. Arès, "Canada 70: Une Enquête du Toronto Telegram," *Rélations* (No. 347), (mars 1970), pp. 77-78.

CHAPTER 9

THE
STRUGGLE
INTENSIFIES

The times of that superstition which attributed revolutions to the ill-will of a few agitators have long passed away. Everyone knows nowadays that whenever there is a revolutionary convulsion, there must be some social want in the background, which is prevented by outworn institutions, from satisfying itself. The want may not yet be felt as strongly, as generally, as might ensure immediate success; but every attempt at forcible repression will only bring it forth stronger and stronger, until it bursts its fetters.

Karl Marx, 1851

Two interrelated ideas, national independence and popular participation in decision-making, had gained a wide following in Quebec by 1968-69. There was also growing impatience and resentment with the socio-economic conditions that prevailed. Still, few active groups expressed these ideas or articulated their frustrations in class terms. It was not yet widely understood that the achievement of these goals was pitted against the interest and will of the ruling class and that a confrontation with the forces of the established order was inevitable. To activate a popular movement for genuine social change, it would be necessary for the program and strategy to express the long-range objectives of the working classes for equality and power. Polarization of this kind had to come and events were moving quickly.

An important step was the election in early 1968 of Michel Chartrand as head of the Montreal Central Council of the CNTU. Chartrand, an outspoken socialist and indépendantiste with a

long history of involvement in Quebec's political battles, transformed the "Conseil Central," which represented the 65,000
CNTU members in the Montreal region, from a relatively dormant organization into the hub of left-wing nationalist activity
in the trade union movement. While its position was distinctly
minoritarian, and sometimes embarrassing to the CNTU, the
Council's meetings became a vital forum for the discussion and
elaboration of socialist indépendantiste goals and strategies, and
it was the concrete decisions taken by the 300 delegates there
which placed the Montreal Council at the center of the movement. In the political struggles which followed, the work of the
Montreal Council was crucial – both because it put its facilities,
public support and staff behind the cause, but also because it
prodded the CNTU, and thus indirectly the other labour federations, to get off the fence and take a stand.

In face of the mounting repression, ostensibly against the
FLQ but actually against all manifestations of the new militancy,
the bureau confédéral of the CNTU, in late 1969, demanded the
resignation of Justice Minister Remi Paul and the immediate
release of Vallières and Gagnon. The QFL Congress, at the same
time, demanded justice for Vallières and Gagnon. It was in this
same period that *Québec Presse,* a decidedly socialist and
indépendantiste weekly tabloid newspaper designed to counter
the propaganda of the establishment press, was launched with
the backing of the trade unions. While in constant financial
difficulty, *Québec Presse* is stronger than ever with 40,000
readers after three years of publication.

The question of immigration and language has been a con-
tentious one throughout Quebec's history. There has existed a
long-standing and well-founded fear that the language and
culture of the Québecois was in danger of being swamped by
the massive English cultural presence. By the sixties, French-
Canadian communities outside Quebec had practically disappeared. Until not too long ago, the French Canadians in Quebec
were able to hold their own in population at least due to a high
birth rate. This is no longer the case: the Quebec birth rate is
now lower than that of many other provinces. Hence it is
understandable why many feared that the resurgence of the
French language and culture of the sixties was threatened by
the large number of immigrants coming to Quebec and having
their children educated in English schools to learn the language
of money.

From our own analytical framework this consideration is indeed a serious one for, as we have argued, it is through the medium of a distinctive culture and language that the formation of an authentic class consciousness can come about. Hence, the language issue is one that is crucial to nationalists of the left as well as traditional "survivance" nationalists of the right; and, indeed, an unlikely coalition formed.

The issue first broke out publicly when the St. Léonard Catholic School Commission in Montreal decided to offer only French language instruction thereby depriving Italian residents of English language instruction for their children.

The bitterly divided Union Nationale government of Jean-Jacques Bertrand, after much hesitation, introduced Bill 63 giving the St. Léonard parents and all others in the province, the right to have their children educated in either English or French. The response was immediate and deafening. The "Front pour un Québec Français" (FQF), a hastily organized coalition of right and left nationalist groups, sponsored a week of mass demonstrations, on one occasion drawing 50,000 Québecois into the streets. Though Bill 63 was eventually enacted, the popular opposition it evoked was astounding. Other demonstrations were held in this same period sponsored by left nationalist groups like the FLP and the CNTU Montreal Central Council demanding an end to the mounting repression, the liberation of Vallières and Gagnon, etc.

At its fall 1969 congress the QFL leadership found itself in an awkward position. Bill 63 had just been presented and the people of Quebec were divided and angered. Laberge, who wanted nothing more than to ignore the issue, found that the executive would be forced to take a stand. On his executive were outspoken nationalists such as Fernand Daoust (formerly of CUPE) and Jean Gerin-Lajoie from the steel workers. Laberge had to work out a compromise position which in fact took no stand on Bill 63, and was aptly described by a sympathiser as "patinage incroyable." This was presented as the position of the entire executive.

To the surprise of all observers, and no doubt to Laberge, the delegates would not buy it. In an unprecedented move they debated the motions, which were supposed to have been quietly ratified and shelved, for hours and hours, refusing to accept the authority of the leaders. They finally forced an amendment insisting that the children of all immigrants to Quebec, even

197

after Canadian citizenship had been attained, must send their children to Francophone schools. The resolution which passed was almost identical to the stand of the PQ.

Because a CNTU congress was not scheduled until the fall of 1970, the battle over Bill 63 took place at the levels of the Bureau Confédéral and the Conseil Confédéral. The first step came at the session of the Conseil Confédéral, the supreme governing organ between congresses. The resolutions passed read: "The CNTU declared itself in favour of unilingualism at all levels in Quebec (the vote was 91 to 30). It is resolved that the CNTU and all affiliated bodies join the common front (FQF) and participate in all action which will be decided upon in this matter by the common front (unanimous vote)."[1]

A few days later Bill 63 was presented and at the Bureau Confédéral meeting President Marcel Pepin was able to win provisional approval for the bill by a vote of 13 to 5. However, faced with opposition at all levels and the realization that there was a contradiction between the Bureau's decision and the policy of the superior Conseil, Pepin backed down, and on October 30th the Bureau Confédéral withdrew its support of Bill 63.

Again the key facts are identical. At the Conseil Confédéral the major issue was unilingualism and the position of the executive was attacked and defeated. Here too this was unprecedented. In addition, the CNTU has become almost fully unilingual in all its business. This does not seem to have incurred resentment even among English-speaking members. The position of the CNTU on unilingualism can by no means be considered moderate, as it sees this question as one of the people versus the establishment. As its brochure on Bill 63 said, "The list of groups and persons favourable to Bill 63 is eloquent. In it one finds all parts of the Quebec Anglo-Saxon establishment as well as the two official political parties, the UN and the Liberals."[2] (This is by no means the last time that we shall see this pattern: the moderation of the leaders challenged by the militancy of the rank and file.)

The third demonstration of widespread working-class support for unilingualism is the survey carried out at the time of the Bill 63 controversy by the Institut de Psychologie of the Université de Montréal.[3] The sample of 4098 Montrealers was stratified according to age, sex, occupation, locale, ethnicity and language. Overall it found 38.04 percent against Bill 63, and 32.58 percent supporting it. Among Francophones only, figures were 46 percent against and 26 percent for.

The breakdown shows some rather interesting features. Looking only at Francophones, of the 10 occupational groups listed the top three read: Students, 10 percent for, 72 percent against, Unskilled workers, 24 percent for, 41 percent against; and Technical and Professional, 30 percent for and 47 percent against. These combined facts suggest that the positions taken by the labour confederations were, if anything, more moderate than the views of their membership and the feelings of the working class as a whole. We should note further that the language issue relates directly to the immediate interests of the workers. Many breakdowns in collective bargaining, and more than a few strikes, can be traced to French-Canadian workers having to speak English on the work floor. This in fact was a specific grievance raised by the Ste. Thérèse local of the UAW in the strike against GM in 1970.

The relationship between the Parti Québecois and the class interests of the working population of Quebec is a complex one – the subject of an important contemporary debate among theoreticians of the Quebec left. In its early days, however, the PQ was little troubled by such questions since working class organizations had voiced few specific political demands and lacked a critical philosophical position. In the late sixties it was still a "radical" step for a trade union member or organization to publicly affirm support for the PQ. And many did. Among the first was the Montreal Central Council of the CNTU.* Because of the CNTU's decentralized authority structure, the MCC and other sub-units were able to take this step though the CNTU itself avoided official support, using as a pretext the law forbidding civil servants to belong to unions supporting political parties.

* The Montreal Central Council of the CNTU passed a resolution on the seventh of April, which included that "in spite of certain omissions and certain weaknesses in its economic program and policy on workers; the CCM-CSN indicates its preference for the Parti Québecois on the ballot of April 29, but makes it clear that the real battle for national liberation for the Quebec workers does not stop at constitutional independence, this constitutional liberation must be taken as a step toward the economic and social liberation of the people of Quebec." Quoted in *Québec Presse* (April 12, 1970).

199

In general, union leaders and militants have unofficially supported the Parti Québecois; the more politically sophisticated have rationalized this position with the comment "sure they're bourgeois, but they're all we've got". The Trade union locals and centrals, particularly outside Montreal, often constitute the core of PQ *constituency* organization and support; this is particularly the case in North Shore communities such as Baie Comeau, Hauterive and Sept Iles. It is their resources that are often used to organize and publicize the speaking tours of Lévesque and other party leaders. Generally, PQ rallies and regional assemblies across the province draw large turnouts in working class regions.

Nevertheless, the organizational and decision-making apparatus of the party is firmly in the hands of new middle class elements – many of whom do not identify with the aspirations of the working class. At its convention during the winter of 1970, the proportion of working class delegates was eleven percent. Lévesque commented: "That's normal. The workers haven't yet acquired the habit of being delegates. . . . They think they have to make delegates of 'those who talk well', the educated." Unfortunately, little was done to counter this tendency through education and organizational change. On the whole the PQ has been careful to be close but never too close to the workers and the trade unions.

In spite of the "bourgeois" nature of its leadership, the April 1970 election revealed that popular support for the PQ came from the working class. We may recall the scare campaign waged by the English corporate interests and the Liberal party when, a few weeks before election day, opinion polls revealed that the PQ was a very close second to the Liberals in popular support.* First, an investment firm, Lafferty-Harwood, "leaked" a letter telling its clients to withdraw their money from Quebec. Next came the "Brinks Show" in which the Royal Trust Company, a pillar of the English financial establishment with close

* Three public opinion polls taken in this period (*Le Soleil,* C.R.O.P., and S. P. Regenstreif) found PQ support at approximately 30 percent. The polls also found that two groups in society supported the PQ more than any other party; these were the 18-24 year olds and those classed as unskilled workers. See V. Lemieux, *et al., Une Election de Réalignment: l'Election Générale du 29 avril du Québec* (Montreal: Editions du Jour, 1970), especially pp. 60-64.

ties to the Liberal party, organized a caravan of armored trucks supposedly carrying large amounts of securities to Toronto. The press was again conveniently tipped off and present both at the Montreal point of departure and the Ontario border. Banks conveniently set up accounts for their depositors in Toronto or Ottawa, and many persons, especially immigrants, were specifically asked if they wished to move their deposit.

The *Montreal Star,* not to be outdone, editorially called for a rejection of the PQ on the grounds that the Québecois were incapable of democratically running an independent state. The English language *Suburban* threatened racial warfare in case of PQ victory.

The result was that the English language and immigrant communities were psychologically terrorized and unable even to hear the message of their compatriots. The Francophone middle class was sufficiently scared off with the result that the PQ was able to gain only enough support to elect members in seven ridings, all of them predominantly French speaking and working class.[4] Of course the maldistribution of the legislative districts also contributed to the outcome. The PQ with 24 percent of the vote, won only 6.5 percent of the seats, while the Liberals with 45 percent of the vote, received 69 percent of the seats. Hence it required 17,000 Quebecers to elect a Liberal and 90,000 to elect a Péquiste.

A detailed analysis of the results shows that the PQ gained the vote of one of every three Francophone Quebecers, and when we add to that total the votes of the pseudo-nationalist Union Nationale, we discover a probable majority of French-speaking Quebec in favour of self-determination. The main point, though, is that it was the workers that provided the mainstream of support for the left nationalist Parti Québecois. (See Table 9-1) Furthermore, it is in those areas of Montreal that traditionally supported the Union Nationale that the PQ was most successful. On the basis of electoral statistics from an earlier period, Pinard argues that: "It is only because they are more likely to identify with the working class that so many workers manifest a strong tendency to support the National Union; not because they lack class consciousness."[5] Simply put, while the UN was undoubtedly not serving the workers' interest, the words and postures of its spokesmen nevertheless manifested the French-Canadian workers' identification with "la nation."

TABLE 9-1

Vote for the Parti Québécois in the April 1970 Election.
Some Francophone ridings in Montreal and the socio-economic characteristics of these ridings.**

Electoral Riding	Parti Québécois Vote (%)	% French Canadians in Riding	% of F.C. voting P.Q.	Education Level (%)			Occupation (%)			Average Annual Income
				Primary School	Second. School	University	workers	office & service	profess-ional	
Ahuntsic	42.9	82.0	51.2	37.0	51.0	12.0	26.0	47.0	27.0	4,520
*Sainte-Marie	42.2	90.0	46.8	63.7	33.0	3.3	50.1	40.5	9.4	3,275
*Maisonneuve	41.9	87.5	47.9	62.0	35.8	2.2	51.2	39.3	9.5	3,585
Fabre	41.5	88.8	46.7	49.9	44.5	5.5	37.8	37.4	24.8	4,706
*Lafontaine	40.7	81.0	50.3	52.7	42.8	4.4	47.5	38.1	14.4	4,200
Bourassa	40.7	79.0	51.5	48.0	47.0	5.0	43.3	41.5	15.2	4,100
*Bourget	40.2	81.0	49.6	51.6	43.2	5.2	40.8	43.2	16.0	4,300
*Gouin	40.9	80.0	51.1	54.4	42.2	3.3	45.1	43.0	11.9	3,650
*Saint-Jacques	39.2	85.0	46.1	65.3	30.5	4.2	43.3	46.9	9.8	2,950
Laurier	38.6	70.0	55.1	48.0	46.0	6.0	42.8	43.3	13.9	3,850
Jeanne-Mance	38.1	72.0	52.9	45.0	49.0	6.0	33.8	43.4	17.8	4,125
Saint-Henri	37.9	80.0	47.4	61.0	36.1	2.9	49.5	41.7	8.8	3,460
Olier	37.7	71.0	53.1	54.0	40.0	6.0	51.1	36.9	12.0	3,805
Mercier	37.3	85.0	43.9	52.8	43.2	4.0	41.4	45.5	13.1	3,560
Dorion	33.3	68.0	48.2	56.5	40.2	3.3	48.4	39.8	11.8	3,520

* Elected representatives to the Quebec National Assembly.
** The socio-economic characteristics were taken from a compilation for *Le Devoir*, April 27, 1970, by Gérald Bernier: the author referred to the 1961 Canadian census for his material on the different electoral ridings, the characteristics of which have not changed appreciably since then.

Source: "The Quebec Elections," *Our Generation*, Vol. 7, no. 2, p. 9.

The Liberals, then as now, were regarded as the party of the English and well-educated Québecois, and were therefore not an alternative. For many workers the PQ likewise, though run by swingers and technocrats, is "theirs."

The results of the spring election caught Quebec by surprise. The PQ had gained popular support but had only a handful of deputies in the National Assembly to oppose the new, powerful, resolutely federalist government of Robert Bourassa's Liberals. Furthermore, if the seven MNA's wished to seriously represent their constituents, their party's policies would have to identify more directly with the working class and its needs. The energy and determination that had been on the streets during the demonstrations against Bill 63 had gone into the election campaign – and the rewards were slim. The psychological terrorism waged by the establishment incurred anger and resentment against a stolen election and a rigged system. While the PQ looked to the courts to rectify the injustices of the electoral system, the bitterness and despair gave way to a more profound and unromantic determination. The summer of 1970 was one of rethinking, the feeling was one of the uneasy quiet before a storm.

The catalyst came with the abduction by the FLQ of British trade commissioner James Cross followed a week later by the kidnapping of the Minister of Labour, Pierre Laporte. Simultaneously, the FLQ published a manifesto (which was read over Radio Canada on October 8 to meet one of the ransom demands). The document, written in simple and stark terms, laid out the class reality of Quebec. It spoke of Westmount, of Eatons, of Power Corporation and the Catholic Church, of Household Finance and St. James Street. It mentioned Cabano, Bill 63, Murray Hill. The April election, it pointed out, had exposed the political arena for what it was – a "Democracy for the Rich."

It was not to the barricades or to an immediate overthrow of the State that the FLQ called the Mr. Bergeron's of Visitation Street; but to "make the revolution yourselves in your neighborhoods, in your work places. And if you do not make it yourselves, other usurpers, technocrats and others, will replace the cigar puffers we now know, and everything will have to be done again. You alone can build a free society. . . ."[6]

The message was heard, the population, and a Church

hierarchy that had evidently much changed, responded. The Pastoral Council of the Archdiocese of Quebec, comprising perhaps one thousand priests, expressed sympathy for the Manifesto. Cardinal Roy and Archbishop Gregoire both made statements pointing to the injustice and inequality around them as sources of the frustration which breeds violence.[7] Speaking for seventeen Gaspé area priests, the Abbé Jacques Banville was quoted in November as saying: "By and large, a majority of the population and of the priests in the counties of Matane and Matapedia are fundamentally in agreement with the social demands formulated in the manifesto of the FLQ. . . . "[8]

The Front d'Action Politique (FRAP), a federation of citizens' and workers' committees who were opposing the Drapeau-Saulnier administration in the upcoming Montreal election, publicly endorsed the objectives of the manifesto, while rejecting the FLQ's tactics. FRAP added that it could not condemn the violence of the FLQ without condemning the violence of the system, and its statement went on to enumerate many incidences of the latter. *Québec Presse* editorialized that the FLQ's analysis of Quebec in its manifesto was "exact," and that the horror of an armed, clandestine movement should be counterpointed to the horror of the better-armed, equally secret, established authority.[9]

A survey of opinions expressed on "hot-line" programs on popular French stations in Montreal during the days the hostages were being held found that over 50 percent of the callers supported the spirit of the manifesto. A CBC interviewer in front of a French Roman Catholic Church found that half the people he talked to expressed sympathy for the ideas presented in the manifesto.[10] Student newspapers, even after the enactment of the War Measures Act, publicly supported the aims of the FLQ.

The manifesto had clearly touched a responsive chord. The new Université de Québec was virtually closed by students and some of its faculty in support of the aims of the FLQ; at the Université du Montréal 1,500 students went out on strike. Similar events were taking place at CEGEP's and even some high schools. The Laurentian and Montreal Central Councils of the CNTU endorsed the manifesto. Michel Chartrand, never a man to mince words, asked why there should be so much anxiety for two lives when, during the previous doctors' strike, little anxiety was expressed for the many people "held hostage" by the physicians. Later he asked, "who's scared of the FLQ? Are the workers terrorized by the FLQ? Are the students terrorized by the FLQ? The only people who are afraid of the FLQ are those who should be scared – the power elite."[11] Chartrand, Gagnon, Vallières and Robert Lemieux addressed a loudly cheering audience of 3,000 at the Paul Sauvé arena on October 15, 1971 – just as the War Measures Act was about to be executed.

The "terrorism" which resulted in the death of Pierre Laporte and Cuban exile for the kidnappers of Cross was the work of perhaps ten individuals. In retaliation, the Trudeau government removed the protection of civil liberties from all Canadians, arrested 450 "suspects," occupied Quebec with 7,500 federal troops and 2,500 "special" police, smashed presses, confiscated documents, and ensured the continuation of the Drapeau autocracy in Montreal.

Evidently this was terrorism not against a small band of conspirators but against a philosophy, against a movement taking Quebec in a direction that Trudeau, Drapeau, Marchand and the others could not tolerate.

Repression succeeded, for the moment, in diffusing the thrust of the movement. There were long and costly trials, money to be raised, a climate of police state fears to be overcome, and a re-evaluation of strategy and tactics to be made. Pierre Vallières' book, *White Niggers of America,* though written in prison four years before, only now achieved wide circulation in Quebec. The authorities had delayed its distribution with harrassment before publication and sedition charges and seizures of copies once published. Like the manifesto, *White Niggers* struck a nerve. Its combination of a powerful biographical statement of the conditions and mentality of a Québecois working class family with a fervent call for revolution made it a topic of wide discussion. Yet its strategic program was already coming into question. As Vallières himself was to point out in December 1971, the FLQ was able to initiate action and to generate group support for its goals, but as a clandestine organization it had absolutely no popular organizing base from which to launch an opposition to the acts of repressive violence it had incited. The state had thus been reached where armed insurrection became counter-productive.

Opposition to the repressive violence of the War Measures Act, such as there was, came from essentially two sources in Quebec, the trade union federations and the PQ. (And federally from the NDP.) The leaders of the PQ, CNTU, QFL, CEQ and UCC, Claude Ryan of *Le Devoir,* and several others formed a common front to prevail upon the government to negotiate with the kidnappers and to oppose the harsh measures taken. While no more than civil libertarian in its aims, this short-lived common front was significant in that its solid opposition to Ottawa's repressive measures posed a concrete alternative to Bourassa's abdication of power to the federal forces. It also reinforced the growing solidarity within the trade union movement and strengthened the link between the workers and the PQ. In the months ahead, as relative tranquility once again returned to the province, the question was whether the alliance between the PQ and the trade unions was to continue and if so under what terms.

As federal elections approached, Canadian politicians and newspapermen discovered the "unemployment problem." In Quebec, of course, everyone knew that unemployment was particularly bad and getting worse. And a new group hit especially hard by the crisis was the CEGEP graduates who had nowhere to go. Bourassa blamed the FLQ for the poor investment climate and hence his failure to provide the promised 100,000 jobs – but not too many were listening. With 10 percent unemployment, up to 25 percent among young people, les Québecois were in no mood for excuses. A strike of non-teaching staff at the Université de Montréal was won because students would not cross the picket lines. The solidarity shown here was a portent of things to come.

This time it was not the FLQ that launched the "fall offensive" but the unions – growing more militant and unified through joint action in the streets and a greater understanding of the class realities of Quebec society. And the PQ grew more uncomfortable. The event that marked the beginning of this new phase of union militancy was the march on *La Presse,* October 29, 1971.

The *La Presse* issue was not a new one. The scars of a bitter and inconclusive strike in 1964 had not healed, and the subsequent political changes in Quebec society only served to sharpen the antagonisms that lay under the surface. When the paper was purchased in 1967 by the Trans-Canada Corporation Fund (which one year later merged with Power Corporation), a new showdown was in the offing. Power Corporation was the epitomy of technocratic capitalism, symbolising the "achievements" of the Quiet Revolution. A conglomerate with interests in many fields, Power Corporation controls approximately 20 newspapers, 10 radio and TV stations, a film company, a publishing house and various other enterprises in Quebec, not to mention its holdings outside the province. Power Corporation is particularly close to the Liberal party and believed to be one of its key financial backers. "Secretary Claude Frenette of Power Corporation was until recently president of the Quebec federal Liberals."[12] The benefits go the other way too with, for instance, the Société de Mathématiques Appliquées, a Power subsidiary, largely and generously supported through government research contracts. During the 1972 federal election, Jean Fortier, president of the SMA was president of the Quebec Federal Liberals.

When the time came to put the brakes on the Quiet Revolution and on the free reign of ideas, it was apparent that a major confrontation would have to take place at *La Presse*. Ever since the heady days of Pelletier, the staff had developed an independence of inquiry and an interest in the political developments in Quebec which, as the developments turned nationalist and socialist, Power Corporation and its allies found more and more impossible to tolerate. Editorial censorship encountered unified staff opposition and tension mounted. Paul Desmarais, head of Power Corporation, refused a relatively normal contractual guarantee to the *La Presse* production staff for job security in face of technological change, thus forcing them into a prolonged strike. In late summer, Desmarais closed the newspaper down tight thereby locking out all employees including the journalists. The strike was on in full force, and the battle lines were drawn.

The issues raised by the dispute were ones with which many workers outside *La Presse* identified. The struggle was for freedom of the press, for job security against "technological necessity," for rights of labour against the imperatives of profit. It united workers in different sectors against a corporate giant and the politicians who served it. The CNTU and QFL (both of whom had affiliated locals among workers at *La Presse*) became directly involved and the CEQ threw in its support. In spite of this, the employer seemed content with the lockout situation and showed little interest in negotiating. There was even talk of closing down this national institution, the second largest French newspaper in the world.

To dramatize the situation, the union common front called a march on *La Presse*. Montreal's Mayor Drapeau refused the "required" permit and, when over ten thousand marchers arrived at the police barricades, fifteen minutes of pushing and shoving ensued; then without warning the riot squad charged. Hundreds were injured, many arrested, one woman was dead. Yet, instead of terrorizing the workers, the repressive violence brought them closer together and trade unionists of the traditional mould, like Louis Laberge, were making public statements against the system and calling for its overthrow.

Four days later, and on 24 hours notice, 14,000 people jammed into the Montreal forum. On the stage were radicals such as Michel Chartrand, FLQ lawyer Robert Lemieux and Women's Liberation representative, Nicole Therrien, as well as the established leadership of the three confederations and many other syndical officers. Yet the split between the radicals and the moderates was nowhere to be seen: speaker after speaker vowed that labour solidarity would win the battle against the capitalists and their allies. Laberge's astounding transformation was confirmed at the QFL convention which was held at the end of November, 1971. Attacking collusion between high finance, government and the judiciary, he called for a struggle on many fronts. "We have examined the political and economic machine which is trying to demolish us, and we have come to the conclusion that there is nothing we can expect from its good will."[13] The positive reception which greeted Laberge's remarks indicates that the shrewd leader had not suddenly become an impetuous militant; the delegates were solidly behind the new direction he was outlining. In fact it was more a case of conforming to a change of mood than of causing one.

A glance at the position papers distributed by the QFL at this time confirms its ideological transformation. In its early 1972 manifesto on employment, entitled *The Rout Must Stop* the QFL described the situation: "All the means of production are in the hands of a few owners who use them only for their own priority, maximum profit. . . . Not only is their priority opposed to our own, but the context is a foreign one."[14]

Accordingly, the workers will never gain full employment or fair working conditions until they take "control of the means of production to orient them to the real needs of the population and to liberate us from this prison that work now constitutes; [and] administer political power which protects the owners of the economy. For the people to take control of the machines, they must also determine the laws so as to protect economic power by political power."[15] Strategically, the document calls for the immediate establishment of a common front of all trade unions, one that would also include the unemployed and welfare recipients.

Another rapidly growing political force in Quebec has been the teachers. The teachers' federation (FNEQ), representing mainly CEGEP level instructors, constitutes a powerful left-wing element in the CNTU. Elementary school teachers who make up the largest segment of teachers are organized in the 60,000 member CEQ. The teachers had waged a hard and unsuccessful strike against the government in 1967. Since then the CEQ, under Raymond Laliberté and Yvon Charbonneau, underwent a radical transformation. A key result has been that teachers in Quebec, unlike elsewhere, are identifying their interests and goals with the working classes rather than professional groups. This development was signalled by the passing of a resolution at the 1971 summer convention which committed the teachers to serving the interests of the Quebec people and to solidarity with the workers.[16] The position expressed in the CEQ white paper which followed was quite precise: "The Teacher is proletarianized. He receives a salary for which he sells his ability to produce at the ideological level. . . . What must be seen in this process of degradation . . . is the implacable logic of a system that concentrates all the means of decision and performance in the hands of a few private owners of the means of production (or a small group of state officials in a state bureaucracy)."[17] The goal of teaching should be to provide genuine and critical education: "Such a project of popular education would of necessity aim at allowing individuals to be autonomous and able to take their activities in their own hands rather than reinforcing those attitudes and practices of a dominant ideology which secures an unsatisfactory consent from people faced with economic, social, and political exploitation."[18] In a manifesto to be studied at the summer 1972 convention entitled "The School in Service to the Dominant Class," the CEQ goes further, calling for a "fight for a radical change in social relations and against the enemy of the workers, the capitalist system." The teachers would carry this fight into the schools themselves, to expose and eventually surmount their class nature. "The school . . . is one of the vital links in maintaining and reproducing exploitative social relations. Its role is no less than to prepare a work force adapted to the needs of capital, a work-force that is abundant, cagey and docile."[19]

The most famous of the recently published documents have been the work of the CNTU. The first, issued in September 1971, was entitled "There is no Future for Us in the Present Economic System." It was soon followed by a lengthy and substantial discussion document, "Let Us Rely Solely on Our Own Means" ("Ne Comptons que sur nos propres moyens").[20] "Ne Comptons Que" is divided into four (actually three) sections. It begins with a penetrating and yet straightforward analysis of the operation of capitalism in Quebec, both in theory and practice. First it elaborates on the structure of the corporation, the importance of profit and the question of monpoly versus competition. It then goes on to delineate the colonial predicament of Quebec's economy. The next section of Part One considers the socioeconomic structure in North America, Canada and Quebec, and how the state functions to perpetuate class stratification. Finally it sets out the actual conditions that prevail in the various economic sectors, and ends with an angry assessment of the extent to which the workers of Quebec are exploited.

Part Two is a more brief but equally powerful attack on the economic strategy of the Quiet Revolution, a strategy exposed as one of buttressing and complementing the capitalist economy with state enterprises which serve its interests Parts Three and Four summarize the exploitation of Quebec's workers and go on to a short conclusion as to what must be done.

> Production capacity, of both men and machines, could be used to the full if production was organized to answer the real needs of the collectivity. In other words, there would be no unemployment. . . .
>
> The field in which the working class could neutralize the American giant is that of socialism. . . .

An economy dominated by workers could only be socialist. By "socialist" we mean:

1) That society (through the state) owns the means of production (factories, land, raw materials);
2) That workers participate directly and collectively in the management of industry and the economy and in setting economic priorities;
3) That economic activity seeks to satisfy the population's needs as much as possible;
4) That economic activity is planned directly by the state.[21]

This CNTU document was not received terribly well in official circles, nor was the PQ too pleased. The labour movement was clearly getting out of hand. Yet the reception among the rank and file of labour was respectful at the very least. Over 100,000 copies were distributed among CNTU members. The workers of Quebec were finally offered an alternative to the present system. The alternative was not complete by any means, but it was a useful tool to enable trade unionists to evaluate the economic system from outside its own framework and ideology.

The growing militancy of the labour movement, both in action and in program, put an end to the easy entente that had existed between it and the PQ. Over the opposition of its left-wing faction,* the PQ refused to endorse the *La Presse* demonstration. The battle was escalated when René Lévesque made statements to the effect that he would rather live in a South American banana republic than in a Quebec controlled by "ranting and raving labour leaders." Yet, to pacify that same left-wing, a mini-manifesto released just afterwards pledged the PQ "to the achievement of Labour's goals – the democratic restructuring of the social and economic system."[22]

In April the PQ published its economic manifesto entitled "When We Will Really Be at Home" ("Quand nous serons vraiment chez nous"), laying out its plans for the economy of an independent Quebec. The program is social-democratic

* This faction first emerged the previous spring. At the 1971 convention of the PQ, a group, based in the unions and citizens' committees, openly challenged the technocrats who lead the party and their concentration on attracting more middle class members. They wanted a party which would act in solidarity with workers and community groups. The rebellion subsided when René Lévesque promised to incorporate many of the group's demands into the party's policies, and committed the party to the goals they espoused.

rather than socialist, relying mainly on regulation of the economy rather than nationalization. The manifesto is on the whole a progressive document and includes radical proposals such as turning over the radio and TV outlets in small and medium-sized centers to community ownership. By spelling out in concrete terms exactly what form of ownership would be required in each sector of industry, the PQ showed some courage and faith in popular wisdom. This is evident when the manifesto is compared to the ambiguous platitudes on employment and economic growth one finds in the tracts of the Liberals and the other established parties. The substance of the PQ's position begins:

> It is necessary to establish several categories of foreign investment in the Quebec economy. According to the nature and activity of the business, it can be permitted or forbidden to be controlled from outside, and in certain cases all outside interests even excluded.
> Exclusively Quebec sectors: The first category deals with sectors where foreign interests would be outlawed in just about all its forms . . . Examples: the mass media, the distribution of printed matter, books, primary steel works.
> Majority Quebec sectors: . . . where a certain portion, even an important one, could be foreign controlled, as long as this participation is below 49 percent. Examples: Banks, trust and insurance companies, railroads and certain manufacturing industries. . . . [23]

The PQ manifesto was harshly criticized from the right, in the *Montreal Star* and the *Gazette* editorials, and by Liberal party spokesmen, etc., as unrealistic and utopian. It was criticized by the left as well, for being state capitalist and basically no more than a continuation of the economic policies of the Quiet Revolution. In any case, the people of Quebec were presented with another set of facts and figures and further useful information on the basis of which concrete and meaningful choices could be made.* What was becoming clear was that to the majority of younger if not yet of all French Canadians,

---

* This is contrasted with the mystification of the consumer and voter, perfected by American advertising and political campaign technology, which removes real choice and leaves only its appearance. See chapter one.

the choice was not between a federalist and a pseudo-nationalist form of capitalism, but rather between a socialist and a social-democratic form of independent state.

Strategically, a clear question was posed. Could individuals committed to a socialist and anti-imperialist Quebec support the PQ, and if so, under what conditions? The debate was grounded on the definition of class and the definition of nation. Without doubt the most important theoretical contribution on the subject can be found in an article written in 1970 by Gilles Bourque and Nicole Laurin-Frenette.[24] The authors directly challenge the thesis they associate with the work of Rioux, Dofny, Dumont and others, which attempts to theoretically justify adherence by socialists to a nationalist party like the PQ. Bourque and Laurin-Frenette maintain that only if one places national divisions as somehow separate from and equal to class divisions can such a position be theoretically justified. In such a case, when a nation becomes aware of its colonized state, its demand for national independence automatically acquires class content because the needs of this "ethnic class" are somehow intrinsically revolutionary. Bourque and Laurin-Frenette reject this contention out of hand arguing that nationalism "is by definition a class ideology" and that "there are (or can be) as many ideologies containing nationalist elements as there are classes in a social formation."[25]

The PQ, like all other parties, must therefore be judged on exactly which class interests it serves and that judgment must not be clouded by the "mystique" of nationalism. As Henri Gagnon pointed out: "Neither Mr. Lévesque nor the péquiste leaders ever claimed the PQ as a workers' party. The PQ never presented itself as the bearer of the great socialist goals. On the contrary, it has always presented itself as the party of the entire Quebec collectivity. . . ."[26] The CAP (political action committee of St. Jacques) put it rather more succinctly: "Disappointed by the failure of the Quiet Revolution, a part of the petit bourgeoisie has moved toward the "autonomist solution." Its project: to regain fiscal resources and power from Ottawa . . . and put a brake on the expropriation of our resources by foreign high finance. But to make its public corporations go, the PQ will have to make its own appeal to the banks, trusts and financiers of Wall Street."[27]

This debate became both current and public in December

1971 when Pierre Vallières, in hiding after jumping bail on his latest charge, sent an excerpt from his forthcoming book, *L'Urgence de Choisir* to *Le Devoir* and another to *Québec Presse*. Apart from his repudiation of the armed insurrection strategy of the FLQ, Vallières came out squarely in support of the Parti Québecois. "It is thus to the PQ that comes at this stage of struggle and perhaps for several years, the responsibility of political leadership of the mass struggle for the interests and aspirations of the masses which have created it and without whose support it could neither develop nor last as a mass party."[28] Vallières offers few fresh considerations to substantiate this position, but the forcefulness of his assertions and his background as a committed activist and tactician have ensured its being given serious and thoughtful consideration. Attacking the structuralist orthodoxy of the left-wing theorists, Vallières asks them to look at the reality of Quebec, to see the PQ, whatever the weaknesses of its current program and composition, as the expression of a truly revolutionary mass sentiment which, because of its historical origins and development, can only, after winning the political battle for independence through the PQ, go on to create a truly independent socialist society.

However, Vallières is unable (or perhaps unwilling for political reasons) to show concretely how this eventuality will come about. In the end the workers of Quebec must take him and the PQ on faith. Because of this Vallières' declaration does not seem to have earned him many followers among left-wing thinkers in Quebec.[29] It was, for instance, harshly attacked in *Le Devoir* by his former comrade, Charles Gagnon. Its reception among the workers is no doubt more positive. The PQ is much admired in working class circles and Lévesque is still regarded as a hero in many working class families in Quebec.* The fundamental question that remains is just exactly what type of support should be accorded to the PQ. Clearly, like the NDP federally, the PQ is in Laberge's terms, "the party closest to the workers," but events have shown, unfortunately, that it is little more. At the strategic level, the Vallières strategy has not been endorsed by the trade unions. The workers and their organizations may work with the PQ and a few militants will

---

* In March 1972 at a mass rally against unemployment sponsored by the three union centrals, Lévesque received perhaps the warmest audience reception.

participate in its left-wing faction – but taking care not to confuse their long-term aims with the objectives of the Parti Québecois as presently constituted.

Events of late spring 1972 pushed ideological and strategic considerations to the background. A direct confrontation between the trade unions and the government was in the offing. The basic issue was the collective agreement of 210,000 unionized public and para-public employees. The common front, which represented them, was the product of the new solidarity among the three federations, its basic goal was to provide decent working conditions for all government workers. It asked for a minimum wage of $100 per week, job security for teachers and hospital workers, and a yearly eight percent wage increase. After many months of fruitless negotiations, strike actions commenced. Seventy-five percent of the members had voted for the strike, but as it proceeded it actually gained support and momentum. The symbol "Nous" (We) was everywhere seen and pickets were strong and well attended. After two weeks, and partially in response to a scare campaign in the English press which exaggerated the seriousness of the situation in the hospitals and maligned the leaders of the common front, the right wing of Bourassa's cabinet led by Choquette, egged on by the party caucus and the English establishment, brought down Bill 19. Bill 19 effectively imposed a collective "agreement" and set heavy fines for any worker, as well as his union local and executive, who did not comply immediately and without protest. This draconian law matched the equally draconian sentences and fines passed out to local union officers for defying court injunctions forcing them back to work. To add further insult the presidents of the three federations, Laberge, Pepin and Charbonneau, were sentenced to one-year prison terms on the same count.

It was clear that the establishment felt threatened. The hysteria of the English media and the severity of Bill 19 and the "contempt" sentences reflected the real issues at stake in the bargaining. It was not, as the government claimed, a question of the workers asking for more money than the state had to give – the unions made it clear in the latter stage of the bargaining that they were willing to keep the settlement to a reasonable figure, revising their basic wage demands, if granted the $100 minimum plus meaningful job security. Finance

215

Minister Garneau admitted it was because the government had to protect the economic structure of private enterprise that it could not accept this proposal.[30] The owning class rightly feared that if such guarantees were written into collective agreements in the public sector, irresistible pressures would build up in private industry. But the bosses depended on being able to pay far less than $100 per week* and fire employees at will in order to maintain the profit margin and control their workers. At a moment of crisis, the government made clear where its loyalties lay: with the foreign owners rather than with the Québecois workers. It was ready and willing to ruthlessly use the machinery of the state, just as Duplessis had done, to keep the workers in their place.

After a day of deliberation and doubt, the three union leaders capitulated to Bill 19 and advised their workers, a majority of whom had voted to defy the law, to return to work. It appeared that the "trouble" was over. Now, beginning with jail for the "big three," the powers that be could punish the "trouble makers." It was, as the English media never tired of pointing out, just a few leaders and ideologues who had forced the workers on this adventurist path.

The facts, however, tell a different story. While the workers with few exceptions, did go back to work, they went angry and resentful, some grumbling of betrayal by their elected officers. There was much talk of a new general strike, this time to include the private sector.

The actual jailing of the three leaders turned out to be the spark that set off the explosion. For one solid week, Quebec was paralyzed by a series of walkouts, strikes and occupations that shook the very foundations of the system. Among those whose actions voiced the growing protest were steel-workers, teachers, journalists, textile workers, printers, hospital workers, non-teaching school employees, construction workers, broadcasters, miners, hospital nurses and physicians, store employees, CEGEP students and municipal and liquor board employees. No total account of the combined size and duration of the various actions has yet been made nor is any fully accurate assessment

---

* The reports of the Canadian Senate's Special Committee on Poverty and of the Castonguay/Nepveu Commission on Quebec Health both set the poverty level for a family of four at approximately $5000 per year or $100 per week.

really possible. Suffice it to say that the events were on an unquestionably major scale.* Report followed upon report of plants closed, factories and even towns occupied.

The spontaneity of these actions, as evidenced by the absence of any call for action by the common front (the organization of the common front had been immobilized by Bill 19 and the jailings), should have made it absolutely clear that what was happening was a movement from the base reflecting a deep-seated dissatisfaction among the working people of Quebec and an unwillingness on their part to passively submit to repression. They acted because they knew that if they did not stand up solidly behind their imprisoned comrades, they would all, sooner or later, suffer the same fate should they dare to stand up for what was rightfully theirs.

Yet the establishment and its media were not ready to accept the truth – for they needed a conspiracy to support their insinuations – just as Trudeau did when he imposed the War Measures Act in 1970. The problem was that the leaders were in jail and it was hard to find any evidence at all of their being behind the actions. So the establishment came out with new warnings: Choquette called it "gangsterism" in the trade unions; the English media discovered "goons." Even on the "liberal" CBC, the news report made constant references to these "goons" who were at the root of all the walkouts; these mysterious non-human creatures of incredible strength who, through coercion and threat, had forced hundreds of thousands of workers off the jobs they loved so dearly. Clearly there were many cases of groups of workers pressuring other workers to join them in some way or another, as might have been expected. Spontaneous actions like these always involve some who initiate and some who follow. There were, no doubt, individuals who joined the actions only grudgingly. The fact remains that the efforts of the working people of Quebec virtually brought the province to a standstill. In certain cases the local trade union executive took the lead; in others (for example, the bus drivers of Montreal) it made sure to keep the men on the job. But the public just heard about "goons," nothing more. Exactly who

---

* The most complete summary of the events as gathered by the Agence de Presse Libre du Québec (APLQ, *Bulletin,* No. 61, mai 18-25, 1972), covers twenty-six legal-size pages.

hired these goons and how they were organized was never made clear.*

When the "goon" scare proved insufficient, the media and the government proceeded to put pressure on the leadership to call off the revolt they hadn't started. Trade union officials found themselves publicly accused of trying to bring down the government: it was suggested that all the actions were actually a covert way of toppling the government and placing themselves (or the PQ?) in charge. Hence they were accused of being anti-democratic, of seeking a coup d'état rather than trusting the people through relying on the ballot box and free discussion. At the same time, the minister of labour intimated that Bill 19 could be amended to allow for a negotiated settlement. The leaders, refusing to permit themselves to be placed in the position of foisting abstract revolutionary content on a popular struggle for simple justice, decided to yield. The three presidents appealed their sentences, were released on bond, and advised the workers that since negotiation appeared still to be possible, no further militant action was called for at this time. Action ceased, for the time being. The movement needed time to consolidate its position and understand the implications of all that had happened.

---

* The "goons" were said to be most active in the construction industry supposedly closing site after site. However, certain facts make it clear that the other side was particularly adept at the use of goons and gangsterism. "An anti-strike meeting of construction workers was organized at the Jean Beliveau arena on Montreal's south shore . . . rental costs for the arena were picked up by the Montreal Association of General Contractors. The Contractors had given non-union personnel and unionized workers who had refused to strike the day off to attend the meeting and later disrupt an official union meeting. At the second meeting, the two groups clashed outside the Paul Sauvé arena. Police separated the two camps and then provided the anti-strike faction with megaphones and loud speakers to harangue the strikers. The leading speakers were small-time contractors, many of of whom depend on the good graces of the party in power to stay in business. At least two of the anti-strike meeting leaders were identified as Liberal organizers. . . .

Early in the week . . . a secret message . . . sent by party president Lise Bacon ordered local Liberal associations to set up, in effect, vigilante committees. They were told to 'gather information on local disturbances, arouse public opinion against the strikers" . . . and swear in 'special constables' . . ." Nick Auf der Maur, "The May Revolt Shakes Quebec," *Last Post,* July 1972, p. 22.

Certain things would never be the same. The idea that radicalism and militancy were limited to Montreal was laid to rest. Instead of militant action being confined to the Montreal area, the reverse almost seems to have been the case. North shore communities, Baie Comeau, Hauterive, Porte Cartier and the one that set it all off – Sept Iles, were occupied and liberated by the workers. In the East the workers took over Murdochville and Thetford Mines. The Laurentian-St. Jerome area was the scene of numerous strikes and occupations.[31] The workers of Quebec made it clear that although labour militancy outside Montreal gets little publicity, it is a grave error to assume passivity anywhere in the province.

Workers learned a great deal from the events of the week of May 11th. One thing they learned was that there are other tactics than strikes and picketting. Attempting to close down institutions and keeping them closed until just redress is rendered is only one of many strategies. They learned about workers' control, about making alliances with other groups in the community, and about ways of setting up cooperative counter-institutions. At Albert Prévost psychiatric Hospital in Montreal, the entire staff, non-medical, nursing, and even medical, simply took over the hospital and expelled the autocratic administration. In those few days before the police charged, not only did the staff realize a new freedom of activity and ease in their work, but the patients, by all reports, benefited therapeutically from the change to workers' control. If the working people of Quebec are someday to institute the socialist society they are increasingly seeking, then it must be through exactly this kind of direct local action that it will come about.

The Parti Québecois was careful to stay firmly on the fence in the dispute. For every attack on the government's insensitivity, there was another, at least as strong, on the union officials' adventurism. The PQ seems to have succeeded in its purpose; it maintained middle class support by placing itself wholly on the side of law and order and established procedure, while it has held onto the allegiance of the working class by making it even more evident that it was the only party at all sympathetic to its needs or demands.*

* A telephone poll of a stratified sample of 490 people in the Montreal area taken during the week of May 11th, revealed that: "About the same number of French speaking Montrealers chose the Parti Québecois

In early June a very interesting and potentially significant event occurred. The official patriotic society of French Canadians, the Société St. Jean Baptiste, went through some remarkable changes at its annual meeting in Quebec. By the time the meeting was over, this traditionally conservative and very Catholic nationalist organization, had changed its name to "Le Mouvement National du Québec," and adopted some rather interesting resolutions. It had declared itself in favour of economic intervention on the part of the state, cooperative forms of production and consumption, community participation, economic nationalism, and the widening of the role of unions. It even extended a fraternal salute to the union federations, recognizing "the importance of their contribution to the liberation of the people of Quebec."[32] A featured guest speaker was Michel Chartrand. He and Fernand Daoust, secretary general of the QFL, were widely applauded when they demanded the abolition of capitalism and the institution of a socialist system in Quebec.

Somehow, it appears to be the Vallières prediction that is coming to fruition. The middle classes, even the traditional middle class as represented by the new MNQ, appear to be moving leftward; certainly it was a very widely defined working class that rose up in mid-May. At the same time, some of the more traditional blue collar elements working in private industry are in revolt apparently against the left-wing stance taken by the union centrals. The new Confederation of Democratic Trade Unions (CSD) founded in June 1972 by three dissident old-line members of the CNTU executive, split somewhere between twenty and fifty thousand workers from the ranks of the CNTU – almost all from the private sector. The ramifications of this turn of events are yet to be seen – though they certainly appear a setback to the radical direction outlined by the labour centrals.

On the other hand, the CNTU will now be able to function with greater effectiveness as a more coherent and unified body.

---

a winner (27 percent) as called for a Liberal victory (29 percent). . . . Some 33 percent of blue collar workers surveyed predicted a PQ government and only 21 percent, a Liberal administration." "Public Opinion Against Union Leaders," *The Gazette,* May 18, 1972, p. 21. The poll also revealed that over two-thirds of respondents, though suspiciously, accepted the government's version of the dispute.

It may also be on its way to being composed almost exclusively of public employees, especially if a proposed merger with the CEQ materializes. (It appears that the major grievance of the dissident workers who joined the CSD was that the CNTU had lost sight of the needs of workers in private industry because of its orientation toward the public sector.) The QFL might then merge with the CSD once its current leaders have retired, with the result that the more moderate elements (social democratic, pro-PQ) would gravitate there; while the CNTU would develop and articulate a more radical workers' party/workers' control position.* But, here we are merely speculating on what may be distant developments.

What is clear is that the CNTU has, to some extent, failed in its goal of creating a common front which incorporates workers from all sectors; it has been unable to successfully counter all the propaganda distributed by the government. There are still some workers who are persuaded that "apolitical" unionism, as practicsed in the U.S.A., best serves its interests. At its own June convention, the CNTU, undaunted, voted to continue the struggle.† Marcel Pepin outlined a short run strategy which entailed the setting up of local political action commitees designed to defeat Liberal and anti-syndical candidates and elect those who share the goals of the labour movement.

The immediate consequence of this strategy is that many union political organizers will continue to work for the PQ without saying so. What it will mean in the long run is unclear. Quebec is still a society in motion, and neither the workers movements nor the Parti Québecois will remain still. The national struggle and the class struggle will continue separately but in coalition. The forms that this struggle will take and just exactly which elements of the population will be involved, and

* See chapter ten below.

† The CNTU's 150 member Conseil Confédéral met in early October 1972 to consider strategy and policy. While the delegates admitted the internal problems of the CNTU were serious and began to deal with some, they unanimously affirmed their commitment to "socialism as the system bringing about economic, political, cultural, industrial, and social democracy in the interests of the workers." They also planned a referendum of the membership on the question of independence for Quebec — "La CSN organisera un référendum sur l'indépendance." *Le Devoir,* 5 octobre, 1972, p. 1.

how, is still in part to be worked out. Certainly, under the right circumstances, the local actions committees of the CNTU could become the nucleus of a new political party, centers of coordination in a movement to win popular control of communities and workers' control of factories. In the concluding chapter, we shall maintain that the historical development of Quebec both permits and necessitates this course of events. One thing that is certain is that there is far more yet to come. The Québecois have not learned to accept their colonized state; they are instead learning what it will take to overcome it.

Footnotes to Chapter 9

1. Dossier d'Information sur le Bill 63, préparé par le Secrétariat central d'Action politique non-partisane de la CSN, décembre, 1969, pp. 3-5. (Authors' translation.)
2. *Ibid.,* p. 20. (Authors' translation.)
3. Reported in *Ibid.,* p. 31.
4. For a detailed analysis see: "The Quebec Elections" (editorial article), *Our Generation,* Vol. 7, No. 2, pp. 3-17.
5. Maurice Pinard, "Working Class Politics: An Interpretation of the Quebec Case," in O. Kruhlak, *et al.* (eds.), *The Canadian Political Process,* (Toronto: Holt, Rinehart & Winston, 1970), p. 221.
6. Quoted in, "The Santo Domingo of Pierre Elliott Trudeau," *Last Post,* (November, 1970), p. 10.
7. Edouard Smith, "Opération Démocratie," *Our Generation,* Vol. 7, No. 3, pp. 101-2.
8. Quoted in Dominique Clift, "The Clergy's New Radicalism," *The Montreal Star,* November 13, 1970, p. 7.
9. "The Santo Domingo of Pierre Elliott Trudeau, *Last Post,* (November, 1970), p. 10.
10. *Ibid.*
11. Quoted in *Ibid.,* p. 6.
12. Nick Auf der Maur, "Power Corrupts, Absolutely," *Last Post,* (December, 1971), p. 15.
13. Nick Auf der Maur, "Quebec Labour Turns Left," *Last Post,* (December, 1971), p. 11.
14. In Michel Pelletier and Yves Vaillancourt, *op. cit.,* pp. 102-3. (Authors' translation.)
15. *Ibid.,* p. 107.

16. Nick Auf der Maur, "No Minority Group is Treated Better," *Last Post,* (December, 1971), p. 25.
17. Quoted in Henri Gagnon, *C'est Quoi L'Etat* (Montréal; Gaetan Piché, 1972), p. 110. (Authors' translation.)
18. *Ibid.,* p. 111.
19. Les enseignants dénoncent l'école, *Québec Presse,* June 4, 1972.
20. "Ne Comptons Que" plus "Le Deuxième Front" were published in English as *Quebec Labour* (Montreal: Black Rose Press, 1971).
21. *Ibid.,* pp. 166-67.
22. Nick Auf der Maur, *op. cit.,* p. 13.
23. Quoted in Ralph Surrette, "The Year of the Manifestos," *Last Post* (July, 1972), p. 29.
24. "Classes Sociales et Idéologies Nationalistes au Quebec," *Socialisme Québecois,* No. 20 (mai, 1970), pp. 13-55.
25. *Ibid.,* p. 25. See also D. Roussopoulos, "Social Classes and Nationalism in Quebec," *Our Generation,* Vol. 8, No. 2, pp. 37-57.
26. Henri Gagnon, *op. cit.,* pp. 68-69.
27. Quoted in *Ibid.,* p. 66.
28. Pierre Vallières, *L'Urgence de Choisir* (Montreal: Parti Pris, 1972). For a partial translation and commentary see, Henry Milner, "The Implications of the Vallières Declaration," *Our Generation,* Vol. 8, No. 2, pp. 27-37.
29. See Bourque's rejoinder: "En réponse à Pierre Vallières," *Socialisme Québecois.* No. 23 (Spring, 1972), pp. 127-38.
30. Nick Auf der Maur, "The May Revolt Shakes Quebec," *Last Post,* (July, 1972), p. 15.
31. *Ibid.,* pp. 18-21.
32. "Les SSJB changent de nom et tendent à se radicaliser," *Le Devoir,* (14 Juin, 1972), p. 3.

CHAPTER 10

NATIONALISM
ON THE
LEFT

The presence of a powerful and significant left-nationalist movement in Quebec is now beyond question. Part One established the existence of objective socio-economic conditions to which this movement is a direct and necessary response. Yet it was not until the sixties and early seventies that a realization of Quebec's colonial economic status expressed itself in the thought and actions of large numbers of Québecois. The information presented in the previous chapters helps to explain why this happened when it did. Chapter six focused upon the traditional elite and its attempts to create and defend a quasi-feudal Quebec state in keeping with Church teaching. Chapter seven dealt with the rise of a new group of well-educated lay persons who wanted Quebec to catch up with the rest of the Western world and thus challenged the old elite demanding less power for the Church and greater democracy for the people. Both of these groups were important in that they interpreted the daily reality of the people in hope of persuading them to conform to certain ideas, principles, and patterns of behavior by promising them visions of a better society. Neither group, however, raised the issues of economic colonization and thereby both served to reinforce the domination of Quebec by a numerically small, essentially foreign, class of people.

When economic discontent, which might have threatened the foreign economic elite and its domestic political allies, appeared in the thirties, this discontent was successfully deflected from the real sources of exploitation toward various symbols and scapegoats. Left-wing groups, from the Communist Party, to some international unions, to the few remaining pockets of the old "rouge" tradition, were effectively stymied from presenting their explanation of events and view of reality to the people by the monopoly over the media and educational institutions maintained by the Church and the intellectuals around it.

In the forties and fifties technological development brought certain institutions (like Radio Canada, the revitalized C.T.C.C. [CNTU], and the Laval School of Social Sciences) to the center of the historical stage. Around these institutions an opposition intellectual position made itself heard and shattered the monolithic intellectual atmosphere of Quebec. In Hegelian terminology this new thinking was the antithesis of the thinking of the thirties. Each contradicted the other but neither was complete as neither threatened the economic domination of Quebec by American and English-Canadian business interests. The new intellectuals, in attacking only the ideas that prevailed and not the underlying socio-economic structure, mistook the ideological self-image of the society for the society itself. The failure of these ideas when implemented during the Quiet Revolution gave rise to a new intellectual position. The left-wing nationalism of the late sixties and early seventies is seen then as a synthesis, or as a more complete, more historically true, consciousness than either of the other two.

It is neither our ambition nor within our competence to provide the complete answer to the question: why did left-wing nationalism develop in Quebec? What is important is that it has developed, and the very process of this development can help us to understand its prospects and possibilities. In this chapter we will outline a few of the factors that we have found to be significant in this forty-year process. An analysis of these factors, it is hoped, will make an application of our work helpful in relation to similar movements in other parts of the world. We have little interest in knowledge for its own sake (or change for its own sake), but rather agree with Marx that interpretation of the world, in its final sense, is at the same time an effort to change it – to reveal, so as to ultimately realize, the potentialities of freedom and justice.

In his study of social class and power in Canada, Professor Porter noted that:

In modern societies it is possible to identify, beyond the economic and the political, several sub-systems, each having a relatively autonomous life. Important among these are institutions such as the mass media, educational institutions, and the Church, which create and propogate the ideas which hold the society together. All of these sub-systems perform essential social functions. All of them must be directed and co-ordinated. It is this need for direction and co-ordination which gives rise to power. The power which resides in all these other sub-systems circumscribes the power of the political system. Power in other words is distributed through these various institutional orders.[1]

Within each of these sub-systems of power, is an elite, which makes decisions affecting the society at large. It is the degree of co-operation among these elites, or the degree to which their long term interests coincide, which determines the openness of the society. For example, if the interests of the elites are opposed, the resulting struggle for power is usually brought out in the open so each side can seek support. Information is distributed by both sides to glorify the virtues of their position, and dialogue ensues. In such cases the intellectuals who direct these institutions which create and propogate ideas (the ideological elite), are divided. However, if the interests of the elites coincide with one another, there tends to be a monolithic ideology which predominates.

The use of elite theories such as Porter's must be tempered with an understanding of the class basis of society. While modern society does indeed contain these autonomous sub-systems, the social pattern which sets the limits of sub-systems autonomy is essentially a class one. The role of the elites in the various sub-systems, and in particular the ultra-essential ideological elites, is circumscribed by the socio-economic class structure. This is clearly the case with Quebec. Because Quebec is not a sovereign state, there is no military elite to consider. Not until the nineteen-sixties is the bureaucratic elite or the labour elite (a questionable term – especially in the case of Quebec) of any significance. Because of Quebec's satellitic position, its economic elite, composed of Anglo-American corporation executives, is the primary source of influence and power throughout the entire period of our study. The complexion and methods of the political elite have changed significantly in the past four decades, but its subordinate position with respect to the long-term interests of the foreign economic elite have remained constant. Apart from technological advances that affected all levels of Quebec society, it is to changes in the third group, the intellectual or ideological elite, that we must look for an explanation for the historical developments described.

There are three basic clusters of factors that we distinguish as crucial in Quebec's evolution toward left-wing nationalism. Each may be seen as a successive layer, and the addition of each layer increases the determinateness of the explanation. It is the combination of the three factors, or successive layers that makes some sense out of this complex but important historical process. We have touched upon each of the factors before, but far too briefly.

The first cluster of factors relates to the collective or national existence of the Québecois. This factor may be taken as an historical given, the outcome of a colonial pattern of settlement and rule. This collective existence, or national consciousness, is at the root of the failure of the techniques used internationally by the American-based corporate ruling class to sufficiently win the allegiance of the people in this particular satellite to its culture, ideology, and social patterns.

The second cluster may be seen as related to transformations in the "forces of production." By this is meant changes in technology, in industrial organization, and in patterns of communication and education. This latter is particularly important in the case of Quebec.

The third cluster of factors, and the most decisive and theoretically complex, has to do with the part played by the intellectuals in the face of changes in the first two factors.

Chapter one described the sales effort through which American industry, aided by the government, endeavors to stimulate market demand in order to maintain overall economic stability. It maintained that this leads to the creation of "new needs" which come to motivate and direct behavior in much the same way as do the needs for food or sex, and that the internalization of these "new needs" results. in a society in which an individual's identity becomes indistinguishable from his material possessions. The consequence of this proliferation of flashy consumer goods and credit buying is a blurring of social class distinctions.

The magnitude of the "blurring of social class distinctions" depends to a very large degree on the class position of the beholder: each strata, except the lowest one, can distinguish a class below it, but it would appear that people on the lower rungs of society are unable to distinguish between themselves and individuals from other classes, except perhaps for the very wealthy.

Thus through the creation of a highly motivated, consumer oriented society and the myths that go with it, the ruling class has been able to protect its economic hegemony. The lower classes are educated both formally and informally to accept the American myth of egalitarianism and disregard their own socio-economic position in relation to the society as a whole.

The first cluster of factors, then, relates to the way in which the American ruling class applies these same techniques for stimulating market demand in satellitic nations such as Quebec. Because of the differences in language, customs, history and values, the mechanisms – resulting in the creation of new needs – which the American ruling class uses fairly successfully at home are far less successful in a satellite where there is a distinctive national culture.

The lower classes are comprised of the majority of the people in a society, blue and white collar workers, the jobless, welfare recipients and students. As consciousness develops this agglommeration congeals into a single working class. The lower classes develop class consciousness as they become aware of the implications of socio-economic inferiority. From this comes a recognition of the class structures of the society and their own place in it. This perception is accompanied by the realization that the worth of the franchise is limited by the inequitable influence of the ruling class upon most of those who hold political power, the information media, and the electoral process itself. The final stage is the attainment of self-consciousness as a class fundamentally opposed to the ruling classes and able to construct a different, that is socialist, society.

One of the ways in which the worker comes to a realization of these things is by recognizing the similarities which he has to other workers, and the features which distinguish them – as a group – from the powerful persons in the society. This process

228

of becoming aware of sameness and difference occurs first at a lower level: it is making distinctions on the basis of very crude indicators. Within the metropolis, the boss drives a Cadillac; the white, unionized worker a Chevrolet. The boss wears fashionable clothes; so do his white collar employees, although they are of poor quality. Both cheer the same football and baseball teams; both see many of the same movies and television programs. They may even read the same newspaper.

Within the satellite, the situation is different: the boss speaks a foreign language. He promotes individuals of his own ethnic group as opposed to those from the majority group. He demands that contracts be written only in his language. The machines he purchases have instructions printed only in his language. His life-style, habits and customs seem relatively strange and unknown. The boss and worker do not watch the same television programs or movies. The newspapers they read are worlds apart. The boss cannot even directly communicate with those who bear the burden of his decisions. In general, class differences are magnified within the satellite because those in positions of power are to a large extent ignorant of and segregated from the ways of life of the lower classes.

This point can be illustrated by looking at some of the ways in which foreign entrepreneurs have related to and treated the French-Canadian inhabitants. In his study of Drummondville in the late thirties,[2] E. C. Hughes described the insensitivity of the English managerial class to local customs and traditions. Church holidays were often ignored. The English looked upon local politics with disdain and held themselves aloof from any open participation in the community. Despite this "separatism," the foreign entrepreneurs always seemed to know which persons in the local power structure to influence in order to gain the needed concessions for their industry. They pulled the strings behind the scenes without having to become embroiled in community politics.

The company towns built mainly in mining areas seem to have been even more brutal. These towns were built to accomodate a relatively cheap, plentiful labour force and to exploit resources at minimal costs. There were few, if any, other considerations taken into account in organizing and constructing these barracks of labour. The owners and managers, for a large part Americans, had no qualms about treating French Canadians very differently than they treated white, American or English Canadian workers. Unionization was violently, brutally, and often illegally blocked. Wages were much lower than those paid by the same company elsewhere in Canada or in the United States.[3] French Canadians were viewed as not quite up to the standards of WASP society; but this fact was not invisible to them nor was the support these foreign entrepreneurs received from Quebec politicians.

A number of authors in recent years have attempted to outline those critical experiences in the development of a left-wing nationalist consciousness. It has been often noted that French Canadians who are forced to interact with English-speaking persons, whether in business establishments, in mixed areas or simply by living in a city like Montreal where there is a large English minority, are more likely to develop this consciousness. In a study of members of the Rassemblement pour l'Indépendance Nationale (RIN), it was found that deeply felt threats to the identity of French Canadians living in English Canada or among the English in Quebec, such as hearing commands to "speak white," constituted critical experiences affecting a change in world view.[4] In addition, French Canadians knew that any advancement in the business world required playing up to "Les Anglais" and in the end becoming Anglais, and they resented it.[5]

Thus, the presence of a different ethnic and cultural group at the top of the social structure facilitates the recognition of power relationships and class distinctions on the part of the lower classes within the population. Added to this are cases of outright discrimination and expressed attitudes of disdain towards the French Canadians and their culture, which aggravate and expose the social class distinctions. Although by the sixties the English were more careful and sensitive than they had been in the thirties, several incidents may be cited to illustrate a still common attitude on their part.

In November of 1962, Donald Gordon, the president of Canadian National Railways, a Crown corporation, declared publicly that he would rather hire English Canadians in executive positions for, in effect, French Canadians were not competent. Then, "N. R. Crump of the CPR inadvertently substantiated the charge of prejudice in an attempt to exonerate his colleague. Crump advanced the explanation that the classical education provided in the collèges classiques was not adequate preparation for a railroad executive. Thereupon an enterprising journalist published statistics on the educational background of the thirty-two top officials of both railroads. Less than a quarter of them met Crump's basic requirement of a university degree in engineering; 50 percent of them, including Gordon, had no university training, and some had not even been to high school. Four had law degrees."[6]

English-Canadian left-liberals demonstrated much the same attitude. A year earlier at a Laval students' congress on separatism, Douglas Fisher asserted that if the French Canadians wanted to leave confederation, English Canada would be glad to see them go for they had produced only hockey players and strip-teasers, and their federal representatives were irresponsible do-nothings.[7] Even by 1971, after English Canadians had been asking "what does Quebec want?" for ten years, Arnold Hart, President of the Bank of Montreal, publicly warned Premier Bourassa that it was not the bombs and left-wing militants that scared off prospective investors. After all, many parts of the world are today plagued with this disease. But, he suggested, it is the linguistic policy of the government: investors want their employees to speak their language and they want their children to attend schools of their language.[8] As Mr. Hart's bank is a kingpin in Quebec's financial structure and involved in the financing of many government activities, this statement must be seen as a more than academic comment on the current political scene.[9]

The political differences between say Fisher and Crump were unimportant. What mattered was that both aroused the national feeling of colonial domination. The reaction to this attitude in the early days had been a turning inwards, "Je me Souviens." In the fifties there were some who told French Canadians to integrate themselves into the North American milieu – so that they would be accepted as being like everyone else. But by the mid-sixties it became clear that les Québecois achieved nothing at all and lost a great deal by turning their back on their national or collective existence. The goal became to re-affirm that existence politically, economically and culturally by creating a real society of the future rather than preserving a mythical one of the past. But because of Quebec's past, because of the social solidarity which developed in response

231

to colonial control, les Québecois had built and would build a collectivity not like the others, potentially free from the subtle chains of the culture of international capitalism.

So emerges left-wing nationalism in Quebec: it is the paralleling of class division by ethnic and language divisions which aggravates and exposes the social class distinctions among the population. Since the Anglo-American ruling class uses Quebec to supply natural resources more than as a market, the effort which goes into stimulating market demand in Quebec is significantly less than within the United States itself. This, coupled with the insensitivity and disregard shown to the French-Canadian population, demonstrated the true motives of the English-speaking ruling class and exposed as false their espoused objectives of aiding the growth and development of Quebec. Thus, it is through the symbols of the nation that the lower classes of French Canada begin to develop class consciousness. The attributes of wealth and privilege which accrue to the English-speaking elite come to be seen not as "rightfully" theirs but as bounty stolen from the French-Canadian nation.

The second cluster of factors affecting the development of left-wing nationalism in Quebec relates, more than anything, to the changed role of the mass media over the past four decades in Quebec, and the liberalization of the education system. An open, free flow of information and ideas allows for the development of a consciousness opposed to the ruling ideology. Within a tightly censored milieu, evidence necessary to demonstrate the failure of government policies to solve social problems can be distorted or simply made unavailable. Corruption can be completely hidden, and grievances can easily be channelled onto scapegoats. But, more significantly, a highly censored environment will keep the people ignorant of the world at large, thus making it difficult, if not impossible, for them to compare their society to others.

The degree to which individuals are able to critically judge information and ideas presented by the mass media depends to a large extent upon the duration and content of their formal education. Until the nineteen-sixties, the education of Francophone Roman Catholics of Quebec was entirely under the control of the Church. The latter's philosophy of education dictated that long years of schooling were only for the elite: for the children of that minority who could afford the classical college.

These children would be trained to take their rightful place as the new generation of professionals; for the children of workers or peasants only the minimum schooling was provided – unless they were exceptional, then they might be trained for the priesthood. The children of Anglophone Protestants could go to high school (tuition free) and then to university, but this channel was open only to those Francophones who wished to obtain a science degree at university.[10] This option was not encouraged.

Between 1939 and 1950, 9,304 students graduated with a baccalaureate degree from Quebec's classical colleges. Thirty-seven percent of these continued to become doctors, 11 percent engineers, 7 percent lawyers, 5 percent obtained commerce degrees, and 4 percent received degrees in applied science. Of the 465 who chose business, only 119 aimed at jobs in industry. The rest became certified public accountants or entered a family business.[11]

Between 1900 and 1950, of the youth between the ages of twenty and twenty-four years, the percentage of boys who had nine to twelve years of education increased from 19.8 percent to 41.9 percent in Montreal. These same figures for Toronto were 25.8 percent and 53.3 percent. The percentage of girls who had nine to twelve years of education in Montreal increased from 26.4 percent to 45.9 percent.[12] It is important to note here that it was not until 1942 that education in Quebec was made compulsory to the age of fourteen years. Of those between the ages of twenty-five and thirty-four years, in the late fifties, 13.2 percent of the men and 6.7 percent of the women of Montreal were university graduates. Of this age group in Toronto, 18.4 percent of the men and 16 percent of the women had acquired a university degree.[13]

The Church's very rigid ideas about what should and should not be taught in school resulted in a very narrowly educated population. The publishing of all French language texts, until 1960, was carried out by publishing houses and printers owned by church congregations.[14] Because the government throughout the thirties, forties and fifties supported the Church's policy, the intellectual isolation of the province was reinforced through control of the types of books which could be bought at stores or borrowed from libraries. In 1942, Ontario had 468 public libraries, Quebec had 27, of which only nine were French.

While Ontario had an illiteracy rate of 2.3 percent, the rate for Quebec was 4.7 percent.[15]

Following closely behind the rural electrification program of Premier Duplessis, was the radio. In the rural parish of St. Denis studied by Horace Miner not one home had a radio in 1936. By 1949 practically every house was equipped with this new form of link-up with the world. With the organization of the Canadian Broadcasting Corporation in the thirties, an outlet for the development of French-Canadian talent and for programming reflecting French-Canadian culture and uniqueness became available. Radio Canada, as we noted, was a federal crown corporation and as such sufficiently outside the grasp of the traditional elite and its political allies in Quebec. Thus radio and, in the fifties, television because of their "global village" nature as media and because of their actual content and relative freedom from censorship, penetrated the ideological barrier that had been constructed.

Once this had happened, the very traditional structure of the press and information network contributed to the overthrow of old ideas. The case of *Le Devoir* merits elaboration in this context. Since its founding by Henri Bourassa in 1910, *Le Devoir* has maintained a fair degree of economic independence. Unlike other newspapers in North America, it has never relied on the good will of capitalist advertisers to stay in business; nor was it ever treated by its publishers as an enterprise whose primary purpose was to make money. Rather, it has relied on the subscriptions of a loyal following to carry on its duty (devoir) of providing information and interpreting reality. During the thirties, *Le Devoir,* like the rest, was trapped within the ideological framework of the old order and its pages gave voice to the same outmoded and quasi-racist explanations and exhortations. When, in the late forties and fifties, the outside world and its reality began to penetrate into Quebec through Radio Canada, returning intellectuals who had been educated abroad, etc., *Le Devoir* underwent a profound transformation. Because the writers and publishers of the paper had no vested interest in the status quo, they could print the truth – even if that truth had changed. This explains the difference between the courageous journalism of *Le Devoir* during the Duplessis Regime – especially the Asbestos strike – and afterwards, as compared to the ignominious hypocrisy of the *Montreal Star* and *Gazette,* two "progressive" English papers.[16]

The case of *Le Devoir* is somewhat exceptional but not isolated. Other newspapers were still less constrained by the capitalist publishing framework, though not quite as independent. Furthermore *Le Devoir* has always been particularly influential in Quebec, affecting other media outlets as well as the ideas of educated Quebecers.

As technological change and international influences altered the basic framework of thought and knowledge, and consequently the message conveyed in Quebec's papers, these institutions nevertheless retained their special social role. It was understood that the journalists and editors of the Québecois newspapers were not just another bunch of hack businessmen but a group of people with a duty to understand and explain the truth, as they saw it, to the people; and this duty was usually taken seriously. Thus the press, which had been a key element in defining and communicating the conservatism that reigned in the thirties and before, became a center of new ideas, a locus for the spread of new perspectives and developing movements.

By the early sixties the ideological sub-system had been fundamentally transformed. Education was being revolutionized, the junior colleges or CEGEP's were equalizing the secondary education available to Protestants and Catholics. The old system under which, as Marcel Rioux described it, "the teaching of religion, of Aristotelian philosophy, and of history contributed, through its dogmatic determinism, to reinforce the fatalism in French Canadian peasant culture",[17] was on its way out. The revitalized institutions of the sixties – schools, media, etc. – negated this fatalism, giving a new meaning and pride to being Québecois.

By the sixties the Québecois had become selective with regard to foreign cultural influences. When the newly nationalized Hydro-Québec needed technical advisors, French-speaking Swiss were sent for. Also, an airmail "delivery service of French newspapers and reviews permitted the French Canadian readers to read Parisian periodicals at about the same time as people in Marseille, Senegal, or Dakar. A great step forward: each new reader of *Paris-Match, L'Express,* or *Marie-Claire* is perhaps a former buyer of *Life, Time* or *Vogue.* In this way he discovers that the world can be thought of and talked about in French. . . . "[18]

In sum, technological change forced the outside world into

Quebec and proceeded to shatter the cultural monolith that had so long persisted. The electronic media, the press, and later the schools, affected this process and new ideas, new world views, were formulated and discussed. By the time these views had reached the stage of implementation, Quebec was beginning to pass into a new stage where new external influences were no longer accidental but instead purposefully sought out to complement the growing positive vision of a truly independent Quebec.

We thus arrive at the third cluster of factors, the social role of the intellectuals or, in Porter's terms, the ideological elite. Because, as is clear by now, our classification of the three basic factors is highly arbitrary and abstract, it is emphasized that it is in fact one integral process that we are describing under these three categories.

We have already pointed out that it is the element of consciousness that we consider crucial in historical change. Given the class nature of our society, it is only through the formation of a unified and conscious collectivity among the exploited classes that the possibility of an end to exploitation arises. We have noted as well that such an analysis as we are attempting must begin to overcome the basic insufficiency in Marx's treatment of the process of coming to consciousness. The first two factors we outlined have made Quebec at this historical moment structurally conducive to the spread of such a consciousness in the form of a left-wing nationalist movement of decolonization. The added factor, and the one we regard as most important, is the role of the intellectuals. In saying this we reject the economic determinist or "vulgar" Marxist position which lays the inevitable mechanisms of history at the root of social developments. We share the perspective of Italian Marxist philosopher and revolutionary, Antonio Gramsci, "in which man and reality, the instrument of labour and the will, are not separated but come together in the *historical act*. Hence Marxists believe that the canons of historical materialism are valid only after the fact, for studying and understanding the events of the past, and ought not to become a mortgage on the present and future."[19]

Marxist analysis after Marx suffered from a determinism that he himself, at his best, would not countenance. The proletarian socialist society was inevitable, so little analysis of the concrete conditions of the existing social structure of a given society was necessary. Nor need much attention be paid to bringing the proletariat to a consciousness of its historical role. The Russian Revolution officially replaced electoralist with revolutionary tactics but the Soviet domination of the third international, especially after the accession of Stalin, in fact contributed to the growing sterility of mainstream socialist thinking on these questions during the first half of this century.

The work of Antonio Gramsci is one very important exception. Gramsci, who died in 1936, was little known outside of Italy, but interest in his thought has risen in the past few years, and his work has noticeably affected socialist theoreticians in Quebec.* Gramsci was virtually unique. From a position within the international socialist movement he grappled with the difficult questions marxist theoreticians chose to ignore; he developed a dynamic understanding of the path through class consciousness to state power which contrasted sharply with the stale determinism of the orthodox theoreticians. We will rely on a few of his more important insights as a framework for the theoretical and strategic conclusions we offer in this the final section of this book.

One example of Gramsci's insight, and one that applies directly to Quebec, is his understanding of the Church as a political force in Italy. While most socialists offhandedly dismissed the Church as obsolete, Gramsci never underestimated its key historical role. After the creation of an Italian national state in the late nineteenth century, the Church was in a position analogous to that of the Church in Quebec during the same period. The Church retained no formal political power but through its control of co-operatives, credit unions, trade guilds, mutual-aid societies and the like, it had vast influence in local economic and social matters, areas the liberal state did not penetrate. Its mortal enemy was socialism (as evidenced by

* For example, Parti Pris, the left publishing house which emerged with the disappearance of the magazine of that name, not long ago published *La Pensée Politique de Gramsci* by Québecois, Jean-Marc Piotte. Parti Pris has restricted itself to books pertaining directly to Quebec except for a few internationally known works such as Che Guevara's diary. The fact that it chose to devote some of its meager resources to printing a work on this relatively unknown thinker is thus quite indicative of the respect now accorded to the work of Gramsci.

the fact that by 1919 the only two parties with mass support were the socialists and the Catholic PPI). However, added Gramsci, this competition with the Church was inevitable and even hopeful. "The Popular Party is a necessary phase in the development of the Italian proletariat toward Communism. It creates 'associationism' and solidarity where Socialism could not, where the objective conditions of a capitalist economy do not exist. . . . Only 'democratic Catholicism' could amalgamate this social group. But in so doing the Church itself was committing suicide: once the peasant masses were organized, Socialism could influence them. When the peasantry became conscious of its real power, it would no longer want priests as spokesmen, but fellow peasants."[20]

In Quebec, the Church's social policy and strategy, which succeeded in eliminating socialist expression during the thirties, paradoxically laid the groundwork for the establishment of a socialist society by evoking the collective interests of the people in relation to their everyday economic and social needs. But it could only be socialism and not the Church that could meet these needs. Gramsci's analysis is useful in explaining why this should be so – but it does not stop there. He realized full well that the existence of such potentiality is insufficient. A conscious and organized mass force is required.

Fundamental change comes about through class action, the overthrow of capitalism will be the task of the working class; but, as Gramsci points out, the working class "scarcely deserves the name until it becomes conscious of its existence as a class."[21] This consciousness entails a world view capable of absorbing and transcending the culture and accomplishments of the past. And it is to the intellectuals within the working class movement or party that falls the task of winning the workers over to this world view. Gramsci saw clearly that the desire for liberation does not somehow flow from the innate qualities of oppressed classes. Resignation, fear, and passivity are as much to be expected. It was incumbent upon the intellectuals to bring the working class to a sense of their own strength and responsibility, and to expose the ideological mask of the society. The proletariat had to be convinced that the interests of the ruling class conflicted with the interests of the society in general and their own interests in particular.

We have contended that the national sentiments of les

Québecois, their coming to know themselves as a collectivity apart from the rest of North America and its mass-consumption oriented capitalism, gives the workers of Quebec a possible linguistic and cultural basis to the development of a revolutionary class consciousness. We have further argued that technological changes affecting the press, the schools, etc., provided a medium for the expression, clarification and dissemination of the elements of this consciousness. Nevertheless this two-layered foundation requires intellectuals united with the working class who can build on it and develop the theoretical underpinnings of the revolutionary movement.

In the last forty years the ideological positions articulated by Quebec intellectuals have changed a great deal, but their importance has remained constant. Intellectuals are vital to the maintenance of all social structures, they provide the personnel for the ideological organs of a society, schools, church, voluntary associations, etc. To describe the relationship between the ideological activity of the intellectuals and their function of winning the loyalty of the masses to the status quo interests of the ruling class, Gramsci elaborated the concept of hegemony:

> Hegemony is an order in which a certain way of life and thought is dominant, in which one concept of reality is diffused throughout society in all its institutions and private manifestations, informing with its spirit, all taste, morality, customs, religious and political principles, and all social relations, particularly in their intellectual and moral connotations.[22]

These words are an apt description of Quebec in the thirties when the traditional elite's control of the educational institutions and the language barrier which protected Quebec, successfully prevented the intellectual expression of opposing ideas. Chapter six described how the traditional elite attempted to integrate itself into the daily lives of the masses via various voluntary organizations such as the labour unions, Catholic action groups, and co-operatives. In these ways the message of the ideological elite succeeded in reaching large segments of the general population while the newspapers and reviews controlled by this elite enlightened the educated elements of the society. This group was instrumental in changing the composition and outward behavior of the political elite in the mid-thirties. But the socio-

239

economic structure was little affected. Duplessis replaced Taschereau but the hegemony over thought was nowhere challenged.

The most outstanding feature of the traditional intellectuals, the writers, teachers and scholars,* is that they represent "historical continuity". They consider themselves autonomous and independent, and their reasonably subtle ties to the ruling class permit them to maintain such illusions.[23]

In the late forties and fifties a new group of intellectuals had arisen in Quebec trying to achieve hegemony for its own concept of reality and the social principles by which it interpreted the world. It was urban, international, and modern in its outlook, in contrast to the traditional, rural and xenophobic attitudes of the old order. By 1960 this new intelligentsia had temporarily succeeded in winning a position of hegemony for its ideas. The new intellectuals were convinced that their own world view was objectively true unlike the biased, ideological doctrine of the traditional elite. Yet their hegemony no sooner arrived than it began to disintegrate.

What is clear is that the intellectuals of both periods played a central role in upholding the social structure. The right-wing nationalism of the thirties was well suited to economic exploitation until a contradiction in the position preached by the traditional elite became evident. While the Francophone masses were told that materialism and big business were un-Catholic and therefore not good, they were also directed to collaborate with, rather than oppose, this foreign economic elite. Whether on issues like the municipalization of hydro-electric companies to provide power at reasonable cost or when it came to the demand for better wages and working conditions, the traditional elite consistently sided with the economic elite.

But the changing world caught up with the old order; the new conditions exposed its inherent contradictions. Modern technologies of communication and transportation, etc. brought with them new facts and ideas. When the Catholic workers at

---

* We have been using the term intellectuals to refer generally to this group that Gramsci refers to as "traditional intellectuals" which he differentiates from the "technical intellectuals", the managers, scientists, technicians and experts. This distinction is a difficult one to make and is particularly inapplicable to French Quebec before the Quiet Revolution, when the role of this second group was negligible at best.

Asbestos responded by demanding a modicum of justice, the elites this time could not contain their struggle to one isolated locality. Instead, "La Grève de l'Amiante" gave birth to a much wider cause. The resulting split within the ranks of the clergy on support for strikers and on the need for social welfare, tended to weaken the legitimacy of the traditional elite. The powers of the Church and political corruption became issues dividing both clerical and lay intellectuals. Because of the changes in the structure and content of the media, dissident intellectuals gained some access to the people. The dissidents, who were usually trained as social scientists, worked from such positions as trade union leaders and journalists in the hope of influencing the Québecois masses. Their approach to social questions was new and different.

Rather than being alienated from the dominant capitalist structure and pretending it did not exist, the goal was to integrate with it so as to reap its benefits, thus catching up with the rest of North America. This entailed limited state intervention, a powerful though moderate trade union organization, and a liberal democratic political system. While elements within the economic ruling class found a move in this direction opposed to their immediate interests in that it led in particular instances to increased wages; in general, it fit in quite nicely with the widest interests of that class.

From this perspective the goals of "rattrapage," and of the Quiet Revolution in general, can be seen as simply the implementation of these long range interests. They were to provide the owning class with a bureaucratic infrastructure which would modernize transportation and government services to meet the needs of an industrial set-up which was becoming far more highly technological and complex, and would provide the up-to-date education and sophisticated public relations to train a population more open to the culture of international capitalism. And without denying some usefulness and value to the new ideas and the reforms of the Quiet Revolution, one can assert that fundamentally this is just what happened.[24] Hence the hegemony of the new intellectuals and their principles in the end served exactly the same interests – though the means by which these interests were to be ministered had assuredly progressed. It is only *because* the new intellectuals believed they were serving the "common good" and not the interests of a particular class that these ideas gained such ready accept-ance among the population, i.e. that they achieved a hegemonic position. But this was exactly the case with the traditional intellectuals. They too firmly believed that they were serving the common good, and many had genuine antipathy for the English business class whose interests they served in the end.

But the hegemony of the traditional elite lasted longer, far longer. The ideology of "rattrapage," like any class ideology, was incomplete; and the people of Quebec, now that they had been given the opportunity to be critical and test the ideas offered to them against the reality encountered in their lives, found the new ideology wanting. The new group itself, which had banded together only to fight the old ideologues and their political regime, was split, some of its members going on to a position far in advance of and opposed to the objectives of "rattrapage."

This then is the point at which we find Quebec in the early seventies. We would be gratified indeed if we could point to a strong identifiable intellectual presence acting within an organized working class movement as Gramsci would insist. In fact we cannot be so certain. What we do know is that the position enunciated by the leading thinkers of the Parti Qué-becois and set down in its economic manifesto is not the basis of a program around which the working class can unite. Its implementation does not entail the abolition of foreign capitalist control. But the PQ platform is also not to be shrugged off as simply the latest restatement of the interests and justification for the economic prerogatives of the ruling class. An electoral victory by the Parti Québecois would entail, at the very least, a redistribution of power within the ruling class, especially away from Anglo-Canadian interests.

Whether it will entail more, depends upon the role played by intellectuals and activists inside and especially outside its ranks. Fortunately, the Parti Québecois is only one element within the Quebec spectrum, though a key one; and it too has its left-wing faction. Then there are numerous other nuclei of socialist intellectual ferment, especially in and around the trade union movement.

One of Gramsci's greatest contributions was his critique of trade unionism from the left, from within a Marxist perspective. Gramsci pointed out that trade unionism is inevitably a contingent part of the capitalist structure playing a defensive or reactive role. It makes the worker see labour as a means for gain, not as a (potentially) productive and liberating process. Hence the concept of a revolutionary trade union is, in the ultimate sense, a contradiction. Instead Gramsci favoured workers' councils. Workers' councils were institutions of the new society within the bounds of the old – democratically organized instruments aiming for workers' control in the factories and shops. The councils were constant threats to the powers of the capitalist class, warning that at the proper moment the producing class would appropriate and run the institutions of production. They united unskilled and technical workers within a unit of the productive process each of which was a microcosm of the organizational structure of a socialist society. In this way workers councils were a source of ongoing political education. Through them the working class could "educate itself, gather experience, and acquire a responsible awareness of the duties incumbent upon classes that hold the power of the state."[25]

It is in this context that Gramsci speaks of the importance of the Communist Party and in this same context that we endorse the call of Charles Gagnon and others for the creation of a workers' party.[26] "In Gramscian terms a political party is an agent of education and civilization – a school in which one studies the life of the state."[27] Hence its function is basically educational and tactical – and it should not be seen as a paramilitary substitute for the prevailing economic and political hierarchy.

To fit into the context of our time and place, the educational aspect of such political work would extend further than workers' control of the institutions of production and commerce – though this arena is still the central one – and apply Gramsci's understanding of the role of councils without too much distortion to community control of towns and neighborhoods. It would include the institutionalization of producers and consumers cooperatives, and of restructured patterns of social life to transcend the nuclear family and advance the liberation of women. These are the kinds of strategies and activities presaged by the May uprisings. All these activities, and. others against racism, etc., would have to be part of an ongoing program of education and action coordinated and informed by the party. Such a workers' party would appeal to a working class defined widely as comprising the large majority which finds itself exploited directly or indirectly under the capitalist system.

Whether the Parti Québecois can yet be transformed into such a party cannot be fully prejudged at this moment – though it would appear extremely unlikely. Nevertheless, if not to be found there, it must be within the trade union movement itself that such a party will grow and transform the trade unions in the process. Certainly enough has been said to indicate that this may very well be happening, particularly in and around the CNTU. Clearly the political action committees launched by the CNTU at its 1972 Congress may, as noted before, become the nuclei of a party constituted and conceived in just this manner. In fact, the entire series of shifts in the trade union movement since the initiation of the "second front" at the CNTU in 1968 can be seen as small but concrete steps in this direction.

The separation of Quebec from Canada, which we take to be almost inevitable, is only a first step though an extremely important one. (It may be an important step for Canada as well, as it could possibly bring English Canadians as a collectivity face to face with their own colonial position vis-à-vis the U.S. with a sense of purpose not clouded by constitutional or bicultural divisions.) It may very well release those energies in and/or out of the PQ that will go into setting up workers' councils, community councils, etc., all over Quebec, and set in motion the popular forces which would build an indigenous socialist system – "un socialisme d'ici."

Footnotes to Chapter 10

1. John Porter, *The Vertical Mosaic* (Toronto: University of Toronto Press, 1965), pp. 201-2.
2. E. C. Hughes, *French Canada in Transition* (Chicago: University of Chicago Press, 1943), chapters 7-15.
3. Mason Wade, *The French Canadians* (Toronto: Macmillan of Canada, Ltd., 1968), Vol. 2, pp. 864, 969-74.
4. G. Parker, A. Lévesque, G. Dozois, G. A. Vachon, *op. cit.*, p. 266.
5. *Ibid.*, pp. 79-85.

6. Robert Fulford, "French Canadiens and the CNR," *Maclean's Magazine,* January 26, 1963, p. 4.
7. Mason Wade, *op. cit.,* p. 1112.
8. Quoted in *Québec Presse,* semaine du 31 janvier au 6 février, 1971, p. 28.
9. See for example, "Ti-Jacques and the Big Boys," *Last Post,* April, 1970, pp. 8, 9.
10. Charles Bilodeau, "Education in Quebec," in Douglas Grant (ed.), *Quebec Today* (Toronto: University of Toronto Press, 1960), p. 407.
11. Edward M. Corbett, *Quebec Confronts Canada* (Baltimore: The Johns Hopkins Press, 1967), p. 188.
12. Norbert Lacoste, *Les Caractéristiques Sociales de la Population du Grand Montréal* (Montréal: La Faculté des Sciences Sociales de l'Université de Montreal, 1958), p. 59.
13. *Ibid.,* p. 60.
14. Dusty Vineberg, " 'Maîtres Chez-Nous' Means Book Control Too," *Montreal Star,* February 18, 1971, p. 39.
15. Stanley Ryerson, *French Canada* (Toronto: Progress Books, 1943), p. 165.
16. P. E. Trudeau, "Some Obstacles to Democracy in Quebec," *Canadian Journal of Economics and Political Science,* XXIV, 3, (August, 1958), pp. 297-311.
17. Marcel Rioux, "Démocratie et culture Canadienne-Française," *Cité Libre,* juin-juillet, 1960, p. 4. (Authors' translation.)
18. Gérard Bergeron, *Le Canada Français après deux siècles de patience* (Paris: Editions du Seuil, 1965), p. 141.
19. Quoted in Eugene Genovese, "On Antonio Gramsci," in James Weinstein and David Eakins (eds.), *For a New America* (New York: Vintage, 1970), p. 291.
20. John Cammett, *Antonio Gramsci and the Origins of Italian Communism* (Stanford: Stanford University Press, 1967), pp. 130-31.
21. *Ibid.,* p. 205.
22. Quoted in *Ibid.,* p. 204.
23. Eugene Genovese, *op. cit.,* p. 299.
24. See B. Roy Lemoine, "The New Quebec State," *Our Generation* (Vol. 8, No. 4, October, 1972).
25. Quoted in Eugene Genovese, p. 293.
26. See Charles Gagnon's rebuttal of Pierre Vallières' Declaration, *Le Devoir,* January 5, 1972, p. 5; also January 6, p. 5. See also Henry Milner, *op. cit.*
27. Eugene Genovese, *op. cit.,* p. 294.

BIBLIOGRAPHY
(arranged by chapters)

CHAPTER ONE: THE AMERICAN METROPOLIS
Paul A. Baran & Paul M. Sweezy, *Monopoly Capital* (New York: Monthly Review Press, 1966)

R. J. Barnet, *The Economy of Death,* (New York: Atheneum, 1969)

R. J. Barnet, *Intervention and Revolution,* (Cleveland: World Publishing Co., 1968)

Fred Cook, *The Warfare State,* (New York: Macmillan, 1963)

Ralf Dahrendorf, *Class and Class Conflict in Industrial Society,* (Stanford: Stanford University Press, 1959)

G. Wm. Domhoff, *Who Rules America?,* (Englewood Cliffs, N.J.: Prentice Hall, Inc., 1967)

G. Wm. Domhoff, *The Higher Circles,* (New York: Vintage, 1970)

David Horowitz (ed.) *The Corporations and the Cold War,* (New York: Monthly Review Press, 1969)

Aldous Huxley, *Brave New World Revisited,* (New York: Bantam, 1958)

Gabriel Kolko, *Wealth & Power in America,* (New York: Frederick A. Praeger, Inc., 1962)

Ian Lumsden, (ed.), *Close the 49th Parallel, etc: The Americanization of Canada,* (Toronto: University of Toronto Press, 1969)

Herbert Marcuse, *One Dimensional Man,* (Boston: Beacon Press, 1964)

John McDermott "Technology the Opiate of the Intellectuals" *New York Review of Books,* July 31, 1969

C. Wright Mills, *The Power Elite,* (New York: Oxford University Press, 1956)

Vance Packard, *The Hidden Persuaders,* (New York: D. McKay Co., 1957)

Wm. A. Williams, *The Tragedy of American Diplomacy,* (New York; Dell Publishing Co., Inc., 1959)

Ellen Willis, "Consumerism & Women", (Toronto: Hogtown Press, 1971)

R. Winter-Berger, *The Washington Payoff,* (Secaucus, New Jersey: Lyle Stuart Inc., 1972)

CHAPTER TWO: QUEBEC: AN ECONOMIC SATELLITE

André d'Allemagne, *Le Colonialisme du Québec,* (Montréal: Editions R-B, 1966)

A Citizen's Guide to the Gray Report, (Toronto: New Press, 1971)

CNTU, *Quebec Labour,* (Montréal: Black Rose, 1972)

Robert Comeau, et. al., *Economie Québécoise,* Montréal: Les Presses de l'Université du Québec, 1969)

Stuart Jamieson, "French & English in the Institutional Structure of Montreal", M.A. Thesis, McGill University, 1938

John Porter, *The Vertical Mosaic,* (Toronto: University of Toronto Press, 1965)

André Raynauld, *Les Croissance et Structures Economiques de la Province de Québec* (Québec: Ministère de l'Industrie et Commerce, 1962)

Report of the Royal Commission on Bilingualism & Biculturalism, (Ottawa: Information Canada, 1969)

Rodrigue Tremblay, *Independance et Marche Commun Québec-Etats-Uris* (Montréal: Editions du Jour, 1970)

CHAPTER THREE: LES QUEBECOIS:
AN OPPRESSED MAJORITY

Diane Cohen, *CBC,* "Viewpoint", October 20, 1970

Rick Deaton, "The Fiscal Crisis & The Public Employee in Canada", *Our Generation,* Vol. 8, No. 4, (October, 1972)

Lysiane Gagnon, *La Presse*, (October 26, 1968)

Lysiane Gagnon, "Les Conclusions du Rapport B.B.: De Durham à Laurendeau-Dunton: Variation sur le thème de la dualité Canadienne" in *Economie Québécoise*, (Montréal: Les Presses de l'Université du Québec, 1969)

L. Favreau, *Les Travailleurs Face au Pouvoir* (Montréal: Centre de Formation Populaire, 1972)

B. Roy Lemoine, "The Modern Industrial State: Liberator or Exploiter," *Our Generation*, Vol. 8, No. 4, (November 1972)

Income Distributions: Incomes of Non-Farm Families Individuals in Canada in Selected Years, 1951-1965, Dominion Bureau of Statistics, June, 1969

Michel Pelletier et Yves Vaillancourt, *Du Chomage à la Libération* (Montréal: Les Editions Québécois, 1972)

André Raynauld, G. Marion, R. Béland, "La Répartition des Revenus entre les Groupes Ethniques du Canada", study done for Royal Commission on Bilingualism & Biculturalism.

Stanley Ryerson, "Social & National Factors in the Quebec 'Awakening'," Paper presented at the Seventh World Congress of Sociology, 1970.

Special Senate Committee on Poverty, (Report) *Poverty in Canada* (Ottawa: Information Canada, 1971)

CHAPTER FOUR: THE SATELLITE AND THE METROPOLIS

André de'Allemagne, *Le Colonialisme du Québec*, (Montréal: Editions R-B, 1966)

R. J. Barnet, Intervention & Revolution, (Cleveland: The World Publishing Co., 1968)

Conseil d'orientation économique du Québec, *Documents de base en vue de la planification*, septembre, 1962

A Citizen's Guide to the Gray Report, (Toronto: New Press, 1971)

D. Drache, "National Consciousness' in Ian Lumsden (ed.) *Close the 49th Parallel, etc: The Americanization of Canada*, (Toronto: University of Toronto Press, 1969)

C. Gonick, "Foreign Ownership & Decay," in Ian Lumsden (ed.) *op.cit.*

André Gunder Frank, *Capitalism & Underdevelopment in Latin America*, (New York: Monthly Review Press, 1969)

Gabriel Kolko, *The Roots of American Foreign Policy*, (Boston: Beacon Press, 1969)

Kari Levitt, *Silent Surrender*, (Toronto: Macmillan of Canada, Ltd. 1970)

John Porter, *The Vertical Mosaic*, (Toronto: University of Toronto Press, 1965)

"The Quebec Liberation Movement" (mimeo) (Toronto: Hogtown Press, 1970)

André Raynauld, "La Propriété des Entreprises du Québec", study done for the Royal Commission on Bilingualism & Biculturalism.

Rapport du comité interministèriel d'étude sur le régime des rentes, vol. ii (mai. 1964)

Report of Royal Commission on Bilingualism & Biculturalism (Ottawa: Information Canada, 1970) Vol. 3.

Gary Teeple (editor), *Capitalism and the National Question in Canada*, (Toronto: University of Toronto Press, 1972)

CHAPTER FIVE: NATIONALISM AND INTERNATIONALISM

Anouar Abdel-Malek, "Sociologie de développement national: problémes de conceptualisation," *Revue de l'Institut de Sociologie*, 1967, no. 2-3.

Gilles Bourque, & Nicole Laurin-Frenette, "Classes sociales et idéologies nationalistes au Québec 1760-1970," *Socialisme Québécois*, no. 20, (join 1970). For an English language commentary & translation see, D. Roussopoulos, "Nationalism & Social Classes in Quebec," *Our Generation*, vol. 8, no. 2.

Fred Caloren, "The War Measures Act and the Politics of Functionalism," *Our Generation*, vol. 7, No. 3.

Ramsay Cook (ed.), *French Canadian Nationalism*, (Toronto: MacMillan, 1969)

Rolf Dahrendorf, *Class & Class Conflict in Industrial Society*, (Stanford: Stanford University Press, 1969)

Horace Davis, *Nationalism & Socialism*, (New York: Monthly Review Press, 1967)

Gad Horowitz *et. al.,* "Nationalism, Socialism and Canadian Independence", *Canadian Dimension* Pamphlet, 1969.

John Leggett, *Class, Race & Labour*, (New York: Oxford University Press, 1966)

Karl Marx, & Frederick Engels, *Manifesto of the Communist Party*, (Peking: Foreign Language Press, 1965)

Quotations from Chairman Mao Tse Tung (Peking: Foreign Language Press, 1967)

Nicos Poulantzas, *Pouvoir Politique et Classes Sociales*, (Paris: F. Maspéro, 1968)

Marcel Rioux "Sur l'évolution des idéolgies au Québec" *Revue de l'Institut Sociologie*. No. 1, 1968.

P. E. Trudeau, *Federalism & the French Canadians* (Toronto: Macmillan of Canada, 1968)

Wm. A. Williams, *The Tragedy of American Diplomacy*, (New York: Dell Publishing Co., Inc., 1962)

CHAPTER SIX: AUTHORITARIANISM AND SELLOUT

R. P. Armchambault, s.j. "Les trois phases de l'Ecole Sociale Populaire," *l'Ecole Sociale Populaire*, no. 269-270, 1936, p.45

Léandre Bergeron, *Petit Manuel d'histoire du Québec*, (Montréal: Editions Québécoises, 1970)

Louis Berubé, "Une Victime de l'Age de Fer", M.A. Thesis, Laval University, 1958.

Gilles Bourque, *Question Nationale et Classes Sociales au Québec 1760-1840* (Montréal: Editions PartiPris, 1970)

"Les Caisses Populaires", *L'Ecole Sociale Populaire*, no. 269-270, 1936

Réal Caux, "Le Parti National Social Chrétien" M.A. Thesis, Laval University, 1958.

Gaston Cholette, "Le Comité d'Action Catholique de Saint Charles de Limoilou", Licence, Laval University, 1943.

Gilles Croteau, "Etablissement et Intégration de l'Institution Co-opérative à l'ile d'Orleans", M.A. thesis, Laval University 1952

J. B. Desrosiers", "L'Ecole Normale de Vaudreuil", *L'Ecole Sociale Populaire*, no. 269-270, 1936

Gérard Dion, "La Doctrine Sociale de l'Eglise dans le Québec" *Perspectives Sociales*, 1962-1963

Evelyn Dumas, *Dans le Sommeil de Nos Os*, (Ottawa. Les Editions Leméac, 1971)

E. A. Forsey, "Politics in Quebec", *Canadian Forum*, June, 1933.

_____ "Under the Padlock", *Canadian Forum*, May, 1938

_____ "Duplessis Marches On, *Canadian Forum*, Jan. 1939

_____ "The Padlock – New Style" *Canadian Forum*, March 1939

Le Goglu, 1931, 1932.

Jean Hulliger, *L'Enseignement Social d'Evêques Canadiens de 1891-1950* (Montreal: Editions Fides, 1958)

E. C. Hughes, *French Canada in Transition* (Chicago: University of Chicago Press, 1943)

E. C. Hughes & M. L. McDonald. "French & English in the Economic Structure of Montreal", *Canadian Journal of Economics & Political Science*, vol. 7., 1941

Stuart Jamieson, "French & English in the Institutional Structure of Montreal", M.A. Thesis, McGill University, 1938.

Gilles Laflamme, "L'Education Syndicale à la Confédération des Syndicats Nationaux", M. A. Thesis, Laval University, 1968.

Michael Oliver, "The Social & Political Ideas of French Canadian Nationalists", Ph.D. Thesis, McGill University, 1956.

Jacques Pelletier, "La Relève: une idéologie des années 1930", M.A. Thesis, Laval University, 1969.

Quebecer (Frank Scott), "French Canadian Nationalism", *Canadian Forum*, May, 1936.

Herbert Quinn, *The Union Nationale* (Toronto: University of Toronto Press, 1963).

Stanley Ryerson, *Unequal Union* (Toronto: Progress Books, 1968).

W. Saint Pierre, "Le Fondateur", *L'Ecole Sociale Populaire*, no. 269-270, 1936.

Frank Scott "Quebec Fascists Show Their Hand", *Canadian Forum*, 1936.

P. E. Trudeau (ed.), *La grève de l'amiante*, (Montréal: Editions Cité Libre, 1956).

"La Vérité sur l'Espagne" *L'Ecole Sociale Populaire*, mars. 1937.

Mason Wade, *The French Canadians*, (Toronto: Macmillan of Canada, 1968).

CHAPTER SEVEN: THE DECLINE OF THE OLD ORDER

Paul Bélanger, "Mutations du Syndicalisme Québecois", *Recherches Sociographiques*, vol. 3-no. 3, 1963.

A Carrier, "L'idéologie politique de la revue *Cité Libre*" *Canadian Journal of Political Science*, December 1968.

Gérard Dion, "The Trade Union Movement in Quebec" *University of Toronto Quarterly*, April, 1958.

Charles Henri Dubé, "La Vérité sur l'Ordre Jacques-Cartier", *Magazine Macleans*, mai, 1963.

Blair Fraser, "The Fight over Father Lévesque", *Maclean's Magazine*, July 1, 1950.

Roger Lemelin, "The Silent Struggle at Laval", *Maclean's Magazine*, August 1, 1952.

Charles Lipton, *The Trade Union Movement in Canada* (Montreal: Canadian Social Publications, 1966).

"Mgr. Charbonneau et l'opinion publique dans l'église", *Cité Libre*, janvier-février, 1960.

Herbert Quinn, *The Union Nationale* (Toronto: University of Toronto Press, 1963).

Maxime Raymond, "What does the Bloc Populaire Stand for?" *Maclean's Magazine*, January 1, 1944.

Marcel Rioux, "Sur l'évolution des idéologies au Québec", *Revue de l'institut de Sociologie*, 1968, no. 1.

Stanley B. Ryerson, *French Canada*, (Toronto: Progress Books, 1953).

Louis Savard, "Cité libre et l'idéologie monolithique du vintième siècle au Canada français", M.A. Thesis, Laval University, 1958.

P. E. Trudeau, *La Grève de l'Amiante*, (Montréal: Editions Cité Libre, 1956).

Tremblay, J. P. "Mr. Raymond & the Bloc Populaire", *Canadian Forum* (November, 1942).

Mason Wade, *The French Canadians*, (Toronto: Macmillan of Canada, 1968)

CHAPTER EIGHT: THE FLOODGATES ARE OPENED

R. Arès, "Canada 70: Une Enquête du Toronto Telegram", *Relations*, (no. 347), (mars 1970)

G. Barker, A. Lévesque, G. Dozois, G. A. Vachon, "Les Idées Politiques des Canadiens-Francais—Four Nationalist Movements", Study done for the Royal Commission on Bilingualism & Biculturalism.

C. Beauchamp, "Le Permanent Syndical de la Confédération des Syndicats Nationaux", *Recherches Sociographiques*, vol. 8, no. 2, 1967.

Paul Bélanger, et. al, "La Rivalité Intersyndicale au Québec", *Recherches Sociographiques*, vol. x, no. 1, 1969.

Jacques Brazeau, "Quebec's Emerging Middle Class", in Marcel Rioux & Yves Martin (eds.) *French Canadian Society* (Toronto: McClelland & Stewart, Ltd., 1964)

Edward M. Corbett, *Quebec Confronts Canada*, (Baltimore: The Johns Hopkins Press, 1967

J. Crispo, *International Unionism*, (Toronto: McGraw-Hill, 1967)

Gérard Dion, "La Doctrine Sociale de l'Eglise dans le Québec", *Perspectives Sociales*, 1972-1973

Louis Favreau, *Les Travailleurs Face au Pouvoir*, (Montréal: Centre de Formation populaires, 1972)

Gérald Fortin, "Le Nationalisme Canadien-Française et les Classes Sociales", *Revue d'Histoire de l'Amérique Francais*, vol xxii, no. 4, mars 1969.

Gérald Fortin, "Transformations et Structures du Pouvoir", in "Le Pouvoir dans la Société Canadienne Française", *Recherches Sociographiques*, 1966

Robert Fulford, "French Canadians & the CNR", *MacLeans Magazine*, January 26, 1963

Hubert Guindon "Social Unrest, Social Class & Quebec's Bureaucratic Revolution" *Queens Quarterly*, lxxi, No. 2, 1964

Peter Gzowski, "The Cardinal and his Church in a Year of Conflict", *MacLean's Magazine*, July 14, 1962

Daniel Johnson, *Egalité ou indépendance*, (Montréal: Editions Renaissance, 1970)

Gaétan Lavertu, "La Participation de la Confédération des Syndicats Nationaux aux Affaires Internationales", M.A. Thesis, Laval University, 1968.

Jacques Lazure, *La Jeunesse du Québec en Révolution*, (Montréal: Les Presses de Université du Québec, 1970)

René Lévesque, *An Option for Quebec*, (Toronto: McClelland and Stewart, 1968)

Hugh B. Myers, *The Quebec Revolution*, (Montreal: Harvest House, 1964)

M. Reid, *The Shouting Signpainters* (Toronto: McClelland and Stewart, 1968)

President's Report, Confederation of National Trade Unions, annual.

Claude Savoie, *La Véritable Histoire du FLQ* (Montréal: Editions du Jour, 1963)

Frank Scott, & Michael Oliver, *Quebec States Her Case*, (Toronto: Macmillan of Canada, 1964)

D. H. Sherwood, "The NDP & French Canada, 1961-1965", study done for the Royal Commission on Bilingualism & Biculturalism.

Smith, F. *Les Résistants du FLQ*, (Montréal: Editions Actualité, 1963)

Charles Taylor, "Nationalism & the Political Intelligentsia", *Queens Quarterly*, Spring, 1965, LXXII, no. 1

Pierre Vallières, *White Niggers of America*, (Toronto: McClelland and Stewart, 1971)

CHAPTER NINE: THE STRUGGLE INTENSIFIES

Nick Auf der Maur, "No Minority Group is Treated Better", *Last Post*, (December, 1971)

Nick Auf der Maur, "Power Corrupts. Absolutely", *Last Post*, (December 1971)

Nick Auf der Maur, "The May Revolt Shakes Quebec", *Last Post*, (July 1972)

Léandre Bergeron, *The History of Quebec: A Patriot's Handbook*, (Toronto: N-C Press, 1971)

Pierre Bourgault, *Québec, Quitte ou Double* (Montréal: Ferron, 1970)

Gilles Bourque et Nicole Laurin-Frenette, "Classes Sociales et Idéologies Nationalistes au Québec", *Socialisme Québécois*, no. 20 (mai, 1970)

Gilles Bourque, "En réponse à Pierre Valliéres", *Socialisme Québecois*, no. 23 (Spring, 1972)

R. Chodos and N. Auf der Maur, *Quebec: A Chronicle 1968-1972* (Toronto: James Lewis and Samuel, 1972)

Dominique Clift, "The Clergy's New Radicalism", *The Montreal*

Dossier d'Information sur le Bill 63, préparé par le Secrétariat central d'action politique non-partisane de la CSN, Décembre, 1969

D. Drache, *Quebec – Only the Beginning: The Manifestoes of the Common Front* (Toronto: New Press, 1972)

"Les Enseignants dénonce l'école", *Québec Presse*, (June 4, 1972)

Louis Favreau, *Les Travailleurs face au Pouvoir* (Montréal: Centre de Formation Populaire, 1972)

Le Front D'Action Politique: Les Salariés au Pouvoir (Montréal: FRAP, 1970)

Henri Gagnon, *C'est Quoi l'Etat*, (Montréal: Gaétan Piché, 1972)

André Laroque, "Quebec et Maintenant?" *Canadian Dimension*, vol. 7, no. 5 & 6, December 1970.

H. Milner "The Implications of the Valliéres Declaration," *Our Generation*, vol. 8, No. 3, (April 1972)

"Ne Comptons Que" and "Le Deuxième Front", published in English as *Quebec Labour*, (Montreal: Black Rose Press, 1972)

Michel Pelletier & Yves Vaillancourt, *Du Chômage à la libération suivi du manifeste de la FTQ*, (Montréal: Les Editions

Québécoises, 1972)

Maurice Pinard, "Working Class Politics: An Interpretation of the Quebec Case", *Canadian Review of Sociology and Anthropology*, Vol. 7, No. 2 (1970)

"Quebec", *Canadian Dimension* kit no. 56 (Winnipeg, 1970)

"Quebec", (special issue), *Radical America*, Vol. 6, No. 5, (October 1972)

"The Quebec Elections", (editorial article) *Our Generation*, vol. 7, no. 2.

"Radio Canada Boycotte le Parti Québécois", *Québec Presse*, 29 Mars, 1970

M. Reid, *The Shouting Sign Painters*, (Toronto: McClelland and Stewart, 1972)

D. Roussopoulos, "Social Classes and Nationalism in Quebec", *Our Generation*, vol. 8, no. 2.

Claude Ryan (ed.) *Le Québec qui se fait* (Montréal: Hurtubise, 1971)

"The Santo Domingo of Pierre Elliot Trudeau", *Last Post*, (November, 1970)

Edouard Smith, "Opération Démocratie", *Our Generation*, vol. 7, no. 2.

James Stewart, *The FLQ – Seven Years of Terrorism*, (Montreal: The Montreal Star, 1970)

Ralph Surrette, "The Year of Manifestoes", *Last Post*, (July, 1972)

"Les SSJB Changent de nom et tendent à se radicaliser", *Le Devoir* (14 Juin, 1972).

Pierre Vallières, *L' Urgence de Choisir* (Montréal: Editions Parti Pris, 1972)

Pierre Vallières, *Les Nègres Blancs d'Amérique*, (Montréal: Editions Parti Pris, 1968)

CHAPTER TEN: NATIONALISM ON THE LEFT

Gérard Bergeron, *Le Canada Français après deux siècles de patience*, (Paris: Editions du Seuil, 1965)

Charles Bilodeau, "Education in Quebec", in Douglas Grant (ed.) *Quebec Today*, (Toronto: University of Toronto Press, 1960)

John Cammett, *Antonio Gramsci and the Origins of Italian Communism* (Stanford: Stanford University Press, 1967)

Edward M. Corbett, *Quebec Confronts Canada* (Baltimore: The Johns Hopkins Press, 1967)

256

Oliver C. Cox, *Class, Caste, and Race* (New York: Monthly Review Press, 1949)

Charles Gagnon, "Je venais de loin quand j'arrivai à Montréal en Septembre 1960," *Magazine Macleans,* juillet, 1970.

Charles Gagnon, rebuttal of Pierre Valliéres declaration, *Le Devoir,* 5 janvier, 1972; 6 janvier, 1972.

Eugene Genovese, "On Antonio Gramsci", in James Weinstein and David Eakins (eds.) *For a New America,* (New York: Vintage, 1970)

E. C. Hughes, *French Canada in Transition,* (Chicago: University of Chicago Press, 1943)

Norbert Lacoste, *Les Caractéristiques Sociales de la Population du Grand Montréal,* (Montréal: La Faculté des Sciences Sociales de l'Université de Montréal, 1958)

"Quebec/Canada. October Events" *Our Generation,* Vol. 7, no. 3

Marcel Rioux "Conscience Ethnique et Conscience de Classe au Québec" *Recherches Sociographiques,* vol. 6, 1965

Marcel Rioux "Democratie et culture canadienne-française", *Cité Libre,* Juin-juillet, 1960.

Marcel Rioux, Quebec in Question (Toronto: James Lewis & Samuel, 1971)

Marcel Rioux & Yves Martin, *French Canadian Society,* (Toronto: McClelland & Stewart, Ltd., 1964)

Pierre Soucier "B & B ou l'inégalité à perpetuité," *Maintenant,* no. 73, 1968

"Socialisme et Solidarité," *Maintenant,* avril, 1972

"Ti-Jacques and the Big Boys," *Last Post,* April, 1970

P. E. Trudeau, "Some Obstacles to Democracy in Quebec", *Canadian Journal of Economics & Political Science,* xxiv, no. 3, 1958

20 Dossiers de Québec Presse, (Montréal: Rééditions Québec, 1971)

Pierre Vadeboncoeur, *La dernière heure et la première,* (Ottawa: L'Hexagon, 1970)